"In Tony Mohr's immersive memoir, *Every Other Weekend*, the Los Angeles of a more innocent time comes to life. Via his quest to understand his two fathers, Mohr illuminates the lives of two vastly different men. Through their personal effects [and] Mohr's research and his astounding memory, intimate portraits of the two men, Tony himself, and a golden era in the infamous city emerge. Highly recommended."

—**Charlotte Rains Dixon**, book coach and author of *The Bonne Chance Bakery*, *The Matchmaker's Temptation*, and *Emma Jean's Bad Behavior*

"Set in Southern California in the early sixties, *Every Other Weekend* encapsulates the life of Tony, a young boy who learns to 'toggle between households' after his parents' divorce. Gerry, the B-movie actor who is as rough around the edges as the characters he portrays, considers his son a pal, while Stan, Tony's stepfather, is a successful businessman who keeps his distance from the boy. While Tony yearns for Gerry's understanding and acceptance, it is Stan who ultimately provides the stability and family life Tony so desires. Anthony Mohr's clever, intelligent writing, with its nostalgic references and inside look at Hollywood, kept me reading throughout the night. I can't wait to see what he comes up with next."

—**Renée Thompson**, author of *The Plume Hunter* and *The Bridge at Valentine*

"One could cut granite with Anthony Mohr's incisive, imagistic *Every Other Weekend: Coming of Age With Two Different Dads*. This memoir is profound in in its distillation and delineation of memory, father and stepfather emerging from these pages as a result of Mohr's honed, crystalized prose."

—**Nathan Leslie**, editor of *Maryland Literary Review*

"Anthony J. Mohr's memoir, *Every Other Weekend*, [recounts] with stunning recollection how he navigated a path between his parents' divorce and his second families after his mother and father remarried. The two fathers couldn't be more different, which he eloquently describes with great detail. His learning to succeed is immaculately shared with the reader. So too are the trials and tribulations of his youth. *Every Other Weekend* is about love, family, perseverance, endurance, and adolescence as well, and a complex window into adult behavior. A truly great and enjoyable read."

—**Carl Borack**, film producer; documentary producer/
director; 1972 US Olympian in fencing; captain (non-playing
team leader) of US Olympic Fencing Team, '88, '92,'96, 2000;
chief of Mission Olympic Fencing Team, Rio 2016

"Anthony J. Mohr has written a must-read coming-of-age memoir for baby boomers lucky enough to grow up in swinging Los Angeles. In easy and mellifluous prose, he captures the flavor of the 1950s and 1960s in the country's entertainment capital. A child of divorced parents, Mohr explores with retrospective grace the heartbreak and possibilities of a life with two fathers. Forced to accommodate to two entirely different approaches to life, Mohr recounts the choices that enabled him to grow into the respected and successful superior court judge that he became."

> —**Robert Post**, Sterling professor of law, Yale Law School, author of *Citizens Disunited: A Constitutional Theory of Campaign Finance Reform,* and *For the Common Good: Principles of American Academic Freedom*

"*Every Other Weekend: Coming of Age With Two Different Dads* delightfully evokes a bygone era of Southern California through the tender lens of a young son growing up between two fathers and two worlds. Mohr paints the fun and freedom of traveling through celebrity-rich Hollywood with his father, a B-list actor, flirt, and crude teacher of life, against the steadier backdrop of his caring but remote businessman stepfather. Like his two fathers, Mohr's touching and tumultuous memoir is equal parts razzle-dazzle and serious life lessons — engaging, poignant, longing, nostalgic but never sentimental. There's just enough mid-century Hollywood name-dropping, the gone glamour of radio stardom and early TV, all as fleeting as his mercurial father."

> — **Lisa Romeo**, author of *Starting with Goodbye: A Daughter's Memoir of Love after Loss*

"Before 90210, there was 1952—growing up in Beverly Hills, Tony Mohr skillfully weaves memories of two fathers through Hollywood gossip and behind-the-scenes tales of the lifestyles of the rich but not famous and famous but not rich. A wry, intriguing look at coming of age in 1950s and early '60s America, and how America came of age through television."

—**Allison K Williams,** author of *Seven Drafts: Self-Edit Like a Pro from Blank Page to Book*

"*Every Other Weekend* not only makes Los Angeles and New York in the 1950s and 1960s come alive, it also sensitively depicts what it feels like to grow up in a fractured, complicated family. Anthony J. Mohr writes with compassion, elegance, and honesty, and this story of his upbringing is such a pleasure to read."

—**Edan Lepucki**, author of *California and Woman Number 17*

"This discerning memoir is at once heart wrenching, thought provoking, and highly enjoyable. Many aspects of Mohr's childhood with two dads—both imposing personalities, albeit in very different ways—were difficult, sad, or confusing, but he also manages to see the positive attributes of both men. Both dads made indelible impressions on his upbringing and character. While many memoirs degrade to tell-alls rife with blame, the author, a retired superior court judge, exudes fairness as he revisits and reevaluates his past. Mohr writes with ease, affability, and a talent for details, especially when recreating a 1950s and '60s childhood in Hollywood and Beverly Hills. And the book offers striking insights into what a child understands compared to an adult looking back. It all amounts to a fascinating read."

—**Ellen Sherman**, author of *Into the Attic*

"Anthony J. Mohr's debut memoir, *Every Other Weekend*, delivers a deftly written story about growing up in Southern California as the child of divorce at a time when divorce was so scandalous it made headlines. Mohr's dazzling writing reveals the challenges he faced while navigating the radically different worlds of his B-list actor father and his successful businessman stepfather. This tender and compelling memoir—part history lesson, part coming-of-age story—reveals with poignancy and humor the sometimes scrappy determination and resolve of a nerdy kid facing two wildly different fathers. At its core, Every Other Weekend is a study in contrasts and, ultimately, a love letter to the two men who raised him."

—**Patricia Glaser**, producer, entertainment attorney; board of directors, Geffen Playhouse; board of directors, Center Theater Group

"Tony shared his manuscript with me on a Friday and asked me to let him know what I thought in the next thirty days. I was done reading on Sunday. Couldn't put it down. His depiction of Los Angeles in the '50s and '60s brings to mind the great shift that took place over the following two decades – from least diverse major city in the US to most diverse major city in the US. Yet, even in its post-war baby-boom growth era, it was a city of dreams—whether you were in industry or in the Industry. The authenticity and humility of Tony's depiction of himself as an awkward (though obviously brilliant) youth is both engaging and heart-rending. Fast read. Must-read."

—**Amanda Susskind,** president of Constitutional Rights Foundation

Every Other Weekend

―◆―

Coming of Age With Two Different Dads

ANTHONY J. MOHR

VIRGINIA BEACH
CAPE CHARLES

Every Other Weekend

by Anthony J. Mohr

© Copyright 2023 Anthony J. Mohr

ISBN 978-1-64663-900-7

Published by

◤köehlerbooks™

3705 Shore Drive
Virginia Beach, VA 23455
800-435-4811

To Beverly. And all the DGs.

TABLE OF CONTENTS

PROLOGUE

Gerald Mohr—father. Stanley Dashew—stepfather. I still compare those two powers, the actor and the businessman, whose lives intersected across one woman and her son: my mother and me. From their respective remarriages in 1958 through Gerald's early death in 1968, they never lived more than a few miles apart, which made it easy for me to see them, but not easy to choose between them.

My father played private eye Philip Marlowe on the radio and enjoyed playing villains on the screen, but he struggled to pay the bills. My stepfather spent over a year cruising the Caribbean and helped introduce credit cards to the world, which earned him mention in a book titled *You Only Have to Get Rich Once*.

My father chain-smoked cigarettes. Stan puffed on a pipe. My father ate steak. Stan ate shrimp. My father's black hair was thick. Stan's brown hair was almost gone. My father's stare could seduce or intimidate, depending on his mood. Stan's blue eyes flashed to life every time he got a big business order, went to sea, or saw my mother enter a room. My father had a broadcast-quality voice. Stan's retained a trace of his New York roots. My father was lean. Stan fought his weight. My father played hearts. Stan preferred poker. My father rented. Stan owned. My father wanted to play villains and spies. Stan wanted to play the businessman. By the time I'd reached the sixth grade, Stan's career was ascending. My father's was heading the other way.

My father never told me how he reacted when Japan

surrendered, but I always imagined him enjoying the victory in some room, kissing a woman—perhaps my mother—while on the nightstand, his cigarette burned in the ashtray. As it turned to ash, I imagined my father whispering the phrases he'd promised to teach me one day.

Stan told me where he was on August 15, 1945—aboard his ketch, approaching New York Harbor. The captain of a Coast Guard vessel yelled to him that the war was over. Stan probably smiled and lit his pipe. He might have allowed himself a glass of wine, just one, but not until he'd returned his boat to port and made sure that every line—bow, aft, mizzen—was cleated to the dock.

My father was a Democrat; Stan, a Republican. Their party identifications cut deep. Adlai Stevenson's loss to "Ike," as our Republican neighbors called him, made my father mope for days. When Senator Robert F. Kennedy ran for president, the campaign asked my father to stump for him. He did, a thrill that caused him to consider a life in politics. I'd seldom seen him so energized as he was at rallies where he urged his audience to "get out and vote." Working for "Bobby" filled him with gusto and verve until, at the Ambassador Hotel, Sirhan Sirhan killed the senator. My father was there, in the ballroom, close enough to hear the shots and struggle through the pandemonium. Devastated and in tears until four in the morning, my father abandoned all political hope and decided to chase one final television series, *Private Entrance*, the pursuit of which led him back to Sweden, where years earlier he'd made his only series that ever actually aired.

Stan's Republican credentials reached back to 1948, to the group of businessmen in Grand Rapids, Michigan, who'd recruited Gerald Ford to run for Congress. Then he helped Richard Nixon. They'd met through their mutual insurance broker, V. John Krehbiel, who'd become Nixon's ambassador to Finland. President Nixon invited Stan to join his administration, a subcabinet post in the Department of Transportation. Stan said no. He wanted to keep working for himself—the quintessential entrepreneur. One night following President Kennedy's assassination, Stan railed against JFK's politics during a discussion with friends. They ought to "chop every one of his programs and *turn off the gas on the eternal flame.*"

"Stanley!" my mother said, grabbing his arm as even his fellow Republican colleagues blanched.

"Well, what I mean is . . ." Stan said.

I flashed to my father. We didn't talk on November 22, 1963. He was in Sweden, working on another project. He wouldn't return for months, and by then, President Kennedy was no longer a conversation piece. As a result, my mourning had occurred at Beverly Hills High School, during the noon hour, with our history teachers scattered across the front lawn and us students clustered around them, desperate for comfort. The faculty tried their best. One or two bent the rules and hugged us, welcome to many who, despite the clear sky, were shivering. The mercury had not made it beyond sixty-five, chilly for the Southland. The republic will stand, another teacher promised. Later in sixth period history, Mr. Dodge, a jolly little man whom we adored, walked us through the vice presidents who had been propelled into the Oval Office by assassinations. Andrew Johnson, Chester A. Arthur, Theodore Roosevelt—"Teddy had been put in the vice-presidency to *get rid of him*"—and now Lyndon Johnson. I listened, rapt and numb. The school canceled the fall play, *Our Hearts Were Young and Gay*, which would have opened that night.

Stan was an optimist, the kind who, if Somali pirates had hijacked his boat and kidnapped us, would have said, "Don't worry, Tony. This will be a great adventure." The deal was always going to go through. He'd get the big order. The investment would pan out. Too often, however, the deal didn't go through, a competitor got the order, and the investment cratered. It didn't matter. The next one would "hit," he'd say. "It can't lose."

My father shared Stan's buoyancy. He always said that the deal was ninety-nine percent done, only to watch it die without so much as a T.S. Eliot whimper. The next season of his television series, *Foreign Intrigue*. The pilot of another series, *Rough Sketch*. And another: *Holiday for Hire*. So this was the price for a life free from steady pay.

I missed the irony—Stan with his multiple cameras, constantly snapping pictures and sending me to the store to pick up two more roles of Plus-X film while my father—a man who made his money in front of cameras, owned nothing more than a clunky Argus 75, which he rarely used. Two-and-a-half months with my mother and father driving through Sweden, Denmark, West Germany, Austria, Italy, France, and Belgium generated no more than fifty black-and-white photos, most of them mediocre, no more than a few of them sharp. Was my father sick of cameras when he came home from a shoot? Stan couldn't travel a mile without amassing fifty photos, many of professional quality. But none of them evoked the blend of reality and whimsy that made up Southern California, a fusion that author Mike Davis called a "new substance, just as copper and zinc become brass that looks like gold."

During his nineties, Stan self-published an autobiography: *You Can Do It*. From what I know, its details are accurate. My father didn't write his life story, but in a 1952 letter, a publicist did—a five-page missive groaning with hyperbole and exaggeration. I guess that's how they did things. I don't know her name, only that she worked at a talent and PR agency called Redoff. It was owned by a man named Red Doff. She sent her letter to Hollywood's moguls at the time: Howard Hughes, Jack L. Warner, Dore Schary, Louis B. Mayer, and Y. Frank Freeman. Hughes ran RKO Pictures then. (Stan would sell his business to one of Hughes' companies.) Jack

L. Warner headed Warner Bros. Studios; Dore Schary, production at MGM. Mayer ran MGM and in 1952 became chairman of Cinerama. Freeman was an executive at Paramount. "Do yourself a favor," she wrote. "Sign up Gerald Mohr. I know it's a flat statement for the old girl to go out on a limb with on a nice, sunny Sunday morning like this . . . but this time, I'll make book. This guy will be a star."

Redoff's publicist included a lengthy description of my father's persona. Here's what she said with, in parentheses, my take on her accuracy:

He goes horseback riding (yes).

He reads everything in print (he did).

He's studied assiduously Freud, sociology, and anthropology (yes for Freud).

He's proud of his Anatole France first editions (I never saw them).

He has perhaps the country's largest private collection of crime literature (I never saw it).

He's fluent in French and German (enough to get by; that's all).

He can beat Humphrey Bogart in chess (he played well; beyond that, I can't say).

He doesn't frequent night clubs, doesn't play golf, doesn't lift weights, and doesn't "collect either old match covers or other men's wives" (yes to all of these; the women he collected were single, widowed, or divorced).

He can't change a tire. (I'll vouch for that).

He chain smokes (you bet).

He guzzles down at least twenty cups of coffee every day (probably ten).

He ignores his mail and hasn't the vaguest idea how to balance a checkbook (right).

She left the most important part for last: "But what the kid can do is act" (yes, without question).

I didn't study my fathers. I watched them in their two worlds, neither of which I could inhabit completely. I lacked my father's looks and charm as well as my stepfather's love of business and the sea. I wasn't trying to learn from them what it was to be a man—the future would take care of itself, I figured—and like most privileged California teenagers during the early sixties, I was sure of a brilliant outcome.

My father died at fifty-four. To compare him with Stan beyond middle age is unfair. Who knows how my father would have behaved at sixty, seventy, eighty, or ninety-six, the age at which Stan died? At fifty-four, Stan acted like a hardheaded businessman with no time for fun. By sixty-four, he'd built a new sailboat—he'd owned several in the past. He had yet to bring under control his gnawing desire to become Southern California's tycoon entrepreneur and premier philanthropist, a goal he never attained, which led to Stan spending his final years depressed, rarely smiling as he tried to launch three more companies, only to see two of them sell for scrap. (After he died, his two children and I sold the third for ten dollars.)

My father may have shared Stan's frustrations along the way, but he died full of hope. "He had three ecstatically delightful months filming *Private Entrance*," his second wife said the first time I saw her after my father's death, which was also the last time I saw her. *Private Entrance* was his last attempt at a television series.

⊙ ⊙ ⊙

"How do you spell Dashew?" asked the restaurant hostess one night at the height of Stan's career. She pointed us to a bench. "We'll call you."

There we sat for over half an hour. Stan could have bought

the bloody restaurant for cash. The hostess used Stan's machine to imprint every credit card that came her way, but none of that mattered to the woman. Had I come there with my father, even if we'd shown up without reservations, a banquette would have opened, just like that, and the staff would have put down place settings, just like that, and handed us menus, just like that. I was learning a major LA truth, so indelible Kevin Starr included it in his multivolume history of California: Hollywood restaurants "thrived on snobbery and selection . . . Nobodies were asked to wait at the bar despite an array of empty tables being held on reserve in the main dining room, all evening if necessary, for Hollywood celebrities."

On a morning after the waiters of a tony restaurant had fawned over my father, Mai stared at me over breakfast and said that they were "nobodies." This wasn't the first time Mai put my father down in front of him, but usually her gibes involved money. It was her worst quality. My mother never did such a thing—to either of her two husbands.

I didn't understand why Mai said that. Rarely did my father and I go anywhere without at least one person asking for his autograph. My father appeared to know everybody, and everybody appeared to know him. Mai's remark made me recall a day in Europe when my father, mother, and I had been dining on the patio of the Albergo Excelsior Hotel in Siena, Italy. *Foreign Intrigue* was in the can. My father spotted a well-dressed man at a nearby table.

"That's a famous writer, Tony," my father said. He took a puff on his cigarette. "He's written great books. *Of Human Bondage. The Moon and Sixpence. The Summing Up.* Go over and ask for his autograph. Say you're my son."

With alacrity, I walked toward the man, a stern-looking gentleman. He was eighty-one that year and looked every second of it, at least to the eight-year-old me.

The man shook my hand, and on a sheet of hotel stationery, he wrote, "For Tony, wishing him a good life and a happy one. W. Somerset Maugham. May 26, 1955."

My father had a flair for writing, and my mother urged him to practice the craft. She thought he could churn out stories between acting jobs. My father never did. He said he lacked the time. Yet, unless he had an early call, he slept till noon.

But once he was awake and full of coffee, our conversations loped along with ease. We talked about the space race, Red China, Indochina, Ronald Reagan ("That bad actor"), the Kennedys ("They're national treasures"), the occult, Shakespeare ("Shakespeare said everything"), Khrushchev, Cuba, civil rights, Nixon ("Jackal Nixon"), psychology ("The abnormal is just an extension of the normal"), girlfriends (his, not mine), the Dodgers ("They're a heart-attack team"), and his quest to land a television series. Usually, Stan limited himself to three conversation topics: business, sailing, and—less often—photography. Okay, politics too—on occasion during election season.

So bent was Stan on becoming known as the master entrepreneur that I doubt he paused to consider how good a man he was. He'd united two families, not just three children, but their aunts, uncles, and cousins. And the alloy remains solid today. He wanted his children to be independent and hardworking. His son, Skip, and daughter, Leslie, are; I am too, I think. Stan pursued sailing and photography to expert levels. He, too, knew everyone. He built a wide circle of friends who, like me, admired him.

But there were times I almost searched for reasons for Stan to come up short against my father. Unlike Stan, my father was catnip to women. Stan's senior prom date stood him up. My father read his lines beautifully. Whenever Stan recited at a Passover Seder, he stumbled through the words, mispronouncing *shema* and the names of the rabbis. Starting in school, people told me I "read beautifully," and for that I silently thanked my father's genes.

⊙ ⊙ ⊙

Then there was the matter of having fun.

At some point during my early teens, Stan said, "Children shouldn't have so much fun," and the statement continues to haunt me. Stan treated fun like caviar, an exceptional treat. Had Stan read Philip Roth's *American Pastoral*—he rarely picked up a novel— he would have related to Swede Levov's father, a workaholic who contemplated the WASPs of his town and asked himself, "What *is* it with them and fun? What is this fun? What is so much FUN?"

In his self-published book, Stan made it clear how much enjoyment his childhood lacked. At fifteen, he was bottling and selling root beer. While still in high school, he helped out at a family summer resort, where he learned to operate and repair machines. He worked for his father, a lawyer, and he never stopped performing household chores.

But God, did my father know how to have fun—swapping industry gossip with his buddies at the Brown Derby, playing hearts through the night, telling jokes on the set. I knew my father had had a good day when he sat down at the dinner table and announced that he'd had fun on the set. And when he did, the rest of the cast probably did as well. In his memoir, *The Garner Files*, James Garner wrote, "Gerald Mohr was the one I had the most fun working with on *Maverick*." Thinking about it now, I'm sure that every time he embraced his leading ladies, my father did more than act. He had fun. He pawed Mamie Van Doren during the 1959 crime movie, *Guns Girls and Gangsters*. A publicity still from *Invasion USA* displayed him and his leading lady, Peggy Castle, lying in the rubble, moments after one of Stalin's A-bombs hit New York. The look on my father's face didn't convey sorrow. It projected lust.

Fun occupied a special place in Hollywood, a quality Joan Didion noticed. "'Having some fun' is also what the action itself is called," she wrote in her essay collection *The White Album*. That's what my father craved: to disappear into a villain and shoot up the town. To become, in the series *Foreign Intrigue*, Christopher Storm, a Vienna hotelier at the time Austria was as divided and dangerous as Germany. To play a travel agent to the rich. In her book *West of Eden*, Jean Stein nailed it: "They didn't do it for the money; money was just a by-product. Now, they also loved to get away from the house in the morning, to be around people with perfect tans and straight noses from Texas who'd dance around them and say, 'It's so nice to be here!' The studio was the family, and someone like Loretta Young was the wife. Not a bad wife. Wouldn't you like to think, this is my wife, Ginger Rogers, rather than the wife at home? So they had it both ways." Or, as Debbie Reynolds said during an interview, "There's more fun in this business than anywhere."

Not surprisingly, I had more fun with my father than with Stan, even when our path to fun detoured through the unemployment lines. At the end, unemployment cash in hand, my father and I would decamp for a game of miniature golf, fish for trout at the Sportsmen's Lodge, or ride horses at the ranchette of one of his wrangler pals. Over dinner not long ago, my stepbrother Timmy put down his wineglass and said, "Gerry would have been great to hang out with once we were adults." Absolutely. I visualize my father and my twenty-three-year-old self sneaking into a club at 11 p.m. and chatting up the women, maybe taking two of them home. I imagine him telling jokes on the set, with me sitting in a makeshift director's chair, looking on.

It comes down to this. At the end of the 1950s (an era which actually did not end until 1965) and then through the 1960s, I eased toward manhood suspended between two worlds. In both I lived a fairly ordinary life, at the margin of what many regard as a fantasy, acquainted with B-list celebrities whom I viewed and treated as regular people. No one forced me to choose between

Gerald and Stan, nor did anyone suggest I do so. While there were times I leaned toward one over the other, for the most part I tried to balance the two.

Both my fathers had their faults, plenty of them, but their positive qualities outweighed them. I know they tried to raise their children and stepchildren as best as they knew how, and it's to their credit that all of us turned out well. Nobody won a Nobel Prize, but nobody failed either. Being a father was hard, I came to realize over the years, frustrating and draining, with as much sadness as joy. Eventually, I grasped that—time for full disclosure—fatherhood was a job I wasn't cut out for. I never had any children, an easy decision in part because I didn't get married until I was sixty-six.

My two fathers helped make me what I became for over twenty-six years—a Superior Court judge—a job that, ironically, required me to balance two or more points of view—and then choose. My fathers showed me what to do, and what not to do.

PART ONE

—◄o►—

Every Weekend

CHAPTER ONE

My Father, in the Dark

After my mother read to me, she dialed up my father's voice on the radio atop the bookshelf in my bedroom. As she fine-tuned that black box, the static and beeps and squeals gave way to an announcer, followed by my father.

"That's Daddy," Mom said, love shining in her blue eyes. She stayed a few minutes before she tucked me in, kissed my cheek, and walked away, her heels click-clicking on the hardwood floor and her dress playing against what adults called her shapely legs. A trace of her perfume lingered after she turned off the light and closed the door, leaving her only child to listen to Gerald Mohr.

In 1949, two years after I was born, *Radio and Television Life Magazine* named my father "Best Male Actor on Radio." Dad performed in some 500 shows—radio plays, as they were known. He was the globe-trotting detective Bill Lance. He appeared on *The Whistler* and *Yours Truly, Johnny Dollar.* He was a regular on Orson Welles' *Mercury Theatre Company, Lux Radio Theater, Hallmark Playhouse,* and forgotten series like *Nero Wolfe, Front Page Drama,* and *Dr. Christian.* They called him "The Iron Duke" because he never missed a line. And he starred in one hundred nineteen episodes of *The Adventures of Philip Marlowe.*

My father played Marlowe during the first four years of my life. Today that makes me proud. Then I just wanted him home more often. I was too young to appreciate the hardboiled plots, and even if he was in the house, my father rarely came into my bedroom to explain them. The radio orchestra's crescendo told me when something was about to happen, because I was not too young to absorb the meaning of the music under the cynical words of noir.

Nor was I too young to recognize authority in a voice. Dad's may have been disconnected from a body, but it was always in charge. His baritone could exude sarcastic skepticism in the "Mmmms," and "Oh reallys?" that defined Philip Marlowe's reaction when his client spun a tall tale. His voice could soothe when Marlowe said, "Tell me about it, baby." And his voice could intimidate an audience: "Get this and get it straight," he snarled. "Crime is a sucker's road, and those who travel it wind up in the gutter, the prison, or the grave."

But during those nights when my father's voice glided across the room to my bed, it failed to comfort. One Christmas episode called for him to console a sick little girl who'd received no presents. She wept and my father cooed to her. It was the first, but not the last time radio made me cry, which I did—alone, under the covers. I got plenty of presents that Christmas, but not enough of Dad. The radio star was not yet comfortable playing the role of a parent.

⊙ ⊙ ⊙

My father's close friends were his radio colleagues, and their kids populated my childhood. Robbie Rubin, two years my senior, taught me baseball (his father Jack wrote scripts for *Hallmark Playhouse*). Valory Mitchell (her father Robert Mitchell wrote for *The Adventures of Philip Marlowe*) and I played pretend games. Pat Woodruff (her father Frank Woodruff was a director for

Lux Radio Theater) and I played hide-and-go-seek. Stephanie Dubov (her father Paul Dubov acted on *The Adventures of Philip Marlowe*) was daring, and her father kept two cheetahs in the backyard. Her daring would last through her life. Stephanie died at sixty-seven, but before she did, a gorilla would teach her to say "dirty gorilla" in sign language, and she would publish an essay about her childhood experience with a trained Bengal tiger.

But my father's twenty-year radio run was peaking when I entered his life. *The Adventures of Philip Marlowe* lost a few more listeners with each Philco television set that entered a household. And while Robbie, Valory, Pat, Stephanie, and I had fun on the jungle gym, our parents struggled to enter this cool new medium.

Although we were oblivious to it, their vocational retraining must have been intense. Radio actors read their lines standing at a microphone. Television actors had to work with props and learn to master movement—space work is what they called it. My father never knew what to do with his hands, which may be why he became a chain-smoker. Radio scriptwriters had to create good dialogue, but little more. Their stage instructions could be limited to sound effects like "MUSIC . . . DOWN AND UNDER" and "SLAP . . . CRY OF NEWBORN BABY." Screenwriters had to describe characters in motion. With cheaply created cues, radio could invite its audience into an alternative universe. Not so with television. "Television has a camera, and the audience expects the camera to show it something real." Playwright and screenwriter Paddy Chayefsky wrote those words in his essay, *The Big Deal— Television Craft*. Part of his work appeared in an English textbook that by the 1960s, Beverly Hills kids—which I'd become by then— were expected to read and know.

I didn't mean to be disloyal to my father when I abandoned radio in favor of television shows like *Howdy Doody* and *Sheriff*

John. Buffalo Bob and Sheriff John spoke to me. Criminals and adults down on their luck didn't. Buffalo Bob and Sheriff John made me happy, and their shows weren't broadcast in the dead of night.

⊙ ⊙ ⊙

I felt nothing when Philip Marlowe went off the air. But with radio's fadeout, my father and his friends no longer worked steadily. At one point between my fourth and sixth birthdays, I remember my father not working at all. I didn't miss the noir, and my mother read to me a few minutes longer at night. But I continued to miss him. Opening his bedroom door before noon risked the wrath of a beast, roaring at me to stay away. Sometimes the door was still closed at two when I came home from kindergarten.

Once awake, my father grumbled as he wandered about the house, starting in the kitchen with coffee and then drifting to the dinette—a circular space with a wooden bench along the periphery and a table that sat up to ten people. There he read the newspaper and ate fried eggs with burnt bacon and burnt toast. After his second cup of coffee, my father moved to what he called "my chair," a green high-back in the living room that was positioned so that he could sit with his back toward our television set. This, I realized later, was not an accident. Whenever he looked up from his book, he could see the fireplace near the bay window straight ahead, and to his right, a natural wood coffee table and our long couch against the north wall. If he sat in either of the other two armchairs facing him, my father would have had to look at the object that was strangling his career.

With my father not working, dinner became a silent meal. The sole sounds were the clink of forks against knives and coffee cups on saucers, stopping only when he lit his Virginia Rounds cigarette and my mother, a Camel. Dessert was a spoonful of vanilla ice cream and a Nabisco cookie. We started eating hamburgers more often, and I remember wondering why, because one of my earliest images was my father's big grin whenever my mother cooked filet mignon, and she used to serve it often. "Baby, no restaurant cooks it better than you," he would say. My father said nothing when she made hamburgers.

Even if my mother served something expensive, I sensed no joy in our dinette. One night when I asked what we were eating, Dad said, "We're having duck." As in, "Get this and get it straight. We're having duck."

"Ducky wuckie," my grandmother said into the hush. She lived in a granny flat behind our house, across a covered patio. Her rhyme amused no one, including me. In her letter to the Hollywood moguls, Red Doff's employee called her "a celebrated singer in Vienna before her marriage." Pure nonsense.

The tension was confusing, so I turned to my comfort food: Ballard Oven Ready Biscuits. The dough Mom pulled from its cylindrical package cooked in nine minutes. I doused my hot biscuits in butter and let the warm goo slip down my throat. I'd eat them until Mom and Dad ordered me to stop.

⊙　⊙　⊙

The word *afford* joined my vocabulary, and I learned to associate it with money. One day when I heard Mom and Grandma saying they could not afford something, I asked, "Want me to give you some of my money?" Mom hugged me and said they didn't need my allowance, so back into the piggy bank went my silver quarter. I was never scared. I still had my wooden train that I pulled along grooved tracks that I could snap together and lay out across my bedroom floor. Mom kept her Plymouth and Dad, his Ford. The living room furniture remained. So did the Kelvinator refrigerator and the O'Keefe and Merritt stove.

My father's transition to television was slow—guest appearances on a few series, including *I Love Lucy, The George Burns and Gracie Allen Show*, and *Four Star Playhouse*—and while Dad's TV work never matched his radio reputation, at least he worked. And we inched closer to each other. Before cruising out the door in the morning, he hugged me good-bye and said, "Now I gotta go make a buck." Dad's voice brimmed with enthusiasm, not a trace of resentment. He was accepting television into his life, and at the same time, he seemed to be accepting me into his life.

⊙ ⊙ ⊙

Years later, after my parents divorced, after both of them married other people, and after I'd turned thirteen, old enough to understand, my father began telling me about his past. By then we'd become pals—his word. He called me *pal* when he was happy. He called me *Tony* when I did something wrong.

My father's eyes sparkled when he described his radio days. He'd started in New York. One night when he was sent to cover some event in Times Square, he invented a melee complete with rocks, bottles, and knives, boosting the ersatz violence until he was shouting into the mic, "Times Square is running with blood." If he lost his job or got disciplined, he never said. He moved to Hollywood. He got parts. Then bigger parts. He said that Humphrey Bogart had been charming to work with in radio's version of *The Treasure of the Sierra Madre*. Often after broadcasting live, my father and the rest of the cast repaired to a banquette in the Brown Derby, a restaurant in a brown-colored building built to resemble a derby hat, where their caricatures hung on the walls and they could "have some laughs" into the night.

I listened, but my father's radio roles seemed as distant as he'd once been. The details had already faded from memory until they became little more than feelings stitched together by hardboiled sentences and musical passages I couldn't hum. But the one stubborn fact I never forgot was that during the opening years of my life, my father's role had been little more than a voice I heard in the dark.

CHAPTER TWO

The Jungle

I was four. I tried to hold the bar of soap my father tossed to me. "Oh. Slippery soapy," my father said after I dropped it onto the pink floor of the tub. The shower was running full blast, which made his voice sound like he was under water. I picked up the soap and tossed it to him; he tossed it back, and again the bar popped out of my hand. "Oh. Slippery soapy," he said again. I squealed and laughed. We kept lobbing the bar, I kept stooping to pick it up, the water kept spurting from the shower head, and he kept saying, "slippery soapy." Our game lasted, I'm sure, no longer than five minutes, but I'll never forget my father chanting, "slippery soapy." An everyday shower, a treasured memory.

◉ ◉ ◉

My father gave up Bootsie, his German shepherd, because the dog was jealous of me. In came Bo, a black and white wire-haired terrier half Bootsie's size, and so friendly that I asked my parents if I could marry her. Next came Sweetie, a parakeet. A lizard joined our menagerie. A cat was on the way. Then goldfish and guppies. But my father wouldn't give me a cheetah. If Stephanie Dubov could have them, I wanted one too. I'd seen them pacing back and forth, purring in their backyard cage, or at least that's what Stephanie said they were doing. Her father wouldn't let me play with them, not because they would attack me—they liked humans, Paul said—but because cheetahs couldn't retract their claws. They're playful, he said, but if they pawed in a display of affection, they'd hurt me. The naive me was sure, that day, that my father would have let me play with them. I was wrong.

My father sided with Paul Dubov. "You're only going to play with safe animals," he said that night.

By then my father understood my desire to play with every type of beast imaginable, a desire due, perhaps, to so many Los Angeles attractions that featured mammals. Horses at Ponyland, where Beverly Boulevard and La Cienega met. More horses at Corriganville (B-Western actor Crash Corrigan's ranch near Simi Valley. Incidentally, in several films, Corrigan wore gorilla suits). Still more at Hoppyland, in Venice, built by the man who played Hopalong Cassidy. The trend would expand into Orange County and last through the late sixties and beyond with Japanese Village and Deer Park—patterned after the deer park in Nara, Japan— and then Lion Country Safari, where you could drive next to lions, provided that you rolled up the windows.

But for some reason, I wanted to play with a monkey.

My father said he would take me to Jungleland.

⊙ ⊙ ⊙

To reach Jungleland required a twenty-five-mile drive to Thousand Oaks over a country road through chaparral-covered hills, but my father liked to drive, and I liked to ride with him. I can still see his left arm resting on the window frame, and how he, with the top down, smiled into the wind.

Somewhere in Tarzana—a place named after Tarzan—before we entered the countryside, my father pulled into a gas station. "Fill 'er up," he said. I remember his pleasure at being able to drive anywhere in what was becoming a nation on wheels. On the days I rode with my mother and she needed gas, she said, "Two dollars' worth"—and that's what she always said. She sounded hesitant, as if the station might not have ten gallons of fuel available. When my father said, "Fill 'er up"—and that's what he always said—it was without the slightest doubt about the outcome. Confidence—a good fatherly quality. While the attendant pumped gas, two more men raced up to us and started wiping the windshields, checking the tires, and looking under the hood.

Back on the road, I stared out the window at the meadows. *Ten minutes to Walnut Grove*, read a sign by the road. It featured a picture of a family smiling outside a new house surrounded by trees. The mother, father, little boy, and—the center of their attention—a baby.

I turned to my father. "Where do babies come from?"

"Well," he said, sounding as though he'd rehearsed for this moment, "Daddy plants the seed in Mommy's vagina. Nine months later, you have a baby."

The explanation made sense to me. I leaned back in my seat. We passed another sign that read "Five minutes to Walnut Grove." The same house, the same trees, the same happy family.

"Daddy," I said, "I want to be a gardener."

"Why do you want to be a gardener?"

"So I can plant lots and lots of seeds in Mommy's vagina."

I can't recall what my father said after he stopped laughing. I could swear he kept on chuckling all the way to Jungleland.

Jungleland covered 170 acres of plains and trees and wild animals. A tram took us across the grounds to the lions. A lady lion tamer appeared in the park's wild animal shows. Jungleland's drinking fountains were made to look like the open jaws of a lion or hippopotamus. Guides made sure to say that many of their animals had appeared in numerous shows. (MGM's mascot Leo the Lion, Bimbo the Elephant from *Circus Boy*, Tamba the

Chimpanzee from *Jungle Jim*, and, years later, *Mister Ed.*) Then there was Susie.

Susie was a gibbon, with fur so thick a boy could lose his way. Her marble-black eyes called to me, or so I thought.

My father wouldn't let me touch her. I threw a tantrum. He didn't say anything. I turned my back on him and watched a set of parents let their little daughter pet Susie. Susie pushed her face against her arm. As the girl giggled and squealed with glee, I kept whining and didn't stop until I heard the scream.

Susie had torn the flesh off the girl's arm, then reached through the bars and mangled the girl's face.

Somehow, the girl's hysterical parents managed to free their daughter. Blood spurted out from what was left of her forearm.

Whoever the girl was, she was not the sole child to be injured at Jungleland. In 1966, when I was home from college, my father told me a lion had mauled (but didn't kill) Jayne Mansfield's son. Three years later, the park closed.

"It was just something about Susie," my father told my mother at dinner. It was "that something" that had protected me from Susie.

⊙ ⊙ ⊙

My father and I went to a party for the children of the stars at the hillside home of Uncle Bernie, owner of the Beverly Hills toy store of the same name, famous for its so-called lemonade tree. (Lemonade flowed from every branch.) In the backyard, statues of elves flanked a hobbyhorse, and a trail passed Bugs Bunny and Elmer Fudd, Woody Woodpecker, and Donald Duck. Once home, I asked if I could have a pet rabbit. "We'll see," my father said. Then he let me sit with him in his favorite chair while he read a script. The rabbit slipped out of my mind.

CHAPTER THREE

Raillery

When I was five, I began to notice that my parents and their friends seemed to have a lot of fun together. Each time the doorbell rang and the guests poured in, there were shrieks of "Great script!" and "You look divine!" and "I loved your scene!" The chatter surged, retreated, then heaved again. Somebody mentioned "the set" and the others laughed.

Even to my young eyes, the women looked glamorous and carefree, hair combed just so, teeth white and straight. If someone snapped a picture, each woman knew which profile the camera preferred and turned that way, posing for the shot.

As for the men, they appeared a tad serious, even stern, as though they were thinking about their next picture. My father's smile, however, signaled to me that all he thought about that night was enjoying himself. He was the handsomest of the group; my mother, the prettiest.

I knew a few of the guests: Joe Ainley and his wife Betty Lou Gerson, an actress who'd played in an episode of *The Adventures of Philip Marlowe*. They lived a block away and let me swim in their pool. Joe enjoyed beekeeping and showed me the hives behind his house; no bee stung me. Dick Mack, a radio and television producer whose son, Johnny, was a year or two older than I. Jeff Chandler (nominated for an Oscar for playing a Native American in *Broken Arrow*) and his actress wife, Marjorie. At six-four, Jeff was one of the few in the room taller than my father.

One night, I slipped out of bed and started down the stairs to the landing. From there, I could see a slice of the living room and the stunning men and women who filled it.

The banter flew, bounced off the beams, and didn't stop until my grandmother called out, "Children, who wants cake?"

They all did, and my grandmother beelined for the kitchen to cut up the bundt kuchen she'd baked that day. I don't remember her making any other kind of cake. Its spongy smell mixed with the scent of coffee to create a sublime aroma, which I breathed in when it reached the stairs. It pushed away the odor from the cigarettes many of the guests were smoking.

As my grandmother passed below, cake in hand, she said to nobody in particular, "I think I've got a little rheumatism." She announced it with bravado, an unnatural tone for her. Normally when she claimed to be sick, she would describe her disease with a morbid tone of voice. But not tonight. Back in the living room, I could swear she was chuckling along with the crowd, something I rarely remember my grandmother doing.

One of the men told a joke that went over well. Another followed. Then it was my father's turn.

"Hey," he said, "You hear about my brother the tailor? Your brother's a tailor? How much would he charge me to make a suit? Thousand dollars. Thousand dollars? He's no tailor, he's a robber. That's my brother—Robber Tailor."

As the guests roared, I pushed my hand against my mouth in order to keep still. Although in retrospect the joke wasn't that funny, the way my father told it—with full-throated merriment—captured the room.

The jokes continued until my mother said, "Who wants more coffee?" One of the guests called out, "Me, please." En route to the kitchen to put on another pot, she passed the stairs and a whiff of her perfume rose up to me. I enjoyed the scent quietly. If she'd noticed, she would have shooed me to bed.

She returned with piping hot coffee in the kettle, and I'm sure she poured it carefully for whoever wanted it. Someone talked about a shooting script. One of the women attempted a joke.

"Not bad," said a guest.

"That's funny," said another.

Then it was back to my father. "Hey, you hear about my brother the dentist? Your brother's a dentist? How much would he charge to make me a set of teeth? Thousand dollars. Thousand dollars? But I've only got a buck. He'll make you a set of buck teeth."

This joke wasn't so witty either, but everyone laughed again. My father knew how to tell 'em. In his memoir, not only did James Garner call my father fun to work with, he wrote that my father "could tell a joke better than anyone, and he had a bunch of them. Never repeated himself. And he was a pro." I didn't inherit that talent. Somewhere during my twenties, I'd try out his two "brother" jokes, with pathetic results.

I yawned. The smoke from the living room overtook the whiff of the coffee and burned my eyes. Up the stairs I went slowly in order to enjoy the party as long as I could. All I heard from my bed were swells of conversation, punctuated by sudden bursts of hilarity. Voices rose and fell, an ocean of sound and smart-sounding sentences. If this was the adult version of fun, I'd take it.

I have pictures of one of their parties. I can't recall, but it might have been a New Year's Eve. I do know that they were taken no later than 1952, because my friend Robbie's father, Jack, appears in the photos, and he died that year, at forty-two. The snapshots display an ebullient group, most of them holding cocktail glasses not yet raised in a toast. One woman acts as if she's about to pour her highball onto Jack's wife, Beulah, who's kneeling below. Jack wears a tie and looks nerdy—a square as they used to say—but not my father. The most dashing of the men, he wears an open-collar shirt and a plaid sport jacket complete with a one-point pocket handkerchief. My father isn't holding a drink. I never saw him drink. He didn't need booze to joke and frolic, just a pack of cigarettes. He owned the best smile in the room. And in the photos, my mother sparkled, the happiest and sweetest of the women.

Even at my age, it was easy to tell this group liked loud gatherings, a chance to hoot and laugh and, I'm sure now, debate the issues of the day. At times, their boisterous fun kept me awake, but I didn't care. Upstairs in bed, it was comforting as well as enjoyable to hear the snips of their banter. I don't remember what they said; it was their snappy cadence and rapid-fire raillery that remained with me—especially my father's. I was learning that he could dominate a room by doing little more than raise one eyebrow, as he did when he wanted to make me smile. I was too young to describe his party persona as a blend of nonchalance, jest, and dalliance, with a dash of Shakespeare here and there, but as I got older, I recognized those qualities.

My parents' gatherings were one subject the author of the Redoff letter to the moguls got right: my home was a place "where good friends, good music, good books, good home-cooking, and, especially, good arguments prevail as the thematic atmosphere." Her comment squared with what Peter Lunenfeld pointed out in *City at the Edge of Forever—Reimagining Los Angeles*: private homes were the town's social center—something no five-year-old would pick up on. Where people lived defined the Southland more than night clubs, monuments, plazas, restaurants, and public art, all of which were relatively scarce back then.

Maybe my parents' suite of friends was still celebrating the end of the war and the onrush of early Fifties prosperity. Or perhaps they were enjoying life in the funhouse that was the film industry. And as they did, I enjoyed the outsized presence of my father. These parties were fantasies themselves I'd realize eventually, stages for his looks and charm and talent, the reasons for his upward spiral, almost twenty movies and TV shows and counting.

CHAPTER FOUR

Invasion USA

It was the spring of 1952. I was five, the sun was out, and my friend Valory and I were playing in her backyard. A fight had broken out, but not with her. I heard about it from a newscaster whose voice came through Valory's den window and said the "fight could lead to a third world war." This had to be make-believe. But Valory believed the announcement. Her hands flew to her cheeks, and her mouth became an oval.

"A war," she said. "People could get hurt."

I was old enough to know what a war was. Our game of Let's Pretend was over.

I ran from Valory's yard and raced up Hazeltine Avenue, past the twelve houses that separated her place from mine, a home that Red Doff's publicist described as "a rambling, informal two-story farmhouse in the San Fernando Valley."

My mother gave me her beauty-contest smile and a hug. A war had not started, she promised, at least not in the San Fernando Valley. She said that Korea, the place the announcer most likely was talking about, was far from California, and I had nothing to be afraid of.

But I was frightened—of Russia, Stalin, communists, A-bombs—words I heard on the radio in my mother's Plymouth and the TV in our living room. Whatever they meant, I was dimly aware, frightened more by the tones with which adults pronounced those words and the looks on their faces as they uttered them. President Truman appeared nervous on our Philco the night I heard him say, "Mr. Stalin," in what context I don't recall. Behind the circles of his eyeglasses, the President's black-and-white face seemed too taut, despite his efforts to sound tough. More than once I heard someone say, "Stalin's A-bombs" (probably Edward R. Murrow, I'd learn) and heard Senator Joseph McCarthy say, "Communist." McCarthy spat it out as "commonist," which made the noun even more menacing. My friend Chuck's father said a communist lived on our block. He gave no details.

Thanks to Mr. Stalin, fear crept around our neighborhood and leeched into my house, affecting even my father, six foot two, the man who'd danced with Rita Hayworth in *Gilda* and whose intuition had saved me from being mauled by a monkey. Normally Dad wasn't afraid of anything.

In my room one night, I heard my father say, "The atom bomb has been dropped on the United States of America." Neither my mother nor my grandmother replied while again and again, my father gave the locations of three nuclear explosions, as though he were delivering a news bulletin. I was too young to know he was tucked into a script and running his lines.

Most of my classmates at Sherman Oaks Elementary School did not seem scared of war. They behaved like the young of a nation that had yet to lose one. Even their playground jargon made combat sound like fun. "Helldivers," one boy said each time he hit the tetherball. Our teacher must have known he was thinking of dive bombers, and she never accused him of swearing. Two other kids played "Bombs over Tokyo" at recess, but it was the bomb drills over the years that I remember. Drop—cover the face with your left forearm, use the right hand to pull your shirt over the neck.

Crouched under my desk, I didn't know what to think. My father was not preparing me to go to war, not with my doting mother and jumpy Grandma Henny in the house. He didn't own guns; he didn't buy me toy soldiers. I never saw a battlefield. Southern California lay far from the Shilohs and Saratogas. My father had been drafted after Pearl Harbor but served his country at an army studio near Santa Ana, where he'd acted in radio dramas like *Wings to Victory*.

Sometimes when it rained and I couldn't play outside, I sat on a window seat in the living room and listened to my father's wartime radio shows, which had been preserved on black glass records. I absorbed the boom of artillery and the howl of planes before they crashed. No one helped me with the history, because no one listened to the records with me. Those dark afternoons, I doubt that anyone knew what I was doing. Dad was at the studio or upstairs studying his lines. Mom was cooking and Grandma lay in bed with her diathermy machine on. That black contraption had more dials and meters than the TV cameras I'd see on sound stages. She said it generated heat for her arthritis.

One night at dinner, in the middle of a boring adult conversation, Dad said, "Invasion USA." His tone shifted with the phrase. Always so suave, my father acted worried. So did my mother, who was normally calm. My grandmother also looked serious, but then Grandma always behaved as though enemies surrounded our half acre in Sherman Oaks, prepared to storm our house and overrun her granny flat. I started to ask if the Russians had attacked, but before the question was out, my father told me to stop interrupting. He was in a bad mood, and so, cycling between confusion and fear, I listened and rolled my green peas around the plate until, moments later, the conversation drifted to another subject.

Several days later, Dad said, "Invasion USA," again and added that Russian planes would bomb New York City. We had relatives there: Grandma Sadie, Uncle Dick, Aunt Nanette, Uncle Carl, and my cousins Jeff and Warren. This time I remained quiet and didn't ask for an explanation. I'd wait until one of those weekend days when my father took me to the barbershop and I watched him get a haircut, or we drove to the location of his latest Western and went horseback riding. Sometimes he took me on the roller coaster at Pacific Ocean Park, where getting scared was so much fun. POP, as everyone called it, was an amusement center built on a pier south of Santa Monica, in Venice. My father tried to take me grunion hunting one night, but I fell asleep before thousands of those little fish arrived on the waves and turned the beach silver as they dug into the sand, the females to lay their eggs, the males to fertilize them. Minutes later, he said, they rode away with the tide.

But when those rare moments with my father occurred, I never raised the subject of invasions. We talked about other things. It was my chance to explain my life, for he didn't seem to have a good understanding of it, and I didn't want Stalin's A-bombs to wreck our time together.

Nor did I seek answers about an invasion from my mother while she read to me. Listening to her mimic *Freddy the Detective* was too pleasant to spoil. Maybe I feared what she'd say. More likely, I was embarrassed to say I was afraid of Stalin, just as I was afraid to admit that I liked Lindsey, the prettiest girl in my class. So, I wondered silently if A-bombs would fall on our house.

I dreamed that they did. Soviet planes appeared over Sherman Oaks, coming on slowly, in formation. They looked like the jets I saw on television, but now each fuselage was thousands of feet long. They obscured the sky and poured out A-bombs like sand from my toy dump truck. Thousands of big-finned ovals with the letter *A* painted on them smashed into the lawn, the slide on my jungle gym, and my tree house in the orchard. The jets whined as loudly as the sirens from fire trucks on Ventura Boulevard. Mrs. Hutchinson, the old widow who lived next door, screamed for help as did Mary and Joy, the two fifth-graders who lived across the street.

But the next morning LA's yellow sky was empty. No bombs had struck the lawn. My jungle gym was unharmed, as was our peach tree, our lemon tree, and the red brick incinerator against the corner fence. No bombers appeared that day, or during the weeks that followed. School let out and summer vacation passed in peace. Chuck and I played baseball in the street. He said his dad was going to vote for "Ike and Dick." My father was home a little more often. He planned to vote for Adlai Stevenson but didn't say why.

One night, my father made a deal with me, I'm sure because I was annoying him: If I let him read in peace for an hour, we'd play with "the invisible monkey" that lived in the drawer of the small desk next to my father's favorite living room chair. When I returned sixty long minutes later, he opened the drawer and said, "Psst," followed by, "There he goes." Dad pointed to the ceiling and kept saying, "Psst, psst, psst." I could have sworn I heard the little creature swing from one beam to another. I was sure he was real. Monkeys appealed more than A-bombs, and this ghost of a primate was nothing like evil Susie at Jungleland. Moments later, it hopped back into the drawer, and my father resumed his book.

During that summer, our lawn took on the sweet smell of cut grass, with moisture blending in when my parents let me run through the sprinklers. Morning cloaks, cabbage whites, and tiger swallowtail butterflies winged about the hedges that separated us from our neighbors. Occasionally a car grumbled down Greenleaf Street. Hummingbirds darted about the flowers. At times an owl hooted. Each day between four and five, when the San Fernando Valley baked and even the metal chains that held my swings got too hot to hold, the Good Humor man drove his white truck past my house. I listened to the fifteen happy notes of his theme song and no longer scanned the sky for A-bombs.

Sometimes after Mom bought me a Popsicle, I'd walk down to Valory's house. Valory had started wearing her light brown hair in a flip. I wasn't too young to notice her flawless olive skin, light eyes, and musical voice. And she still liked to pretend. A day with Valory was a good day. We played in nearby vacant lots and created little neighborhoods in her backyard, laying out the streets with pebbles and building houses of twigs and wood chips. She made sure to include a school. I added a gas station. I took pictures of our work with my Brownie camera. One afternoon, in a nearby vacant lot, Valory and I found a concrete block. It must have weighed a ton. We lugged this piece of rubble back to her yard and imagined it was the tallest building in our little world.

Shortly after school resumed, Robert Rinaldo, another boy on our block, came over to play with Valory and me. He was tall, a couple of years older, with sandy hair and an open face. He liked telling stories and he assembled words in a clever manner that made Valory laugh and made me jealous. Robert put his vivid imagination on display on Halloween night. Valory, Chuck, and I knocked; his front door creaked open—Robert must have used a string because he was hiding somewhere—and all we saw was darkness. His disembodied voice said, "Come in and get your treats." Chuck, Valory, and I felt the threads that hung low across the entry to the dining room, where Robert had placed the candy bowls. We took our Snickers and Mars Bars, and into the black void, Valory said, "Thank you, Robert." Later, after we returned to Chuck's Cotswold cottage house and gushed to his father about the experience, he warned us not to go back there because Robert's father was the communist he had warned us about.

They blacklisted Robert's dad, Frederic Rinaldo, and also

his writing partner Robert Lees. That term would not enter my vocabulary until the fifth grade, and I wouldn't absorb the full story until at least the eighth. Robert never discussed the subject. Thanks to that smear, Frederic Rinaldo wrote "only occasionally" according to the Online Archive of California. He became a salesman for a wholesale paper company until 1984, when he retired. Lees continued to write, under a pseudonym. Not until I was older did I start to appreciate the cruelty of what happened and how the blacklist was another reason so much fear permeated my neighborhood.

My parents assured me that Robert's father was not a communist. He wrote comedies, including three movies that had starred Abbott and Costello. One was familiar to me: *Bud Abbott and Lou Costello Meet Frankenstein.* I wanted to believe my parents, but if Robert's father wasn't a Red—the label Chuck's father had used—why couldn't he write scripts anymore? I saw Robert after that night but not often, and I never met his dad.

My father was lucky. Few relished a good political debate more than he did, and he didn't hold back his liberal thoughts. But he never praised Russia. He thought the Soviet Union was every bit as evil as Nazi Germany. Maybe that's why he never drew attention from the red-baiters.

⊙ ⊙ ⊙

The day before Thanksgiving, 1952, a black-and-white photo lay on the coffee table when I arrived home from school. In it, my father was hunched up against a wall. His eyes were closed, his face was blood-smeared. The blonde who clung to him with her fleshy white arms was not my mother. Next to them, a huge piece of concrete tilted, blasted out of the building. Yet the woman's lipstick remained perfectly outlined on her parted lips. She wore an evening gown; Dad, a pinstripe suit. His tie was loose. At first, I thought my father was in agony, but the expression on his face could have been a smile. Something told me the picture wasn't real, but I couldn't be sure, and seeing him with this woman confused me.

◉ ◉ ◉

My father's world was just as fictive as Valory's and mine. *Invasion USA* was a B movie about an A-bomb attack on America. My father played a newscaster in it, the starring role. Maybe I should have known my parents had been discussing a film. After all, make-believe pervaded our house, right down to the invisible monkey. But I had yet to make a reliable distinction between fact and fiction. Earlier that year I'd seen *The Duel at Silver Creek*, a movie in which my father was killed, and it took at least an hour for my mother to calm me down. When Dad talked about bombing New York, I thought he was describing a real war as opposed to—what? A bad set of rushes that day? That was it. I mistook the Russians for the rushes, the unedited film the crew watched after a shoot. But Dad said, "the Russians" again several nights later, clearly this time, and then he said "invasion."

Of course, the eight-and-a-half-by-eleven glossy on our coffee table was a studio publicity shot for *Invasion USA*. Maybe Mom told me that when she came into the living room and saw me gaping at it. Whether or not she did, the image lasted. You don't forget seeing your father bleed when you're a child, even if it's only in a movie. Looking at that picture from the vantage point of half a century later, I'm certain my father enjoyed playing in the rubble with his costar, Peggie Castle. But when I first saw it, I thought that one of Stalin's A-bombs had hit him. Or did I? The image tangled my childhood mind. Was Dad really hurt? He never appeared wounded at dinner. I always wondered why he failed to explain what *Invasion USA* was or, at least, hide that photo. But such thoughts occur to today's parents, who give their kids more attention than we received back then. We children of 1952 were left to figure out the real world on our own, and having an actor as a father made that task harder. As I was beginning to learn, reality and make-believe didn't always collide; they blended.

Invasion USA opened two weeks later, on December 10, 1952. My parents never took me to see it—a wise decision. Columbia's advertising strategy for the movie had been to frighten the life out of people. *It will scare the pants off you,* screamed their posters. The studio lifted the phrase from a column by Hedda Hopper, one of Hollywood's best-known journalists. They even tried—unsuccessfully—to have the City of Los Angeles turn on the air-raid sirens before the premiere.

◉ ◉ ◉

Years later, after A-bombs had been upgraded to H-bombs, after the Cold War passed and so did my father, I saw *Invasion USA.* Its plot was simple: the Russians win their war against the United States, but the moment they do, the war turns out to be a dream, make-believe. The movie is full of stock World War II footage and miniature sets that blow up. Safe at home, surrounded by friends with whom I'd spent a good day in the sun, I chuckled at the actors who portrayed the Russians as ugly uniformed thugs spouting propaganda with overheated Slavic accents. "The People's Government of America vill take the vealth from the greedy, the speculator, and the capitalistic bourgeoisie." The campy script also gave my father come-on lines such as, "The last time I met a girl I liked, they bombed Pearl Harbor." Then my grin evaporated. I may have been in my fifties, but I relived the role of a confused little boy when Dad broadcast the bulletin that I believed: "There have been official reports of three A-bomb drops . . ."

I wish my father had told me what this movie was all about when I was five. Maybe then we could have pretended together. While Valory and I built ersatz towns, my father reported that cities had been leveled. Indeed, both our worlds were make-believe, mine in pictures taken with my Brownie and his in theaters.

⊙ ⊙ ⊙

In the spring of 1954, I ended up watching parts of the Army-McCarthy hearings but had no idea that I was doing so.

"Sorry Tony," my grandmother said sadly—my grandmother who always did my bidding—"I can't play with you because we're going to watch the morning session."

"We're busy now, Tony," my father said sternly. "We're watching the afternoon session."

Until boredom set in and I walked away, I sat with my parents and my grandmother in the living room watching black and white images of a room full of men in suits droning on about what, I had no idea. The proceedings wouldn't become riveting until the eighth grade and beyond.

⊙ ⊙ ⊙

Maybe my father's patriotic role in *Invasion USA* helped insulate him from being hauled before the House Unamerican Activities Committee. Would he have obeyed an order to name names? Based on the courage he displayed on the screen, I'd say no. But that's the wishful thinking of a son who at five, perceived nothing short of perfection in his father.

I know at least one classmate whose father found himself ensnared by the House Unamerican Activities Committee. At first he tried to evade them, but ultimately cooperated in order to avoid a contempt citation and continue feeding his family. He wept the day he explained his choice to his daughter. She held back tears the day she described the ordeal to me. Many think he provided names, but the story he told his daughter differs. He said they put him in a hotel room, presented him with a ready-made list of names, and asked him to corroborate them. He did. Would my father have given up his friends in order to save his career? The answer doesn't matter; as far as I know, he had no names to name.

CHAPTER FIVE

Half Pint Panel

M y father's phone call surprised me, coming as it did moments after I'd arrived home from my first-grade class. "How would you like to go on television?" he asked. Al Gannaway, a family friend, wanted me on *Half Pint Panel*, a children's talk show he was producing in Los Angeles.

I shouted back an eager "Yes!"

A couple of days later, I settled into my father's Ford for our drive to the studio. He asked if I was enjoying the first grade.

I told the truth. Yes.

"Are you in 1A or 1B?"

"B-1," I said. B-1 was the right term for the first semester of a grade. I felt a little surprised at the question. My father lived with me; he should have known the proper label.

My father kept saying how much *fun* he had at studios and how much *fun* I was going to have on *Half Pint Panel*. I'm sure I nodded along, eager to see the universe that lay on the other side of our Philco TV, the place where my father traveled to "go make a buck."

When we reached the ABC Television Studios on Vine Street, just south of Hollywood Boulevard, I felt the change from reality to a controlled environment where fantasies, like those my father acted in, existed. The sleek building suggested something whimsical waited inside. Atop, next to a neon sign that read *American Broadcasting Company*, was a replica of a microphone, rectangular with a bulge in the middle. On the ground floor, the studio shared space with a camera shop and with Sy Devore, a clothing store frequented, I'd learn later, by television and movie personalities.

A sense of excitement swirled as an assistant led me to a back room. In front of a mirror framed by lights, a woman applied makeup to my face. The brown sponge she used produced a cool, moist sensation, pleasant; and it remained pleasant even as the mixture caked and dried and made moving my cheeks a challenge. Someone combed my hair. Someone else dabbed on more stuff. On occasion, my father talked of being *in makeup*, and now I knew how long *makeup* lasted. Too long.

They said I was ready, finally. A lady led me to the sound stage.

The sound stage was a cavernous place, dark except for a small area where lights glared and baked us in heat. They shone in from all directions, from walls and trusses suspended across the ceiling. This lit area constituted the set, a warm spot in the middle of a space so dark I could barely see the rows of empty seats where the audience would sit.

I must have been the last to get out of makeup. Seated on folding chairs, their faces glistening, my seven copanelists, who all seemed near my age, wore little dark suits or little white dresses selected by parents who, like mine, knew that solid colors looked good on the black-and-white screen. Some must have been child actors. They looked so calm. A few stood up and started to explore, like puppies learning their way around a new home. I joined them. We behaved politely to everyone who approached us, be it to point out something interesting or warn us away from a thicket of cords.

A San Bernardino newspaper, which I'd eventually read, described Al Gannaway as a "relaxed young man," and he was. I sensed an immediate connection with him. No stranger to the camera, Al would go on to produce the successful TV series, *Stars of the Grand Ole Opry*. He also was a songwriter who'd written music for, among others, Nat King Cole, Frankie Lane, and Bob Hope.

Al signaled us to gather near *the box*, where we'd sit during the show, chairs and tabletops bearing our first names. Thanks to the sound stage's immense size, the box resembled a piece of dollhouse furniture. But the cameras didn't look like toys. They were silent creatures that glided on dollies. Their lenses resembled snouts with a cyclops eye that turned red whenever they took a test shot. From their rear hung a thick black cord that piled in a loop on the floor and connected to a box containing a miniature screen and a slug of dials. Fascinated, I stared at these contraptions until Al asked us to quiet down.

"This is not like a test in school," Al said.

He'd introduce each of us to the audience, then ask where we went to school, if we had brothers and sisters, and "what you want to be when you grow up?"—questions whose purpose was to encourage us to talk.

The group listened without saying a word. My Sherman Oaks School classmates weren't like them. If these kids were nervous, it didn't show, and amazingly, I wasn't jumpy either, even when Al reminded us that "we're going on live," like much of television in the early 1950s. Maybe my father's cool style was rubbing off on me.

While the audience trickled to their seats, Al gave each of us souvenirs—circular tin badges imprinted with the name of the show and its logo: a drawing of a boy with tousled hair, freckles, and an overgrown smile. Then, before sending us into the box, he gave us his one rule: take off your shoes. Why he said that I don't know.

"Have fun," Al said. "Talk to each other. Jump in whenever you have something to say."

Taking my place to Al's left, between two other panelists, I leaned forward, hands on the table, unlike the good-looking children on both sides of me. They sat upright, hands folded in their laps, their perfect faces calm and beatific as they waited. On came the lights, so strong they made the kids next to me look as if they glowed. The temperature in the studio soared, but that didn't faze me or any of us. After the announcement— "*Live* from Hollywood, it's *Half Pint Panel*"— I tossed my head and smiled through the jingle. *It's Half Pint Panel time, panel time, panel time* went the theme, one of those tunes that plunge deep into the brain, there to remain forever.

"Here's your first question," Al said. Then he asked something along the lines of, "It's Saturday morning. Your mom has three dollars for you and your older sister, but your mom has to leave right away and can't make any change. She won't be home until tonight. Who should get most of the money?"

As I started to consider the problem, another panelist leaned into the microphone, opened his eyes as wide as they would go, and said the sister should get most of the money because she's older. He sounded adult despite his falsetto voice, and under the lights, his hair glistened.

It made sense to me. Even though Al said we shouldn't be afraid to disagree with each other, I couldn't think of a reason to do so, so I remained silent.

Al called on me. "What do you think, Tony?"

"Maybe next time," I said, "Mommy will give most of the money to the boy." Nobody laughed at me, and Al said that both of us had come up with solutions that were fair.

Another question, another problem to solve. I knew an audience was out there, among them, my parents, but the lights made them invisible. It didn't matter. I was enjoying the banter.

Several times, Al paused to talk one-on-one with us. The reporter for the San Bernardino newspaper described most of what I had to say:

"The son of Gerald Mohr (radio's tough private eye, Mike Malloy) blurted out his father's unlisted telephone number in the interest of promoting the sale of his guppies and later on in the evening said that between pictures his father could make lots of money selling parakeets at six dollars apiece."

The reporter, however, missed the final exchange:

"Tony, what do you want to be when you grow up?"

I said I wanted to be a gardener.

"And why do you want to be a gardener?"

From the first or second row, my father's voice bellowed out, "No!"

For a microsecond, Al looked startled, but he was too much of a pro to remain flustered. "Ah, well, that's nice, Tony, thank you. And now, hi, Judy, where do you . . ."

Who knows what my mother and father and I talked about on the way home besides how much fun I'd had. But I do know we didn't talk about planting seeds in vaginas.

⊙ ⊙ ⊙

Half Pint Panel aired on a Sunday. The next day, the bungalow where my first-grade class met became a riot of shrieks the moment I walked in. My classmates had seen *Half Pint Panel*, and now they swarmed. Some of the girls tugged at my shirt. Before I could say anything, Mrs. Christian called the class to order.

She wanted to know why I hadn't told the class that I'd be on television. After all, *sharing* was one of her favorite class activities.

I don't remember what I said beyond babbling something incoherent.

Mrs. Christian turned to the class and asked, "How many of you saw Tony on television last night?"

Almost thirty hands shot up, shocking to me. Before my father told me about the show, I'd never heard of *Half Pint Panel*.

Mrs. Christian turned to me. Behind her, on the green chalkboard, she'd written the words *father, mother, brother, sister*. "Promise," she said gently, "that you'll tell us the next time you're going on television."

Every head in the room nodded. "Yes, Tony," one of the girls said. "Promise us."

A redheaded boy with freckles piled on. "Yeah, Tony. We wanna know."

Then the whole class chimed in.

I didn't know how to react to Mrs. Christian's thirty little sunrays focused on me, but since I didn't expect to appear on television again, I promised.

I exhaled as we returned to our routine—the Pledge of Allegiance followed by our reading lesson—*Fun with Dick and Jane.*

⊙ ⊙ ⊙

That week, just because I felt like it, I drew the television camera from *Half Pint Panel*, a crude pencil sketch, inaccurate but laden with details. What arose from memory consisted of dials and switches and lenses and cords until the device looked more intricate than I'm sure it was. After dinner, I showed it to my parents.

"May I borrow this?" my father asked.

Of course. He put it on a shelf and returned to what he was saying about how Adlai Stevenson could help the country and "Tricky Dick" couldn't.

"I showed your drawing to Al," my father said a day or two later. "He wants you back on the show." Not to be a panelist again, but to talk about the drawing.

I was ecstatic at the chance to see a television camera again. To this day I don't understand why Al found my mediocre sketch worthy of TV time. Was he doing my father a favor? Did he honestly think his viewers would care? Whatever his motive, the return excited me except for one aspect: the promise to notify my class if I reappeared on television.

I had no choice. The next day, after walking from the playground up the steps to enter the single-story orange-brown bungalow that served as our classroom, I forced myself to keep my word. While my classmates giggled and fidgeted, waiting for the bell to ring, I approached Mrs. Christian at her desk. She was a large grandmotherly type with wide facial features and a friendly nature.

"Mrs. Christian," I stammered, "I'm going to be on that half pint show again—"

Instantly, Mrs. Christian clapped her hands. "Class," she said, "Tony's going back on television."

All eyes on me again, eyes that saw me in a new light. Our best kickball and tetherball players came up and shook my hand. Then there was Lindsey, with ice-blue eyes and blond hair in a ponytail, stunning even at age six and probably knew it already. Her sole comment to me before this moment had been, "You're scrrreeewy," uttered as she pointed her index finger at her ear and traced a circle. What prompted her remark, I have no idea. Had I botched an attempt to flirt with her? Or tossed an eraser at her? Or snubbed her because I liked her? Who knows anymore? All I know is that this particular morning, Lindsey beamed and said I was "neat-o." I'm not sure I knew the word *popular* yet, but that morning, I discovered what popularity felt like—warm, bracing, empowering. I'd become special, an object to admire, like my father.

During almost all of the second broadcast, I sat away from everyone, far from the lights and the cameras while Al Gannaway led his new group through their exchange. Next to me, mounted on an easel, was a giant blowup of my drawing, which I had trouble seeing in the dark. Then, near the end of the show, my area of the soundstage lit up, and a beast of a camera—a real camera—rolled toward me. My drawing looked nothing like it.

Al told the audience why I was back. He called my work "imaginative" and "creative," then asked me to explain the knobs and dials I'd included on my contraption.

I can't remember my explanation other than, full of enthusiasm, I pointed to a circle and said, "This knob does___," then to a button and said, "This does____," and so on. I'm sure I mislabeled every grip and dial. I called one part of the camera "the sound barrier," but instead of laughter, my half-pint lecture generated applause from the audience, plaudits from Al, and more superlatives from Mrs. Christian and my classmates the following morning.

"You were great," said Beverly, the tanned daughter of George Fenneman who, like my father, worked in radio and television. Beverly's father acted as Groucho Marx's sidekick on *You Bet Your Life.*

"Here he is," he'd announce, "the one, the *only* . . ." and then the audience would holler, "GROUCHO." Anyone who watched *Dragnet* also heard his voice, for George Fenneman was the person who said, "Only the names have been changed to protect the innocent." Beverly's brother would coproduce the late 1970s nighttime TV soap opera *Dallas.*

As I looked at her and the rest of the class—our two kickball stars, the class brain, the budding bodybuilder who'd brought a Charles Atlas pamphlet to show-and-tell and who'd learned to play the accordion, all of them fawning and fussing—it dawned on me: my first-grade class may not have known whether what I said was true, but saying it on television made it true. Had I given the same disquisition, word for word, in the classroom, they would have realized it made no sense and laughed. But now my currency soared, and even miserable performances in kickball and tetherball failed to mar my standing—all because of the power of television.

I made no new friends on *Half-Pint Panel*. What six-year-old would have viewed that show as a networking opportunity? I can't blame myself for failing to collect names and phone numbers, but now I wish I'd connected with some members of, in the words of that San Bernardino newspaper, this "group of intelligent moppets" whom Al Gannaway had collected and aired "across the board" on KTLA.

Who were these kids? I'm sure a few were the offspring of Gannaway's friends. Others, I'm certain now, belonged to stage mothers and fathers, eager to shoehorn their darlings into show business. Thanks to Google, I know one of them was Charles Herbert, among the most sought-after child actors of his time, "a storybook character come to life," as one reviewer described him. In a period of six years, he'd appear in twenty Hollywood features, including *The Fly* and *Please Don't Eat the Daisies.* He starred in *Houseboat* with Cary Grant and Sophia Loren. Charles was born in 1948, almost a year and a half after me, yet his Wikipedia page claims he appeared on *Half Pint Panel* in 1952, the same year I did. He almost matched the face on the tin badge Al Gannaway gave to me. There are two chances in forty-five that we appeared on the same show, because according to *Billboard*, forty-five is the number of episodes the station ordered.

Maybe failing to bond with my copanelists was fortunate. "Hollywood Eats Its Children," read the title of an interview with Charles Herbert. Like so many child actors, he failed to transition into adult roles. One person wrote that "he felt secure and confident when the cameras rolled, but like many child actors, he faced difficulties adjusting to the real world beyond the controlled environment inside the studio walls." In other words, the Hollywood-created fantasy that Charles Herbert radiated on the screen became his reality, safe and full of laurels, while reality turned into a scary place. The fantasy, intended by its creators to manipulate the viewers' emotions and, by the way, make a profit, manipulated Charles as well.

Charles Herbert crashed. By 1969 he was through with Hollywood, or stated more accurately, Hollywood was through with him. Since he had no other training and since his parents had mismanaged his money, Charles started doing drugs and rambling through life to nowhere. It took forty years before he became clean and sober, an achievement that must have made him proud. He died in 2015, shortly before his sixty-seventh birthday.

CHAPTER SIX

My Father Died Fifty Times

My father died of a gunshot wound when I was five. I saw him scream and clutch his chest and crumple to the ground. I couldn't help him, couldn't even kiss him good-bye. I just had to watch his six-foot, two-inch body bite the dust.

Everyone else cheered. Their applause soared and banged and didn't subside until all my father's friends had been led away in handcuffs and the pretty girl asked Audie Murphy for his real name, because "I can't go through life being Mrs. Silver Kid."

Then the lights came on in the giant La Reina Theater on Ventura Boulevard in Sherman Oaks, with its slightly musty smell. A thick red curtain slid down in front of the screen, and everyone looked happy. But I couldn't stop crying, even after Mom picked me up and told me Daddy was still alive and waiting for us back home.

My father died some fifty times before dying for real. He started his acting career as a minor gangster in a play called *The Petrified Forest*. He was a villain in his first starring film role in Hollywood, in the campy *Jungle Girl* (1941). But *Duel at Silver Creek* (1952) was the first time I saw him die.

My father played the leader of a gang of claim jumpers who forced victims to sign over their mining rights before killing them.

He was so wicked that he shot a woman at point-blank range, killing her without a trace of emotion on his rugged face.

Marshal Lightning Tyrone chased my father on horseback, but Dad made his horse run faster. (Dad loved horses; no stunt man needed to do his chase scenes.) He galloped down a road to a hiding place among rocks that looked vaguely familiar.

The law won. Even though Lightning's trigger finger didn't work right, and he was oozing blood from a wound, he tricked my father into the open and shot him.

Mom insisted that those cheering girls and boys idolized my father, but I didn't believe it. Really, she said, they love him because he's such a good bad guy. That's why they yelled and clapped when the sheriff got him.

I couldn't understand, so my mother tried again. "You know Jerry Lewis; he and Daddy are making a movie together." (They were—the slapstick *Money from Home*—Dad played a villain in that one too.) She said that Jerry Lewis had a son who became upset because everyone laughed at his father. His parents had to explain that the audience was laughing *with* Jerry Lewis, not *at* him.

⊙ ⊙ ⊙

Early one morning a week or two later, Dad drove me north to Vasquez Rocks. The moment we arrived, I knew why the location looked familiar. This was the place where Lightning Tyrone had shot my father.

Dad and I walked along the dusty road where the chase had been filmed. It ran between outcrops of sandstone slabs, layer upon layer, at an angle gentle enough for us to climb with ease, until we were over a hundred feet above the road, higher than where Lightning had stood when he pulled the trigger.

Dad did not talk about the movie, and I didn't want him to. I was just happy to be with him. Outings like this were rare during the first nine years of my life. When he wasn't working, Dad seemed busy with other things, exactly what I didn't know. Most of our father/son time lay in the future, after his divorce from my mother—it was only then that my father consciously decided to become my *pal*.

He led me along the ledge to a place that had not appeared in the movie. An overhanging rock created a perfect hiding space with a commanding view of the road. We heard voices below, a group at a picnic table.

The rocks got their name from an outlaw, my father said. It was a new word for me. "It means a criminal," he said, "someone outside the law who should be in jail." Tiburcio Vasquez was his name. A posse had lost him among these rocks because Vasquez knew where to take cover.

"Right here," Dad said in his baritone voice. "And his horse was right behind him!" Tiburcio Vasquez and his horse silently waited out the sheriff's men.

My father brushed some dust off his brown jumpsuit. I probably did the same with my overalls. We lingered on this perch until the high desert air made us thirsty.

We headed down the hill and across the road to my father's Ford, then drove to a nearby restaurant—I think the phrase "ranch house" was in its name—and ate a breakfast of steak and pancakes, chased with orange juice for me and coffee for him. Everyone knew my father there, and they must have liked him, because the pancakes and coffee kept coming.

Who wouldn't have liked him that day, with his sunburst smile? He said "ah" when he sniffed the piping hot coffee and a more lingering "aaah" after his first sip. He acted so—good. Yet Dad had fought, or would go on to fight, Bat Masterson, Roy Rogers, and the Rifleman, and he would lose every time, not just to these heroes, but to many others as well. He never triumphed, and it wasn't just physical. He couldn't fool Perry Mason either. It was a wonder no one ever teased me about this. Maybe my classmates grasped the difference between celluloid and the real world long before I did.

⊙ ⊙ ⊙

I wished that his shows could have ended with my father befriending the heroes, and that finally happened when I was ten. Dad played Doc Holliday, a dying gambler and quasi-outlaw, on *Maverick*. But the camaraderie between him and James Garner failed to comfort me. I knew Dad did not have tuberculosis, as Doc Holliday did, because he never coughed at home the way he did on television. But to watch Holliday try to get himself killed—"When I drop my handkerchief, you go for your gun"—wrenched my gut.

Then it dawned on me: my father might be having fun playing the heavy. It gave him a license to disobey, to break the rules. So in junior high, I started auditioning for the antagonist in school plays, but no one picked me for those roles. Our eighth-grade musical was *The Hither and Thither of Danny Dither*, a Depression-era show whose antagonist was Lucifer, the devil. The student body vice president got the part and played it perfectly; they cast me as one of his victims. I auditioned for Ebenezer Scrooge in *A Christmas Carol*, and they offered me Bob Cratchit. It wasn't right. I knew I could portray a nasty Scrooge but was totally unable to act like his shrinking clerk. Worse yet, how could I handle the loss of Tiny Tim?

It took a whole afternoon, but Dad, a man whose movie deaths delighted thousands, taught me how to be the good guy. Sitting in my grandmother's bedroom, we went through the script line by line until I caught his tones.

"Be extra timid when you ask Scrooge for Christmas Day off," Dad said.

I tried again: "Well, sir, tomorrow's Christmas and—"

Dad stopped me. "You're saying it too fast."

"Well." Pause. "Sir."

"That's it," he said. "Now lower your head and round your shoulders."

"Well." Pause. "Sir. Tomorrow's Christmas and—"

"Read it again."

I did, until I became the shy little clerk begging Mr. Scrooge to let me spend Christmas with my family.

Next, as the setting December sun slanted through Grandma's venetian blinds, we attacked Tiny Tim's death, and the claim jumper who had calmly murdered a woman taught me how to mourn.

"Tiny Tim was your son," my father said. "You're devastated beyond words. Now say it quietly this time: 'My little Tim. My little Tim.'" Dad spoke the lines faster than I had, and he whispered them with bowed head, the second "my little Tim" softer than the first and the final "Tim" barely audible.

I never could copy the grief that he put on his face, but I mimicked the pitch. No one giggled the night of the performance, and my father said he was proud of me.

In high school I stopped trying out for baddie parts or, for that matter, any parts at all. By then I'd realized I was not much of an actor. Whatever theatrical ability I might have possessed was channeled into forensics and debate and, years later, into the courtroom. The divide between fact and fantasy became well established in my mind, and I had made peace with having a bad guy for a father. Or so I thought.

"I got a new part," my father told me one Sunday morning during my junior year of high school.

"Do you play the villain again?" I asked between bites of my scrambled eggs.

"Yep."

"Do you die in this one, too?"

He grinned and lifted one eyebrow, an endearing trait. "Yeah, but it's a really good death."

CHAPTER SEVEN

The Boy in the Park

Forty years before I became a judge, I told my father I wanted to be a spy.

It was an afternoon in 1954. We were sitting in my father's favorite armchair. Flames crackled in the fireplace against the far wall. A winter rain pounded on the pitched roof above the exposed beams. My father wore a jumpsuit, popular attire for actors back then. On his little finger was a black stone in a gold band he called his *pinkie ring.* The smell of his aftershave lotion blended with the smoke that curled away from his cigarette. A script he'd been reading lay on the side table, next to an ashtray.

"I want to spy on the Russians," I said.

My father said, "They'll kill you."

Was my father thinking about a role he'd played on the radio or in some movie?

I said, "Won't America rescue me?"

My father shook his head. His lanky frame remained still in the high-back while I fidgeted. "We'll say we've never heard of you." My father spoke in his Philip Marlowe tone of voice—neutral, impassive, as though I were a stranger.

His attitude made me wonder whom I could trust, but I said nothing more than "Why?"

"Because that's how it works. If we catch one of theirs, the

Russians say they've never heard of him. We do the same thing."
With that he stubbed out his cigarette and lit another.

"It's not fair," I said.

My father said, "That's the way it goes," one of his trademark
lines, often a way of ending a conversation, which I think he
wanted to do, because he stole a glance at his script.

He must have felt that spying would be suicidal for someone
so opposite to his traits. Maybe my father knew me better than I
thought.

◉ ◉ ◉

My father longed for an edgy life overseas, if not the real thing,
then at least to play the international man of mystery. He got his
wish in 1954, when I was seven. A Swedish production company
offered him the lead in the third season of *Foreign Intrigue,* a
television series set in Vienna during the early 1950s, when
Austria's capital brimmed with espionage. The victorious World
War II powers—Britain, France, the United States, and the Soviet
Union—had split Vienna into four sectors, the same way they'd
chopped up Berlin. They wouldn't leave until 1955. My father's
character, Christopher Storm, owned the Frontier Hotel, a place
where gangsters and spies from both sides of the Iron Curtain
frequently checked in. My father seized what he called "my big
break." To do so, he turned down the lead in *The Life and Legend
of Wyatt Earp,* a decision I didn't learn about until I'd turned fifty.
Hugh O'Brian became Wyatt Earp.

Thanks to budgets and politics, the producer filmed *Foreign
Intrigue* in Sweden, where Stockholm stood in for Vienna. We
spent a year living in a suburb of Stockholm, where I attended a
school—Nockebyhovsskolan—and they taught in Swedish.

One fall afternoon—darkness came in earlier than I'd

experienced in California, and there was a touch of snow on the ground—several of us were playing in a nearby park. Deep among the birch trees lived a boy named Tommy, a husky kid with the face of a pugilist and fists to match. Without warning, Tommy showed up, punched me hard, stepped back, and waited for me to do something.

I did something. I ran home. My father was there—filming must have ended early that day—and the moment I told him why I was crying, he took hold of my soft upper arm.

"You have to fight him," he said.

I cringed. In her Hollywood mogul letter, Redoff's publicist had written that I "can lick any kid on the block in any department"—no way. If anything, I ran from fights.

I'm not sure where my father had perfected his command voice—playing Philip Marlowe on the radio, playing the rogues on Westerns, playing gangsters in noir crime movies. But when he used it, I knew arguing was a waste of time. My father marched me back to the park.

The group, who hadn't left, stared at my father and me, expressions neutral except for Tommy's, who, despite my father's presence, looked eager to fight. My father gave me a little push in Tommy's direction. Then without a word, he stepped away, toward the trees.

Who punched first, I don't know. I know that Tommy swung, and so did I. His blows hurt, stabs of pain across my upper body and against my head. I'm sure I struck back and hit him somewhere. At one point we clutched each other, and I recall the rough feel of his shaved blond head that I tried to scratch as we struggled and grunted and spun in a grip that I thought would go on through the night.

It didn't. After I managed a sock that made Tommy stagger backward, he ran to the side of the clearing and crouched down to grab a handful of rocks.

Up to that point, the other boys hadn't cheered or catcalled. Now they chorused as one. "Tommy, *ingen stenar*." Tommy obeyed them and dropped the stones. Then as now, Sweden played by the rules.

Tommy glared at me. His mouth became a slit. I looked for my father, but he'd disappeared among the birch trees.

The fight continued, for hours it seemed, but probably not for more than another minute before the rest of the boys stopped it. Once they did, my father emerged from the woods and took Tommy's hand in one of his and mine in the other. Then he raised our arms and said, "Bra Tony. Bra Tommy." My father was right: good for both of us. Better yet, my father said my name before he said Tommy's.

Bra Tony. Bra Tommy. The compliment didn't stop me from crying once I got home. I cried from relief. I'd been scared but I survived. I cried because I ached all over, and I cried because someday somewhere, I might have to face another bully.

My father didn't leave my side. "Cry it out, Tony," he said. "You'll feel better."

My father delivered those words in perfect pitch, laden with compassion. I don't recall him holding me in his arms, but I felt as though he was, rocking me to sleep during the fifteen—or was it thirty?—minutes that I continued to cry. He waited a beat and said it again. "Cry it out, Tony. You'll feel better." It was as if he'd rehearsed these lines, then held them in reserve for the right moment.

It turns out, he had rehearsed them. I learned this half a century later, when for the first time I saw a movie he'd made in 1952. *The Ring* starred my father as a boxing manager who, while driving down a street, sees a young Mexican boy beating up two men because they'd discriminated against him. With the police blowing their whistles and running toward the boy, my father yells for him to get in the car. He does so, and my father speeds away. Then, safe from the racists, my father parks and introduces himself. Still shaking from the incident, the boy gives his name—ironically, it's Tommy—before he breaks down in tears.

"Cry it out, Tommy," my father says. "You'll feel better."

I may have been an adult, but the moment I learned the source of my father's words, I felt it odd that to comfort me, he'd recited a line from a script. Was that deliberate? Did he even realize what he'd done? Was it okay to use a phrase that wasn't your own in order to show you cared?

Tommy—the Tommy in the movie—knew how to fight. My father took him on. Tommy Kansas became his moniker in the ring. He boxed professionally, at least for a while, before maturing into what the storyline promised would be a fulfilling life—unlike my Tommy. I was told that as an adult, he committed suicide.

While my father calmed me, was he thinking of me, or was he thinking about fiction, the Tommy Kansas who'd fought to prove himself to White people and gain the type of respect my father had ordered me to earn that day in the park? Maybe both.

My fight didn't become a dinner topic. *Foreign Intrigue* did. My father described an incident about the day's shooting, funny enough to make him laugh and to make me ask the question I'd been thinking about for several weeks: could I have a part in his series?

"Let's see if we can have you walk through a scene," my father said. A walk-through meant that I'd remain in the background, saying nothing, but the prospect was exciting enough to make me forget that someone had socked me.

The scene took place in a square somewhere in downtown Stockholm, a cobblestone space surrounded by four-and five-story buildings with pitched roofs and colors ranging from red to yellow to brown. It was noon and sunny. The director gestured at

ANTHONY J. MOHR

a stone drinking fountain in the center of the square, near a series
of long, wooden benches.

"Go over there. Start drinking and keep drinking," he said.

The moment a voice called for "Lights. Camera. Action!" I felt
as though everyone was staring at me, which made me nervous.
I drank and drank and drank the cold water and kept going even
after someone said, "Cut!" I slurped to the point that my father
and the director said I looked as though I'd been washing my face.

Later we gathered in the studio's theater to see the rushes. That's
when I realized that the camera had been focused on a menacing
thug who'd been sitting on the bench. In the background, I was
barely visible. Even I, caught up in the story, ignored myself and
concentrated on the goon. He was supposed to be a communist
infiltrator. He had a flattened face with dead eyes, ready to throw
a punch, or to kill. He resembled an adult version of Tommy.

The scene worked. In other words, I didn't do anything to ruin
it. Maybe that's why within a week, they wrote me into another
episode, this time with lines. Its official plot summary read as
follows: *While resting in a Viennese park, a cryptographer finally
breaks a difficult code but mistakenly uses a small paper plane he
finds on the ground for his calculations. Then he suffers a heart
attack, and the paper plane falls to the ground, to be picked up by
a small boy playing in the park. Oblivious to the state secrets on the
paper, the boy takes it home. Christopher Storm is sent to retrieve
it.*

I wouldn't play the boy who took the formula home. That part
went to a Swedish actor my age, Bo Hannergren. I played one of
his friends whom my father would ask for help.

A studio assistant drove us to a nearby park, where they
inserted me near Bo and several other boys. Someone called,
"Action!" but when my father walked up to us, Eugene Lourie, the
director, yelled, "Cut!"

"Tony," my father said, "don't smile at me. You don't know me." He said it in the same time-to-grow-up tone of voice he'd used to tell me to fight Tommy. But today I felt happy and expansive and put out my hands.

"Ridiculous," I said. I'd heard my parents use that word over dinner. "You're my *father*."

The director was not amused. He frowned and said, "Act like you've never heard of him."

It took all day, but take by take, I turned my father into a stranger. I didn't grin. I didn't cock my head. I didn't extend my arms. I delivered my lines in a voice as polite and neutral as Cold War Sweden. By then it was about three thirty, and we'd lost the light. I'd have to return tomorrow.

No one told me to wear the same clothes I'd had on the day before, and that included my father, who didn't react to the gaffe. Was he so ensconced in his own life that he didn't realize the embarrassment of arriving the next morning and listening to a man scold me in his Swedish accent, "You came to your job in different clothes? That is not good." Now for continuity, they would have to reshoot the first scene.

I muddled through the day, and when we finished, a husky woman named Mai Britt Dietrich introduced herself, said she was the "script girl," and complimented me on a good job. For some reason, her remark made me nervous, a sensation that worsened when she said she had two sons, Tommy and Timmy, who were three and one. "Come to dinner so you can meet them."

Next, my father taught me how to ask for my pay in Swedish. At the bursar's office, a tall woman smiled and handed over what seemed like an astronomical amount of money for my work. I stuffed the Swedish krona and öre into my overcoat and sauntered back to my father, feeling rich, but not eager to act again. Mai Britt was standing next to him and praised me again. Now I grew even

ANTHONY J. MOHR

more nervous. There was something about the way she looked at my father.

She popped into my world with increasing frequency, visiting our house often as the weeks rolled on. At Christmas, she handed me a present, an illustrated book, written in Swedish, titled *Peter is a Babysitter.*

"Look," my mother said. "She's translated the entire book."

Mai had penciled the English text above every line.

"How lovely," my mother said as I thumbed through the pages. She sounded grateful to Mai, which puzzled me. I was too young to frame the words, to search for the real reason Mai had taken so much time to translate, in elegant printing, a forty-one-page children's book.

⊙ ⊙ ⊙

They titled my episode "The Boy in the Park," but in the version that aired on television, my voice was missing. A narrator led the audience through my scenes. They changed the sound track to preserve the European atmosphere, my father explained, because I was the one boy in the park who spoke English without an accent. I still wonder if that was the real reason. Had I sounded so unconvincing that there had been no choice? No one ever said, but then nobody, including my father, suggested I return for another episode. Whatever the truth, the loss of my lines didn't upset me. Just watching myself on the screen, wearing my heavy gray coat, cavorting with the other boys, my hair a mess, conveyed enough satisfaction—*lagom* as they say in Swedish. Thinking about it now, my father let me flop. He didn't encourage me to act. He didn't warn me against it.

Shortly before *Foreign Intrigue* wrapped, Mai said to me, in her singsong Swedish accent, "I loved you from the first moment I saw you in Sweden." The morning my father, mother, grandmother, and I piled into Dad's jaguar and left Sweden for a road trip through Western Europe and then home, I whispered to my grandmother, next to me in the back seat, that I was glad I wouldn't see Mai again. My Grandmother hugged me.

⊙ ⊙ ⊙

After we returned to the San Fernando Valley, my father's career drifted downward, from leads to feature appearances, mostly on Westerns. He longed for another series, but none materialized. Despite an Emmy nomination, *Foreign Intrigue* lasted only another year. *Wyatt Earp* would run six years, from 1955 until 1961. "Big break" indeed.

CHAPTER EIGHT

Mohr v. Mohr

During the winter of 1956, my father flew to Sweden to film another pilot. When he returned, my mother took my grandmother and me to the airport to greet him.

After the propellers stopped, my father appeared at the top of the stairs. Under his arm was a film container.

A moment later, Mai, the "script girl" I'd met on the set of *Foreign Intrigue*, emerged, beaming. If my mother or grandmother flinched, I didn't notice.

I was too surprised to think as she preceded my father down to the tarmac and embraced me. I must have offered Mai a perfunctory hug back despite my shock that she had reappeared in my world. Call it intuition, but I felt as uncomfortable as I had the day we met.

My confusion intensified when my father tapped the container he was holding, looked at Mai, and said, "Here's our baby." He cradled the metal as though it were indeed an infant.

Later, at baggage claim, my father signaled Mai, pointed to the container, and said it again. "Hey, Mai. Our baby."

I let it go, a nine-year-old shaking off another puzzling exchange between adults.

"Our baby" referred to the pilot my father had completed, titled *Rough Sketch*. Its central character was an artist who got himself into some sort of trouble. Mai's first husband was an artist, and while in Sweden, he and my father had become friends.

Once we arrived home, my father set up a screen in the living room, hauled out a projector, and ran the film. It bored me. I couldn't follow the story. I fell asleep.

Rough Sketch never made its way onto a television screen.

⊙ ⊙ ⊙

Late one April day in 1956, while my father was at the studio, my grandmother lay in her room next to her diathermy, and I fiddled with my Lionel electric trains, my mother slipped into my bedroom.

"You know how special your father is," she said without a prelude, eyebrows knitted and a cheerless expression. She didn't look as pretty as usual. She sounded almost as if she were trying to convince herself.

She added a slew of accolades about my father: wonderful man—talented, brilliant. Then, still staring at me, she said, "quite a guy." Her last three words came out slowly.

I didn't understand why she said these things, nor did I know what to say. I nodded and said, "Yeah," and once I did, she walked away, maybe into the kitchen to make dinner.

My mother repeated this litany several times over the next few days, always ending her comments with "quite a guy." Confused, I stuck to my monosyllabic replies.

"Tony," she said a few days later, "when your father comes through the door, run and give him a big hug and kiss." It wasn't a command. It felt like a plea to become exuberant the moment I saw him, the excitement of a puppy that had spent the day alone. My answer remained the same. "Yeah."

When my father rolled up in his Jaguar and closed the garage door, my mother beckoned me to the foyer, her lips pressed together. His footsteps approached the door.

I hugged him, a quick embrace, not what my mother had asked me to do.

My father asked, "How's my boy?"

"Okay," I said, my usual answer.

He turned to my mother and said something about a hard day on the set, and as they talked, I returned to my room.

⊙ ⊙ ⊙

For my ninth birthday, my parents took eight of my friends and me to an afternoon show at the Moulin Rouge, a Hollywood nightclub. Every Sunday they staged a family matinee featuring a kiddy circus complete with balloons, toys, and clowns who sang, danced, and cracked jokes. The *package deal,* they called it, and they charged $5.50 per person.

Along with my mother and father, my guests (seven boys, one girl) and I walked into a room full of rectangular tables, some quite long, with a large stage at the far end. So, this was a nightclub, I thought, a place my parents mentioned often at home, a place that attracted me because of the word *club.*

One of my friends and I started wandering down another aisle.

"Here's our table," my father said, his attitude stern.

We turned back and saw that our table bumped up against the stage.

I have a picture of the party, thanks to a photographer who came to our table. He couldn't pose us, because most of my friends kept talking and fidgeting in their seats. Most, but not all. The one girl I'd invited, my neighbor Peggy, remained still, and so did my parents, especially my father. He knew what the camera wanted from him. Once the club's photographer managed to get our group as still as he was going to, he snapped his photo.

In the black-and-white picture, the boys are dressed in coats and ties, although my knot is crooked. So are my teeth, but I don't seem to mind, because my smile is more expansive than everybody else's save one boy whose name I no longer remember. My left hand rests on the edge of the stage. Across from me sits Peggy, calm, almost serene, dressed in white—a princess cap sleeve, princess neckline, and a headband holding back her black hair. Next to me is Mark, my favorite third-grade classmate, the smartest boy in the class. The photographer may have been a professional, but he couldn't control Mark, who was captured laughing as he looked at something or someone who had diverted his attention from the camera. The grins continued down the line. Robbie's looked beatific. There were David and Rolly and four more, their names lost in time. At the far end of the table, my mother and father struck a placid pose, elegant, with my father in a dark sport coat and my mother with her hair up and wearing a V-neck dress. My mother managed a proper smile, less than joyful, but sufficient to signal satisfaction with the event. A sliver of my father's teeth was visible, but he wasn't grinning. Hands folded on the table, tie tucked into his shirt, he offered the camera the image of an ultra-suave man who may have been present in the scene, but declined to enter into it. Maybe, knowing what I know now, he was thinking of what and who lay in his future.

⊙ ⊙ ⊙

Fall weather arrived sooner than usual. By mid-September, I came down with a cold.

It wasn't serious, nothing more than one of those scratchy throat jobs that make you drag around the house, which is what I did all morning and into the afternoon. Outside, it was gray and cold by Southern California standards. Inside, the place was hushed. I was probably lying in bed reading a selection from the

Freddy the Pig series when one of my parents asked me to come downstairs—which I did, in my pajamas.

They sat in the living room, in the corner farthest from the foyer and farthest from the television set, next to the bay window that looked out on the patio where we barbecued. One parent sat on the couch; the other, in a chair that faced it across the coffee table. I don't remember where I ended up, whether I remained standing, or whether I sat.

To hear my father use my name at the beginning of a sentence unnerved me, but this time he wasn't angry.

"Tony," he said, "sometimes people decide that they shouldn't live with each other any longer. Then they move apart."

I didn't know what he was talking about.

"There are times when married people decide not to live together anymore."

I still didn't understand.

In a neutral tone, my father said that he and my mother would not be living together anymore.

I still didn't comprehend. The discussion—it sounded more like an announcement—was taking place on some higher, abstract plane that had nothing to do with me. I don't remember my mother saying anything, although she must have. Before I'd entered the room, she probably had told my father, "Gerry, you want this. You tell him." And since my father was not skilled at intimate communication, she sat back and listened as he stumbled through his lines.

Yes, I'd still have a father, he said, just as I'd still have a mother, and yes, both parents would still love me.

I'm sure I listened, my throat scratchy, my nose running, but my eyes still dry.

At first, when this little talk was over, it was as though nothing had happened. Outside, the sky remained gray. The house was as silent as it had been several minutes earlier. I returned to my bedroom. To do what, I have no idea. I didn't know what to make of what they had said.

⊙ ⊙ ⊙

In her Hollywood mogul letter, the Redoff publicist wrote that my father's "home life is good enough to put under glass" and labeled my mother "his boyhood sweetheart." No longer. According to court documents, my father moved out on Monday, September 17, 1956, two days after Yom Kippur, the Jewish day of atonement. Although my parents were Jewish by birth, that event meant nothing in our house. I'd never heard of the High Holidays, let alone seen a service. I had never heard of a divorce. Nobody told me where my father went.

My father may have been gone, but his mother remained in the granny flat. Now at every meal, three people filed into the dinette, down from four. At breakfast, my mother put the eggs in front of me, as always, and my grandmother probably said she was going to make a *bundt kuchen* for dessert. When I finished my cornflakes, I went outside to the corner to meet the carpool, and as they approached, I waved my metal lunch box like a semaphore, as always. The pail was pretty to look at, with cartoon characters painted on it and slits in the sides to let in air. At lunch, I peeled back the wax paper to find a peanut butter and jelly sandwich or a tuna fish sandwich or a bologna sandwich or a chicken salad sandwich. As always, my mother had packed the carrots in their own wax paper. The same with an apple or banana. After my meal, I played dodgeball or tetherball or kickball, as always. And when the carpool dropped me off at my front door, I went inside to find my mother and grandmother there, as always.

But now they remained quiet, and when my father failed to come through the door, we slipped into our places on the bench that ran the perimeter of the dinette, and my mother served dinner to my grandmother and me. Though small, the space felt cavernous. I sat farthest from the sliding entry door, against the windows. To my left was my grandmother; on the right, my mother, in a position closest to the door so that she could get up and go to the kitchen. The fourth space was vacant.

During our year in Sweden, I'd started drawing cartoons. Looking at them now, I must have sensed that my parents' marriage was in trouble. Not one scene in them contained a civil discussion between an adult male and female. All my adults yelled at each other ("Now look what you did. You woke up the baby," one hollered in the first panel. "Well, shush it up," the other replied in the next. "YOU shush it up. It's your kid."), and as they did, they breathed fire.

At the table on the patio between our house and the granny flat, I continued drawing cartoons. Thanks to my wretched artistic ability, the characters never graduated beyond stick figures. Peggy helped me. I'd tell her the stories; she'd draw. Her adults resembled real people, and the flames they emitted looked menacing.

One Saturday morning a few weeks after my father left, I woke up and within seconds began to cry. I couldn't stop. I washed. Brushed my teeth. Got dressed. Came downstairs. Ate breakfast. Cleared the table. And never stopped crying.

I cried through Sunday too. At bedtime, I looked at my mother as she tucked me in. Her face was drawn, her mouth narrow. She must have been struggling to maintain her composure.

"Why am I crying?" I asked.

My mother didn't understand, or claimed not to understand, the question in order to buy time.

"Why do I keep crying?"

Now the reason is clear. The house felt incomplete, empty. My father may not have spent much time with me while he lived within its walls, but he'd been there, ensconced in his favorite chair, reading a script or a book with a dull-sounding name (*The Brook Kerith* was the last title I remember), and shooing me away whenever I edged toward him, hoping for attention. "Go amuse yourself," he said more than once.

And even if he ordered me to bed in advance of one of my parents' dinner parties, I didn't realize how jolly my father's industry friends had made the house. Their banter provided wonderful background noise, which in turn made me feel content, even safe, as I lay in bed or sneaked down the stairs to watch them. Now there were no more screenwriters sprawled on the couch, tossing out clever lines. No more actors who swept across the living room, arms extended as they ad-libbed more lines. In his book, a high school colleague, Hawk Koch, who'd become a producer, referred to his trade as "Magic Time." It was. Now I'd been kicked out of that world. No, that's wrong. The magic world had moved away. Ironically, before he left, my father was just beginning to teach me magic tricks.

There were no more jokes. No scripts. No copies of *Variety* among the ashtrays on the coffee table. Gone from the household lexicon were words and phrases I'd grown to like. Such as *stills*, pictures that didn't move. *Chunks*, the portions of a TV show between commercial breaks. *Cuts*, which could be rough or final. *Frames*, which had nothing to do with paintings, and *freeze-frames*, which had nothing to do with freezers. *Lobbies*, which were publicity posters. *Cans*, which were not containers for Campbell's Soup, but rather circular metal containers for reels of film, and when the movie was complete, everyone went somewhere to drink cocktails and smoke cigarettes and congratulate each other because the movie was "in the can."

They called it a wrap party although no one wrapped gifts. You shot with cameras, not guns. You didn't become a pilot. You made a pilot, and it had nothing to do with airplanes. My father worked at a studio, except when he went *on location.* He ran lines, not a company. Someone called an agent figured large in his life, although I never met the man and never quite understood what he did. He'd telephone my father, but not often enough to please my father. The word deal had become as familiar as any word in *Fun With Dick and Jane.* "Make the deal," or "We have a deal," or "The deal's ninety-nine percent done." (If someone said the last phrase, there was no deal.)

Someone removed the caricature of my father that hung at the end of the hall, over the table on which our one telephone sat. Titled *Gerald Mohr—As I See Him*, it had been part of my home since the early to mid-1950s, the years I'd chased the Good Humor truck, ogled a cow brought to my school, yearned to meet the Mouseketeers, heard about the world's first four-level freeway interchange near downtown, pulled my Radio Flyer wagon around the backyard, and learned about "Stalin's A-bombs." The artist who drew that caricature had caught my father, script in hand, during his radio days, a white handkerchief in the pocket of his sports coat, a mischievous grin on his face, his hair combed back, and one eyebrow raised. On the oversized microphone in front of him were the letters CBS, and—hanging over a control booth in the distance—was a sign, lit up, that read, *Silence—on the air.* I'd failed to notice, let alone appreciate, the unique life that had surrounded me. Now it was gone. I lived in nonstop silence, but still failed to link the loss with my tears.

One afternoon, I rummaged through the storage shed in the backyard and found clips. A chirpy squib by Hedda Hopper announcing my birth—"The Gerald Mohrs," she wrote, "(he's the screen's "Lone Wolf") have named their new baby Anthony James." Then, at the bottom of a box, the divorce stories from the trades. Less chatty, more matter-of-fact. Actor Gerald Mohr had separated from his wife, Rita. I fastened on the last sentence: The separation caused great anguish—or was it grief—to "their son, Anthony." How did the writer know that? He hadn't watched me cry. He hadn't visited our hushed dinette night after night. He'd never been to our house. I know now the reporter would have scored a far better story—a scoop I was too young to appreciate at the time—if he'd known that the divorced woman still lived with her ex-husband's mother.

Nobody told me it was inappropriate for my grandmother to remain in the house.

"Let's go outside," she said one Saturday, after I'd cried all morning.

I asked to play checkers. She set up the board on the wooden patio table. I beat her, or perhaps she let me win. We played again, I won again, and broke out crying again. I didn't move from the wooden bench. I remained seated as my body heaved.

My grandmother left her bench, walked around to mine, and hugged me.

"Have I told you that I love you very much?"

I blubbered that she had.

"You are my darling, precious grandson. I will always send you oceans of love with a kiss on every wave."

I kept sobbing.

I saw my father, every second weekend. We'd spend a day together, but never the night. I don't recall what we did together. All I remember is that he said, "I'm still your father." He said it more than once, followed by, "We're pals." I didn't cry when I was with him. I reserved the tears for my mother.

⊙ ⊙ ⊙

My mother and I were driving in her Plymouth to the post office after she'd picked me up from my fourth-grade class. She asked what we were reading in school.

"*Johnny Tremain*," I said. One of the characters was engaged—I didn't know the word for that status—and then the engagement was called off. I didn't know the word for that status either.

"A fiancée," my mother said. "And then she was single," she said.

I nodded and looked out the window, at the one-and two-story buildings and the sidewalks with hardly any people on them. Then I said, "Like you."

"I'm a divorcée."

"A what?" This was another unfamiliar word.

"A divorcée is a woman who was married but isn't anymore."

My mother said it with such a matter-of-fact attitude. I'm sure she was trying to get used to her new identifier by using the word, rolling it over on the tongue, trying to accept it graciously into her life. She seemed to be talking to herself as much as to me.

I didn't say anything more. Now I wonder if anyone my mother knew had ostracized her, worried that a divorcée would threaten their own marriage or burden them with grief.

⊙ ⊙ ⊙

One morning, my mother's face was drooping. Her left eyebrow. The bottom part of her left eyelid. Her cheek on the same side. She didn't say good morning; she shooed me out of her bedroom. My grandmother was running about. The phone started ringing as often as it used to. Moments later, my mother was out of the house—gone.

No one told me what happened. My grandmother said my mother was taking a trip for a couple of days, and that evening she offered to play as many games of checkers as I wanted and then gave me an elephantine lump of *bundt kuchen*. We sat in the dinette, checkerboard between us. I jumped her men and wolfed down her cake.

For several days, my grandmother took care of me. That time is a blur, now. My mother came back, looking as comely as always. She declined to talk about this episode, and I had no reason to ask about it. It would take another three years before I learned that my mother had an attack of Bell's palsy.

But my fleeting image of her condition had burrowed its way into my mind—the frozen brow, eyelid halfway down, half a lip reaching for her chin. The picture became my image of a divorcée. It may have lasted at most a second, but it never went away.

◉ ◉ ◉

I started watching television so often that I learned by heart all the theme songs from *Disneyland, Zorro*, and the *Mickey Mouse Club*. Thanks to Jiminy Cricket's ditty, I'd never forget how to spell *encyclopedia*. I longed to be as attractive and cheerful as the well-adjusted Mouseketeers, wondering at times whether they were the children my father wished he had.

One night in 1956, at the end of the *Mickey Mouse Club*, my mother said dinner was ready. I didn't move. I remained in the high-back chair closest to the TV and watched whatever came on next. Maybe, on a subconscious level, I thought if I stared at our Philco long enough, I'd see my father more often.

My mother let me stay in the chair.

I remained still through the commercials—ads for cigarettes, cars, and candy. All good for you, the spokesmen promised, but the prices of some items were "slightly higher west of the Rockies." I waited until 6:30, when *Engineer Bill* came on the air and played "Red Light Green Light."

"Get a glass of milk," he told his viewers. "Drink when I say, 'Green light.' Stop when I say, 'Red light.'"

I always played.

A few days later, I waded into primetime: *I Married Joan, Cheyenne, The Lone Ranger* (I was surprised to hear my father on that show. He was one of their announcers), *Sergeant Preston of the Yukon, The Dinah Shore Show*. True, I had to sit through fifteen minutes of Douglas Edwards and the News ("Let's Hopscotch the World"), but it was worth it, especially Wednesday nights when *Disneyland* came on (7:30 on Channel 7) and Thursday nights with *Zorro*. Actually, what I watched didn't matter. I needed to see electrons move.

TV dinners entered my life because, I imagine, my mother figured that instead of staring at me in our dinette with nothing to say, I could eat in the high-back while she cried in the bedroom. Maybe my grandmother was doing the same thing in her granny flat, with her diathermy turned up high. Eyes on the screen, I slit the tinfoil cover and pulled it back to reveal my evening meal. Meat loaf tonight, swimming in gravy, with green peas in one of the pockets and mashed potatoes in the other. In the middle, a dollop of apple sauce.

Time for another theme song. *I married Joan. What a girl, what a whirl, what a life.* I dragged my fork across the bottom of the tin plate in order to scoop out the remaining goo. Absorbed in my comfort food, I failed to grasp, at least consciously, the loopy wraparound plot line of several *I Married Joan* episodes in which her husband, a judge, helps a divorcing couple reconcile. *I Married Joan* may have been a sitcom, but it didn't make me laugh. Nor did the episode make me think about becoming a judge when I grew up. I wasn't ready to help anybody, assuming I knew how.

☉ ☉ ☉

The day came that I couldn't wait until 5 p.m. I needed the little screen sooner. At 4:30, on came *Do You Trust Your Wife*, a game show only couples could win, couples who understood each other. In one episode, Jack and Pat, the contestants, took their positions at separate lecterns. Above them hung a banner for the show's sponsor, L&M cigarettes. In a dark suit and narrow tie, Jack could pass for the consummate organization man, tall and thin, speaking in a mousy Midwestern tenor. Proudly, he announced that he sold fiberglass for Owens Corning. Fiberglass, a "thriving new industry," he said, useful in plastics, filtration devices, and now in the home. Owens Corning was going to manufacture fiberglass drapes, women's shoes, and possibly quite soon women's swimsuits. His wife beamed at him. Pat was short and stout, and she couldn't stop talking about Flip, their dog, who loved their children even though he was jealous of them.

The show's host, Edgar Bergen, sent them to separate easels where they couldn't see each other. "Let's see how much you know about your wife, Jack. Write down yes or no. Jack, did your wife fail any subject in high school? Pat, did you fail any subject in high school?" Both wrote "no" on their easels. Their consistent answers earned them a hundred dollars.

To answer the next question, the emcee asked Jack, "Do you trust yourself, or do you trust your wife?"

Jack said he trusted his wife.

"Question: What do the initials TVA stand for?"

Pat cast about for help, but of course Jack couldn't say anything, and finally Pat stammered, "Television—no, Tel Aviv."

"Wrong. It's the Tennessee Valley Authority."

Based on his expression, I'm sure Jack knew the right answer.

Once again, the emcee asked Jack whom he'd trust, himself or his wife, to get the next answer right. This time Jack said he'd trust himself. A gentle laugh rose from the audience. Edgar Bergen asked him for the oldest university in the country. Jack made the right choice—Harvard.

I didn't ask myself, at least consciously, whether my father would have trusted my mother. It was academic now. Neither was eligible to compete, for they were—I sounded out the new word, my voice a whisper—divorcées.

I discovered morning programming, *Captain Kangaroo*, on the air before I left for school. The captain was not dashing like my father. His sidekick Mr. Green Jeans acted foppish. The stories sounded foolish, but that's not why I watched. I'd become the quintessential person for whom the medium was the message. And when I started waking up even earlier, I padded downstairs to gape at the *Morning Farm Report*, on at 5:40 am, with its soothing musical theme and image of a newborn lamb sucking on the nipple of a baby bottle.

The Mickey Mouse Club remained the series that affected me most deeply. I gawped at this ideal ensemble of California boys and girls who were always having fun. Cubby and Karen and Johnny and Sharon and Mike and Nancy and Lonnie and Darlene and Don and Doreen and Bobby and Annette and Cheryl and Jay Jay and Mary. They sang together. They danced together—tap dance, ballet, square dance. They went on hayrides. They watched the circus, bounced on pogo sticks, and rode bicycles, always together. They were delightfully thin and looked so carefree, beaming and exclaiming, "Boy, what fun." They couldn't possibly have divorced parents. They were too happy.

⊙ ⊙ ⊙

My mother told me, "Grandma Henny will be moving away." Another loss; I didn't want her to go. Nor did my grandmother, but at some point, my mother managed to reason with her, to explain that it just wasn't right for her to stay in the granny flat, living with the woman her son had left.

The next time I saw my grandmother was in her ground floor studio apartment at 1211 North Detroit Street, a two-story stucco in a humdrum section of Hollywood, a block west of La Brea Avenue. At least the apartments in her building surrounded a swimming pool.

◉ ◉ ◉

On July 1, 1957, my mother and her actress friend Betty Lou Gerson got in the car, crossed the Santa Monica Mountains—the range that bisects Los Angeles—and drove to the courthouse in Santa Monica, where both were sworn and testified. California was a fault state in 1957. To win a divorce, one needed grounds, which were limited to seven: adultery, extreme cruelty, willful desertion, willful neglect, habitual intemperance, conviction of a felony, and incurable insanity. What did Betty Lou and my mother say under oath? The only clue comes from the pleading, drafted by my mother's attorney, a good one who'd won generous alimony orders for the wives he represented. "Complaint for Divorce – Extreme Cruelty." That's the stone my mother's lawyer picked to throw at my father. Not adultery, which had to have been easier to prove. Nor habitual intemperance. My father didn't drink.

On July 2, 1957, *Variety*'s column "The Hitching Post" announced two marriages, and then the following, under the subhead "Unhitched," a single entry: "Actor Gerald Mohr was divorced yesterday, by wife Rita."

The *Los Angeles Times* offered a few more details. Their reporter quoted my mother as telling the court, "He just wanted his freedom." After many years, I read those articles, on microfilm. My mother didn't keep them.

The judge let my father keep his 1952 Jaguar, a snazzy car with semaphores for turn signals and varnished wood in the interior. My mother got the Plymouth. My father got the rights to the *Rough Sketch* pilot, which would never go on the air, and the series *Foreign Intrigue*, which would soon leave the air. My mother received all the cash except for five thousand dollars. She kept the furniture in the house. My father moved to an apartment at 7200 Hollywood Boulevard, a place I never saw.

CHAPTER NINE

Pepe and The Ring

I stopped paying attention in class. I ignored my homework—especially social studies. While my third-grade report card had contained almost all As and rated me *outstanding* in all ten qualities of conduct, things changed the following year. In February 1957, five months after my father had left, my fourth-grade teacher dropped almost all my conduct ratings to *satisfactory* and lowered my grades.

In December 1957, my fifth-grade teacher disappeared. The principal said Mr. Skovern wouldn't return, but never told us why. Now I'd have to put up with a substitute teacher.

The next morning, Mr. Hernandez walked into my classroom. He was short and lean, with a tan face and thick black hair. He looked younger than Mr. Skovern, who'd been pale and doughy, portly and balding. But he had also been tall—six-two, like my father.

I was ten, but the school still required a naptime after lunch. "What story do you want to hear when you wake up?" Mr. Hernandez asked us.

Someone answered *Zorro*, Walt Disney's newest series, which had become my favorite television show. Zorro, Spanish for fox. Zorro, the expert swordsman who "makes the sign of the Z." I decided I wanted to fence, the sport I'd take up in high school.

"I have lots of *Zorro* stories. Now, put your heads down for a few minutes."

Like everyone else, I placed my forearms on the desk, laid my head on them, and struggled to remain still. I never could sleep in class, let alone in that position.

Suddenly, Mr. Hernandez yelled, "*Ho!*" loudly enough to make Beverly Fenneman shriek. He followed up with, "Lancers! Stupid ones, why can't you catch Zorro?"

Beverly started to laugh.

Then, in a Spanish accent, "Sergeant Garcia, we tried but couldn't . . ."

I laughed, and laughed again the next day as Mr. Hernandez told another *Zorro* story. Each day he regaled us with more episodes. Thieves had stolen gunpowder from the fort. Someone was smuggling jewels. Two thugs were demanding protection money from Theresa, who sold the best tamales in Monterey. Zorro caught all of these fiends. At the end, a girl asked Mr. Hernandez how he knew these tales.

"I worked on *Zorro*," he said.

Two episodes, it turned out. So, besides teaching, he acted. His stage name was Pepe Hern. No wonder he had a sense of humor. Like my father, every actor I met did.

"Now it's time for history," Mr. Hernandez said.

The next day, after waking us from our naps, he used a softer tone to describe a character. "The Eagle's feather. The way it's clipped. It must be a message." Then he looked at me. "The Eagle is afraid of being alone." I'd seen that episode. The Eagle was a villain, but a villain with a reservoir of sadness. That's why I sympathized with him.

⊙ ⊙ ⊙

One warm January afternoon, as the kids ran down the steps and out to the playground, Mr. Hernandez gestured for me to stay behind. We lingered on a small landing outside the yellow-colored bungalow that served as our classroom. The San Fernando Valley sky was clear, and because there was no smog, a trace of odors from the nearby oak trees reached us.

Mr. Hernandez said, "I know your dad. Gerald's a wonderful actor."

I said something neutral, like "Oh."

So he knew who my father was. Maybe he guessed it from the attendance sheet; my surname was not common. This wasn't the first time a fan had claimed to know my father.

"I worked with your dad on a movie called *The Ring*."

My father had never mentioned the film, the story about a fictional boxer, Tommy Kansas. I wouldn't connect it to my fight in Sweden until I saw it, decades later.

"Your dad starred in it," Mr. Hernandez said. He raised his bushy eyebrows as he spoke.

Pepe Hernandez had had a minor role in *The Ring*, which he didn't describe to me, nor did he say that his film credits included *Broken Arrow* and *Cheyenne*. Three years later, he would appear in *The Magnificent Seven*.

From the playground came the shouts of my classmates—the boys playing tetherball and dodgeball, the girls jumping rope. But I was happy to remain with my teacher.

"Your dad is a great guy," he said. "I'm so sorry."

He knew about the divorce. He must have read the trades and the *Los Angeles Times*. Divorce was a mammoth event during the 1950s, scandalous, especially in the entertainment industry. On some level, I'd already learned that people were quick to assign blame. As *Vanity Fair* reported, "When (Frank) Sinatra left his wife Nancy for Ava Gardner, Danny Thomas's wife, Rose Marie, a friend of Nancy's . . . refused to play his records for a time." According to what Robert S. McElvaine wrote in *The Times They Were A-Changin'*, even as late as 1964, "Divorce was still remarkable— and people remarked at length about it when it happened in their neighborhood, although they generally did so in hushed tones."

Mr. Hernandez's sympathy made me wonder if the end of my father's marriage was the reason he was scrambling for parts. Was divorce a disgrace, the reason many of our family friends refused to speak to my father?

My teacher must have sensed how lost I felt. I think he was struggling to find a way to make me happy again. There was a caring quality about him, this man who'd acted with my father and whose Zorro stories made me laugh.

He never consoled me in front of everyone, as Mr. Skovern had done, or in a tone that embarrassed me. Mr. Hernandez didn't have to. One look conveyed his empathy, and he did it in a way that the other students didn't notice when it passed between us. The one kindness I could return was to pay attention in class and try to enjoy school again.

Several nights later, while watching *Engineer Bill*, I opened my history textbook to the chapter about the Revolutionary War and read, "Answering the call, 'To arms! To arms! The British have attacked the Americans!'" I stopped when Engineer Bill was about to start a game of Red Light Green Light, but then I thought about Pepe Hernandez.

What shone through was his bearing, which was—I wouldn't have used this word at the time—fatherly. Pepe Hernandez convinced me that learning was fun and had value. I got up, walked over to the Philco, and turned it off.

School became a pleasure, the way I'd remembered it before my parents separated. I can still recall Pepe Hernandez's smile, his powerful, yet friendly voice and the way he moved his arms as he taught. What's a fraction? Why do you like the *Freddy the Pig* books? How does matter shift from solids to liquids to gas? Sadly, we wouldn't finish the school year together. In January 1958, my mother announced that we were moving away.

PART TWO

Every Other Weekend

CHAPTER TEN

New York

In late February 1958, my mother and I exchanged our half-acre in the San Fernando Valley for 1,700 square feet in New York City. She'd grown up there, and her mother, brother, and sister had never left. Naturally, she didn't tell me about the minor visitation kerfuffle she and my father had about her decision to take me out of California. The lawyers worked it out without a court battle.

The apartment my mother's brother, Uncle Dick, found for us—paid under the table to rent, I learned later—was on Lexington Avenue and 88th Street, a dark affair with two bedrooms, a living room, and a dining room, spacious by Manhattan standards, but to me a cell. He picked it, he said, because its location—the Upper East Side—would allow me to attend PS 6, allegedly the city's best public elementary school.

They inserted me into a class with delightful girls, shy boys, and a refugee from Hungary's uprising against the Soviets. We all became friends, a defense mechanism of sorts, because our teacher, Miss Haber, was a disgustingly nasty martinet. My second week there, a visitor came into the class, why I don't recall. What I do remember was that Miss Haber referred to us as "my pack of stupid idiots." On one occasion she brandished a ruler at the Hungarian boy, who spoke almost no English. "You're not from Hungary," she shrilled. "You're from hunger." The boy collapsed into tears. Like the others, I sat at my desk frozen, not knowing what to say or do.

A classmate raised his hand and said something, what I have no idea anymore, but I remember Miss Haber's answer.

"Rude boy," she said, and then, "I shall write that in your anecdotal record."

The class gasped. I didn't know what anecdotal meant. I'm sure the others didn't either, but the way Miss Haber said it sounded terrifying.

PS 6 published an annual yearbook called *The Quill*. While almost every other class rated multiple photos and mentions, the editors gave Miss Haber's class, officially called 5-3, one picture—all of us in the gym, under a basketball net. The camera was set so far back that even with a magnifying class, it was almost impossible to recognize anybody. The caption said that we were learning about "teamwork." Bullshit.

A map of the school district, shaped like an amoeba, hung on the wall in the main office. "It's pretty," the woman behind the counter said when I asked why the district looked so squiggly. She didn't give the real reason, that PS 6's boundaries had been drawn to keep out Puerto Ricans.

Our Lexington Avenue apartment building lay at the end of one of the amoeba's slender tentacles, which reached down 88th Street from Park Avenue to include us but miss the seven-story eyesore across the street with fire escapes in front instead of the rear, like ours. Technically the building wasn't a slum, but for a person from the San Fernando Valley, who was used to single family houses and large backyards, it looked like one—shabby, smelly, and dilapidated. A bar and a mom-and-pop market flanked the entry, which fed into a narrow, drab hall. Odors from bad cooking poured into the street. One night, screams came from the bar. From my fourth-floor bedroom window, I watched two men in

ANTHONY J. MOHR

T-shirts tumble onto the sidewalk and slug each other, first on the curb, then in the middle of Lexington Avenue. A dumpy woman screamed at them to stop. They didn't. Crouched, heads down, the men kept swinging, and when a blow went home, the recipient reeled backward, hollered an obscenity, and then charged in with more punches. A crowd gathered; the dumpy woman wailed and cab drivers honked as they swerved to miss the pugilists. I couldn't stop looking.

The fight ended when the man in the striped T-shirt hit the man in the white T-shirt so hard that he doubled up and hollered, "Oh, God."

My mother told me to draw the curtain and get into bed; it was late. Frightened, sick, I dreamed that I was trying to fall asleep.

I despised having to walk three long blocks, from Lexington Avenue to Central Park, in order to see a lawn. I loathed playing indoors at the 92nd Street YMCA, which reeked of sweat and deferred maintenance. The kids might as well have spoken a new language, so thick was their accent.

"All right," a pale boy with pimples said at the locker room entrance. "Pay da man some money."

Money or no money, my mother said it was scarce. The Circle Line, a boat that carried tourists around Manhattan, cost too much. We rode the Staten Island Ferry, which charged five cents. The museums we visited were free, which included the Metropolitan Museum of Art. Outings there with my mother ranked among my favorites. Everything about the museum called to me, from its Beaux-Arts Fifth Avenue facade to its mammoth collection of paintings and sculptures. My mother knew which works to linger by, the paintings I should see and the artists I needed to recognize in order to be cultured. "I want you to be able to look at a work and say, 'Oh, that's a Renoir.'"

None of Renoir's paintings became my favorites, but one

work—far from Renoir's style—did: Charles Demuth's *I Saw the Figure 5 in Gold.* The painting featured a giant numeral five on a city street. It dominated the canvas, and behind it, two more number fives receded with perfect perspective into the distance. Demuth had meant to illustrate a poem by William Carlos Williams about a fire truck speeding through the night "among the rain and lights," but thanks to the skyscrapers Demuth placed at the painting's edges, I viewed his quasi-cubist work as emblematic of New York.

I returned to the painting repeatedly, catching my breath each time, unaware, then, of the number five's significance to me. I was staring at, up to that time, a symbol of the first of the happiest two years of my life—five years old, six years old. Especially five. The last year *Philip Marlowe* remained on the radio, the penultimate year my family was stable with me a happy half-pint, safe in Southern California's golden bubble, playing in the backyard with Valory, climbing fruit trees in our orchard, riding my Schwinn through the neighborhood, daring the roller coaster and the diving bell at Pacific Ocean Park, and opening Christmas presents beneath the loving looks of my family. Demuth had displayed my own personal figure five, racing into the dark.

⊙ ⊙ ⊙

One afternoon, I spotted a windup toy in a store window—a small globe with an airplane at the end of a wire tether, in apparent flight. I said I wanted it.

My mother led me away. "It costs seventy-nine cents," she said. "Do you realize that's twenty-one cents less than a dollar?"

I looked down at the sidewalk and pulled my jacket tightly around me to resist the wind. The snow in the gutter had turned to muck.

Manhattan's buildings closed in like a vise. There were no palm trees, no houses, and no Good Humor men. There were no sprinklers to run through and no orange blossoms to smell. There was hardly any sun. And I missed my father. He'd only written twice; his phone calls, almost as rare.

I also missed my father's film industry friends, faces of the fantasy world from which I'd been expelled. My mother and I had moved away as I was beginning to appreciate them. They carried themselves in a manner distinct from the rest of the world. They handled their fame, such as it was, with a yep-I-guess-that's-me approach that kept them from being haughty while still setting them apart. They may have been adults, but their behavior made me laugh. Like the night one of them had jumped on a chair and hooted out lines from some TV show. At the end of that stunt, another actor picked up a cushion from the sofa and tossed it across the living room. Many had children who could invent great stories. Like Richard Adamson, son of TV writer Ed Adamson. Every playdate became a story about space invaders, docile or hostile depending on his mood. Did Richard compose his yarns while his father banged out scripts for *Schlitz Playhouse* and *Highway Patrol*? David Essex had come to the house armed with a superb collection of shaggy dog stories and practical jokes. Did he get them from the *Creature from the Black Lagoon* or *It Came from Outer Space*, both written by his father, Harry?

And then there was Melville Shavelson.

Melville—Mel to his friends—possessed a comedic wit and an Academy Award nomination for best original screenplay. (He'd receive a second nomination in 1959.) A writer for Bob Hope, he would become president of the Writers Guild of America West. Like almost everyone, Mel and his wife Lucy picked sides during my parents' divorce, and they chose my mother.

When Mel attended high school, north of New York City, he

and a classmate, Stanley Dashew, had come close to expulsion for publishing an underground newspaper titled *The Wasp – The Newspaper with the Hidden Sting*. After the school banned the paper, they borrowed Mel's father's car, parked it across the street from campus, and put a sign on top of it: "Get your *Wasp* here." They sold every copy.

Mel and Stanley stayed in touch after high school, and both relocated to Los Angeles. In March 1958, Mel called his classmate, who had recently divorced.

He said something like, "Stan, I should have told you about Rita Mohr before she moved back East."

The following month, Stan got stuck in New York during a business trip and called Mel for my mother's number.

⊙ ⊙ ⊙

Stan met my mother and me on the morning of Sunday, April 27, 1958. He was heavyset. He lacked my father's broadcast quality voice, and he was quiet. Every so often, a tinge of a New York accent slipped out. He wasn't into sparkling, flippant talk. He never would have matched the raillery that came from the crowd who filled my parents' living room. Because he didn't stand up straight, he didn't look as tall as my father, though he was.

For this, her latest blind date, my mother wore a simple, yet tasteful dress in spring colors, but with a warm dark coat because late April in New York could still be cold. I'd met a couple of her set-ups but remember only one: Dr. Glass, a mousy little gnome with eyes too close together and a reedy voice. I was sure that after they saw him, his patients became sicker.

My mother smiled as she greeted Stan, which I knew was an effort, like all of her smiles that year. My mother was so lonely. Sometimes at night I heard a sob from her room. Her sadness made me want my mother to remarry as soon as possible. She could have wed Godzilla for all I cared. I might even have been willing to gag down Dr. Glass.

Stan took my mother and me down to the Battery and onto the Staten Island Ferry. Leaning against the rail with the Statue of Liberty in the distance, Stan smoked a pipe which, despite the wind, didn't go out. My mind drifted to my father, who owned several pipes, including a meerschaum, but never smoked any of them, at least in front of me.

Without warning, my mother looked into Stan's blue eyes and asked, "Are you Jewish?"

"Yes," he said and took another puff on his pipe.

I recall the question because, coming from my mother, it seemed strange. I thought religion wasn't important to her. She'd never discussed having me bar mitzvahed. She hadn't discussed religion at all, Jewish or otherwise. I didn't learn about Hanukkah until, at eight, I'd visited a friend and asked why they didn't have a Christmas tree.

Stan asked how I liked being on the water. My answer was neutral. The first time I'd boarded a boat—fishing, around age six—I became seasick. When we'd sailed home from Europe on a passenger/freighter, I'd spent two days in a deck chair green with nausea. At least the Staten Island ferry was cruising through the smooth waters of New York Harbor.

"Well," he said, "you'll feel different on a sailboat."

Stan said that in 1949, he'd quit his sales job with a business machine company, bought a seventy-six-foot schooner, and for the next year and a half, had taken his now ex-wife and two children from Michigan down the St. Lawrence River, down the Eastern Seaboard to the Caribbean, through the Panama Canal, and onward to Los Angeles, there to resettle. His son, Skip, had been seven. His daughter, Leslie, had been an infant. As he talked, the pipe never left Stan's mouth.

We reached Staten Island and walked about the terminal.

Tracks led out to the left, and I wanted to board whatever train ran on them. When Stan said we didn't have time, I didn't complain. We took the next ferry back to Manhattan. The ride across the water lasted twenty-five minutes, plenty of time for me to notice that my mother appeared content.

Stan dropped me at home and took my mother to dinner.

Ten days later, he returned.

We walked south on Fifth Avenue, below 57th Street, an area full of travel agencies. I darted in and out of them, scooping up maps and pamphlets of islands and countries I wanted to visit. Each time I bolted, my mother and Stan had no choice but to wait for me to return.

Stan said, "You'll never be a sailor on my boat if you keep running off like that."

He took us into a Horn and Hardart's Automat for lunch where, instead of waiters bringing your food, you put money in a slot, opened a transparent plastic door, and pulled out whatever you'd chosen. Between bites of a sandwich, I leafed through one of the travel brochures.

"So, what have you learned?" Stan asked between puffs on his pipe.

I said something about islands, each of which, I was sure, offered a unique world. From our arrival on Manhattan, I'd memorized the names of islands in the Pacific, the Caribbean, the Indian Ocean, the Mediterranean, any place I could escape to. Now I was working on Indonesia.

Stan put out his pipe and turned to his sandwich. He ate slowly and ran a hand through the remains of his hair, as though trying to recall something.

I finished my sandwich and chased it with potato chips. Around us customers withdrew their meals from shelves behind the doors that lined the walls, then brought them to tables and started to chatter.

Stan said, "We visited a lot of islands on our trip." He mentioned Monhegan in Maine, the outer banks of North Carolina, the Bahamas, the Virgin Islands, Martinique, Grenada, Trinidad. I got the impression he was trying to impress me.

After I ate my last potato chip, I asked in a bratty tone, "Okay, where's Navassa Island?"

"Off the coast of Haiti." He answered without hesitating. Stan was the first person I'd met who knew the location of that guano-covered rock. He also knew it was a US possession.

"We dropped anchor there," Stan said.

And that's the moment a glimmer took hold someplace deep, the inchoate perception that I was looking at a man different from Dr. Glass and my mother's other blind dates. Stan had voyaged to an edgy place, in this case a rock that—because of its location, shape, name, and link to America—intrigued me. I glanced at my bag of maps and folders—I'd grabbed them so fast I hadn't stopped to read the destinations—and then I looked back at Stan. A smile was starting to form, not as wide or expressive as my father's. His receding hairline and double chin made his face seem less defined than my father's, but the smoke from his pipe smelled sweet, unlike the nasty odor of my father's cigarettes, and it drew me in.

"What's it like?" I asked.

How much can one say about an uninhabited rock that covers one-and-a-half square miles? Navassa Island hadn't been worth more than a night's stay, and who wants to go ashore only to trudge through bird dung? The place must have stunk, but it didn't matter. I sat rapt through the minute or so it took Stan to answer my question, and after he did, I still wanted to travel there—with Stan.

☉ ☉ ☉

In mid-May 1958, a letter arrived from my father, the first of only two he'd write during my time in New York. I know the number was two. My mother said so in a letter to my father: "He is quite hurt, as he none too subtly suggests, that you've only written two letters to him. He doesn't feel that the cards mean anything."

"My, my," wrote my father, "but you are eleven years old. Next thing I know I will have to get you a copy of Benjamin Franklin's *Advice to Young Men.*"

I figured my father would send the book when the time was right. He never did, and I'd reach adulthood before discovering that my father had not revealed the full title of Franklin's work: *Advice to a Young Man on the Choice of a Mistress.*

As I read my father's letter, I heard his voice, the voice that said, "That's my boy," the first time I'd managed to ride a two-wheeler; the voice that had assured me that our house was solid following the 7.7 Tehachapi earthquake of July 21, 1952; the voice that—when I was four—had made a child actress on one of his radio shows stop crying at the same instant it made me cry. The letter was my father at his rare best, neither impatient nor angry, willing to commit lucid thoughts to the page, something I wish he'd done more often.

◉ ◉ ◉

The next time Stan came to New York, the three of us strolled along the Hudson River. The scent of the water blended with the grass and trees of Riverside Park. Up the hill behind us, cars sped along the West Side Highway. At the 79th Street Boat Basin, we walked out on one of the wooden docks. My mother trailed behind.

"Want to learn something about boats?" Stan asked, in a tone that indicated I had no choice.

I nodded while I recalled the days I'd vomited over the side of a fishing boat off San Pedro and all over the deck of a passenger-freighter in the English Channel.

Stan sat down on a bench and took out a pen and a small notebook.

"There are three main types of sailboats," he said. "A sloop, a yawl, and a ketch."

I sat still while he puffed on his pipe and sketched three hulls.

"A sloop has one mast." He added a mast to hull number one. "There's a mainsail and a jib." He drew those. "A yawl has two masts. The smaller one is well aft. Now a *ketch* also has two masts, but the second is forward of the steering wheel." Stan concentrated on his drawing, his body hunched forward, his big head low, toward the paper. He had hardly any neck. He looked absorbed in the vessels he'd drawn. My mother hovered somewhere near, out of sight.

Whatever I said in reply to his efforts wasn't much. I wasn't interested.

Maybe that's why Stan halted the lesson. He didn't press on to explain a schooner's rig, odd because his eighteen-month trip through the Caribbean had been aboard a schooner. We stood up and continued our walk.

Stan tried again during his next visit to New York. As before, pipe in mouth, he sat me down and drew the distinctions between sloops, yawls, and ketches. I didn't say that he was repeating himself; I'd forgotten the differences. Later, as the three of us walked through Central Park, I did or said something—I don't recall the details—which made him say, once more, "You'll never be a sailor on my boat if you keep doing things like that."

I thought of my father, who'd never said any such thing—"You'll never be an actor in one of my movies if you do that again." It was weird that I compared my father with a relative stranger, but that's what I was doing. I didn't fault Stan; my father had no say over who'd act with him. Stan apparently had more control over his life because he worked for himself. He'd started a business machines company shortly after settling in LA.

Over ice cream at Schrafft's, Stan said he'd wanted to make a film about his trip. He'd run classified ads in *Variety* to find a cameraman to sail with him and then planned to sell short documentaries about his adventure. They shot footage of, among other things, a voodoo rite in Haiti and a storm at sea that almost sank the ship. By journey's end, Stan and his group had amassed 800 color slides and over 18,000 feet of color film. Stan turned his product into a movie, *The Tides of Imamou*, got it released in 1951 into several theaters, and learned what it was like to have a flop. As I listened, I wondered if Stan was telling me this because I had an actor for a father.

Somehow Stan's business kept bringing him to New York every couple of weeks. A meeting. A trade show. A potential customer. He always had a reason to show up and take my mother, and sometimes me, to dinner. What I didn't know was that Dashew Business Machines was about to team with the Bank of America and launch the BankAmericard, the forerunner of Visa. Stan would manufacture the embossers that would produce the credit cards, and his company would also make the machines merchants used to imprint the purchase drafts.

◉ ◉ ◉

Late afternoon on July 19, 1958, I walked into the apartment to find my mother looking dejected.

"I need to tell you something," she said.

I held my breath. *Something* told me it was bad.

"Daddy got married."

"Who?"

"Mai."

The answer shocked me. I was too young to have caught the clues, like the scene at the airport in 1956, two years earlier. No one had mentioned Mai's name all year, and that included my father. But now she was back, which meant that for the rest of my life, I'd see her whenever I'd see my father. Call it a child's instinct, but I'd never cared for her. She seemed snippy, quick to anger and then too eager to please.

My mother handed me the newspaper article. "Actor Takes Bride," read the headline with a picture of the couple below. The last sentence read, "This is the second marriage for both."

I still didn't understand that Mai was the reason my father left my mother.

My father and I had talked several weeks earlier, one of our rare phone calls, which, as usual, lasted no more than three minutes because long distance wasn't cheap. He'd said nothing about Mai. But he had told my mother—in his bad handwriting. "I have written a dozen letters to Tony," he said, "and tore them all up because somehow the written word has a way of becoming terribly blunt. Mai and I are getting married and unfortunately, I am unable to sit down with Tony and talk things out. I think it would be far better if you explained it to him so that he would have a beautiful impression rather than a cold newspaper account. For his sake, I would rather you prepare him."

Well, a cold newspaper account is what I got. If my mother prepared me, I blocked it out of my memory. If she didn't prepare me, how can I blame her? I didn't find my father's letter until decades later, along with my mother's letter back to him, explaining what happened:

He cried and was obviously hurt, but he was able to verbalize —in essence, Gerry, his fear is that you will not have time for him now that you have the other boys. I reassured him that this is not so and that you are and always will be his Daddy and that you love him very much. In the past he would ask if such and such a child is divorced—remembering this, I talked to him at length and explained to him that in spite of the fact that parents can be divorced, children can never be. I presented the news as simply as possible and told him that we want Daddy to be very happy. He immediately wanted to know when I was going to be married— obviously he too wants to find a place for himself.

I felt abandoned, once again. Before making such a move, shouldn't a father alert a child himself? What kept him from doing so? Was he afraid of what I'd say? Maybe living so long with his mother made him immature.

Maybe my father's marriage spurred my mother to speed up her plans, because within a week or two, she announced that we'd be spending the end of the summer in California with Stan in Newport Beach. She and Stan had known each other three months. I was too dense to understand that this was a test, an experiment to determine if they could successfully blend their families.

Stan installed me in his son Skip's bedroom in a house he'd rented on West Bay Avenue. Its window overlooked Newport Bay, so much more beautiful than the decrepit building I faced every morning in New York. My mother stayed down the street at a small motel. Kept secret, of course, was that each night, after his kids and I had fallen asleep, Stan slipped away, down the street, to join my mother.

Stan's house came with a small private beach and a dock on Newport Bay. On the sand was *Glub Glub*, his daughter Leslie's Sabot-class sailboat, and next to it, a weather-beaten rowboat. The living room was furnished with bamboo chairs, couches, and a glass coffee table. A slight salty odor lingered, delightful after months of smelling refuse and exhaust fumes on the streets of New York.

Skip arrived. At age sixteen, he looked, at least to the eleven-year-old me, like the textbook California teen—tan, sturdy, and athletic. He was gracious to my mother and me before saying something about his eighteen-foot Thistle-class sailboat named *Closh Ma Claver*. Then the talk turned to Leslie's Sabot. Apparently, she rarely used it, which is perhaps why he referred to Leslie as "the brat."

"Three hundred bucks," Skip said, glaring out the bay window at his sister's orange-colored boat minus its mast, which was stored in the garage. I was surprised at his pique.

Leslie showed up later, from the San Fernando Valley, where she lived with her mother. Like me, she was chubby. I wondered if divorce added pounds to kids. When I said hello, she tilted her head down and coaxed her eyes toward me.

"Hi," she said, her voice barely audible before she turned and went, I assume, to her room. She was nine, two years younger than I. I was nine when my parents separated.

The next morning, before he drove somewhere, Skip said something to Leslie and me about going rowing.

Later that afternoon, Leslie and I lingered on the dock. The sun and the air felt soothing, so different from New York's wet heat. Whatever we talked about gave way to a riff about Skip. She was seeking payback for something he'd done, and before long, she found it.

She removed the oars from the rowboat. Skip would never notice, she said. We could sit at the end of the dock and watch Skip shove off before realizing the oars were missing.

"He'll start swearing, and we can yell out, 'What's the matter, Skipper? Can't you row a boat?'"

I laughed, but the prank never happened. Either Skip changed his mind and didn't use the boat, or he spotted the oars, propped against the side of the house. Or maybe my mother and Stan walked onto the dock and Skip decided to stay and study them together.

Leslie, Skip, and I got along. (But once we reached adulthood, I learned that Skip and Leslie had decided *I* was the brat because I never helped clear the table or wash the dishes. My grandmother and mother had always handled those tasks.) We spent the two weeks sailing in the bay, where I didn't get seasick, and riding the Balboa Island Ferry, which carried three cars at a time. We passed the evenings either at home or at the Fun Zone, where we ate corn dogs on a stick, rode the large Ferris wheel, with its open seats, and the small Ferris wheel, with seats enclosed by red, blue, and green wire cages.

◉ ◉ ◉

My mother and I returned to New York. During the ride from Idlewild (now JFK) International Airport to our apartment, the rain began. Everything was gray. The closer we came to our apartment, the grimmer and grimier Manhattan looked. The fire escape on the building across the street was rusty, something I hadn't noticed before. On the sidewalk, a man in a ratty overcoat cursed at someone nearby. The air smelled of wet trash. I turned on the TV in time to hear the station identification: "Channel Seven, New York." It sounded wrong. I'd always heard, "Channel Seven, Los Angeles"

Then my mother showed me a newspaper article. It read that the following morning, New York's children would "shake the sand from their shoes" and return to school. No one told me I'd be back in class so soon. In tears, I begged to return to California.

"Everything is going to be all right," my mother said as we trudged into my bedroom. Her voice caught as she said it; then she hugged me.

My mother was correct. PS 6 became a delightful experience. Since the campus was a block away from the Metropolitan Museum of Art, many of us went there during the noon hour.

Classmates began to hold parties. I was asked to become a hall monitor, with the right to wear a white sash and a tin badge. My sixth-grade teacher, Miss Vanaria, was the polar opposite to Miss Haber. She was sweet and indulging—never a cross word. If we misbehaved, she scolded us gently. On one day, during our Spanish lesson, we all said, "Me gusta España." She stopped and bowed her head.

"Oh," she said, "I forgot. I'm supposed to teach you the Castilian pronunciation. I'm sorry." It was clear she didn't agree with that dictate. "Me guthta . . . . Ethpaña," she said, and all of us, still smarting from Miss Haber's torture, assumed looks of sympathy.

My mother was right for another reason. On December 21, 1958, in the penthouse apartment of a distant relative, she married Stan. She never stopped smiling the whole afternoon. I'd never seen her so happy. She told me we were moving back to California, this time to Beverly Hills, where I'd attend school.

The next day, Mom and Stan left New York for their honeymoon, and I left New York for good. I spent the holidays at my grandmother's Hollywood apartment. My father and Mai rented a place across the alley from her, but only for a few weeks before they moved into a house they'd rented on North Arden Boulevard in Hollywood. But, for those few weeks, every morning my grandmother and I heard my father's whistle—a five-note tune he said he'd composed for one of his radio shows.

"Yes, children," my grandmother would shout with glee. She'd pull back the drapes, open the kitchen window, and there they would be, Dad and Mai leaning against a concrete wall between their building and my grandmother's. Dad would wear one of his jumpsuits, beaming, his arm draped across Mai's shoulder, a posture I'd never seen him assume with my mother. Grandma would call them over for breakfast—eggs, burnt bacon, and burnt toast. Perhaps for the first time in years, I realize now, both my parents were happy.

⊙ ⊙ ⊙

Decades later, Mai's son Timmy gave me a scrapbook of studio publicity shots of my father—pictures of him and Mai together and at parties—often with fellow actors including Burt Lancaster, Barry Sullivan, Omar Sharif, and Humphrey Bogart. On one of the photos, my father had written to Mai, *Let's not take so long in the next life to find each other.*

Despite the years that had passed, the pain came in hard. I felt as though my father had tossed away half his life, the half that included me. I wondered when he wrote those words—at the beginning of the marriage when he brimmed with hope, in the middle when he hoped the fighting would end, or in 1968, when, with hope ebbing away, he might have sensed the next life drawing near. Whatever the timing, the words hurt, tempered only by the knowledge that my mother may well have told Stan the same thing. I know Stan told her so; I still have his love letters.

CHAPTER ELEVEN

Radio, in the Light

One January morning in 1959, perhaps the morning Fidel Castro entered Havana, my brand-new older stepbrother Skip hollered "Outta the sack!" and turned on the radio atop our nightstand to KFWB—*Color radio*, as the station labeled itself. (The label was meant to suggest color television, which had yet to become commonplace.) For the first time in over a year, I awoke not to my mother's voice fighting to sound happy, but to joyful disc jockeys—they called themselves The Swinging Gentlemen— and their Top Forty music. Skip goosed the volume up good and loud until Stan said, during a song by Fabian, "Turn that down."

"Aw come on," Skip said.

"How can you stand that?" That question was from my mother, already downstairs in the kitchen. Despite the remark, she sounded happy.

"We're hip, man," Skip called from upstairs.

Then Skip and I laughed. From downstairs, so did my mother. At that moment, the song ended, giving way to one of KFWB's numerous jingles. "Mr. Weatherman, take the cue, and tell us what the weather's gonna do-oo-oooo."

"Moderate to heavy smog," came the forecast, delivered with a carefree voice.

I'd last spent time with a radio somewhere between three and five years old. The medium had invaded my life at night, with morbid stories featuring my father's voice. His Philip Marlowe episodes displayed a dangerous world full of people willing to kidnap and kill, and under these modern versions of Grimm's fairy tales came the sounds of organs and other instruments at their lugubrious best. My father was in danger, or my father was comforting someone. My bedroom lights were out, and I was alone.

Everything changed with KFWB. Its format let in the light. The Swinging Gentlemen were always joking. They played drum-your-fingers-and-tap-your-toes stuff like the "Guitar Boogie Shuffle," catchy tunes like Floyd Cramer's "On the Rebound," and wacky numbers like Pat Boone's "Wang Dang Taffy Apple Tango." Better still, they played these songs often, making it worthwhile to wait for them. And wait I did, through commercials for Preparation H and Mrs. Paul's Fish Sticks, until my mother yelled that some meal or another was getting cold.

Outside the Beverly Vista School at 8:55 one morning, a boy held a transistor radio in the air as we lined up on the playground and started for homeroom. "The Angels Listened In" was playing, and despite the damp chill of the marine layer, the line bobbed and swayed as The Crests sang their song. This boy was not my friend. Built like a bulldozer, Chris had a trace of the pugilist in him. But this morning he held his transistor high so we in the back could hear, and he turned his head toward us and beamed, a wide, open smile that made him look affable. Thanks to Chris, I finally felt connected to every one of my classmates. Old Eva Gross, the English teacher with a sandpaper voice, had never heard of the Crests or KFWB, nor had Mr. Sullivan, our avuncular geography teacher with his crew-cut white hair, nor Miss Lester, the spinster who taught science and turned red the morning someone asked her to define a zygote. During the walk between the playground and the classrooms, my classmates and I frolicked in our virtual world.

One night I realized I could put radio to use. Starting in January 1961, the eighth grade, KFWB launched an on-the-air gossip column. You'd phone an ersatz lady named Kay at HOllywood 1-9511 and dish about your school. Then, according to the flyer the station sent to the record stores, "To 'get the message,' dial KFWB Channel 98—every evening from 6 p.m. on."

Sure I still watched television—less now that my mother had remarried—but TV hosts didn't ask their audience to participate. The Swinging Gentlemen did; they wanted to hear from me, and so on the night of March 20, 1961, I picked up the receiver of the rotary phone in my bedroom and dialed—me, an eighth grader calling a radio station with a factoid about my school: "Beverly Vista's two love triangles," I told Kay, "are Lisa, Mike, and Ron, and Mark, Irit, and Penny."

The next morning, after back-announcing Bobby Vee's "Stayin' In," Bill Ballance read my scoop over the air, read my exact words at the very moment that Lisa, Mike, and Ron, and Mark, Irit, and Penny—all of us—were brushing our teeth and getting dressed and hoping to hear Chubby Checker's "Pony Time" before we left for school. I may not have belonged to the party crowd, but I'd nailed their latest chatter and reveled in the aftermath. They shrieked about it in homeroom and hollered through the halls. Who called the station? How'd he know? What's he gonna say next? Aaack!

A gleeful sense of power came in. I'd claimed radio as my own, the medium that made my father famous. What's more, I realized that my peers and I were sharing a social experience at a virtual watering hole where we gathered to enjoy ourselves. Radio meant joy, not tears.

But I'm ahead of myself. Returning to breakfast in January 1959, Skip called his civics teacher an old fossil. My mother said she had a bridge game at noon. Stan described a big order he was chasing. As I ate my scrambled eggs and the juicy brown sausages my mother knew I loved, I thought how different this breakfast was from the silent meals my mother and I had endured in New York. I sneaked a look at the contented expression on her face as she read through the women's section of the *Los Angeles Times*.

My mother was happy, and so was I. Stan may have still been an unknown quantity to me, but at least in the house was a father once more.

"Is Stan home yet," I asked the first, the second, and probably the third days I returned from school, anxious questions because part of me feared that Stan wouldn't come home.

My mother's answers came out in breezy sentences. Naturally he wasn't back—yet. Stan worked long hours, but he'd arrive in time for dinner. Then Skip came through the door and fired up KFWB, and I relaxed as, together, we grumbled through our homework while listening to the Everly Brothers and Ricky Nelson until Stan did come home and yelled, "Turn that down," and Skip and I laughed before we turned it down.

⊙ ⊙ ⊙

We almost always dined together. My mother set the rectangular table just so, with salad fork and soup spoon in the right places, along with the dessert fork and coffee spoon. She sat closest to the kitchen; Skip, across from me, back to the living room; Stan, opposite my mother. Stan described his latest business machine, which my mother nicknamed Emma. Skip rhapsodized about his Thistle and his souped-up 1946 Ford. It was the Ford that caught my attention, starting with its faded black paint job with dabs of gray primer. Its interior smelled musty. Its sound deafened. But it hauled ass and he loved it. So did his girlfriend Eve, who wrote a magazine column and happened to live in our garden apartment building a block south of Wilshire Boulevard, at the corner of Charleville Boulevard and Rodeo Drive in Beverly Hills.

"Half the school's after her," Skip said, but he'd won her away, even from the varsity quarterback. What was it about Skip that attracted a girl like Eve? With his good looks, with Eve (sister of teenage heartthrob Troy Donahue), with his sailboat and his souped-up car, my invincible older stepbrother had easy access to everything Southern California offered. *Photoplay Magazine* featured him, Eve, and Troy in an article about dating. Skip was reluctant to let the magazine run his picture with Eve. I would have killed for that chance.

We lived in our two-story apartment until my mother and Stan could find a house. Its subterranean parking garage offered ideal acoustics for amplifying Skip's motor when he gunned it. The sound boomed out of the vents and through the courtyard, reverberating against our neighbors' units. They didn't appreciate it, especially Harry, a producer who insisted he was just an old man who needed his sleep but who enjoyed chorus girls and kept a closet full of fur coats for them, coats of all sizes.

As usual at dinner, Stan crabbed about Skip's car. He said it was dangerous; it was too loud; it was ruining his grades. Then to be safe, Skip and Stan usually reset their conversation to sailing, about which they conversed calmly, yet with gusto. That's where father and son bonded while I listened and struggled to understand their nautical patois.

"I want chrome stanchions on the new boat. Also chrome turnbuckles and cleats."

"We were hard on the wind."

"I had to reef the main."

"We'd just come about, and I called starboard tack."

At least I didn't think about heaving over the side.

Before dinner was over, they were teasing each other.

One night when Skip said he wanted a catamaran, Stan said, "I have a name for your new boat: *Alley cat.*"

When Stan described the catamaran he wanted to build, Skip said, "Father, you're getting a barge. I'll beat you home from Catalina every time."

Before dessert, Stan turned to me. "What did you learn today?"

I searched for an answer and settled on life in Red China. As long as I offered an answer, Stan was happy.

"I asked Zelda and Harold for dinner next week," my mother said.

Harold Kress was a film editor and a friend of many years. He and his wife Zelda had picked my mother's side in the divorce and had bonded with Stan.

Skip said the kids at Beverly Hills High School were rich snobs. Stan didn't disagree with him, which made me nervous. We'd moved into Beverly Hills for the schools. I'd have to learn to get on with such people when I started high school, three years from then.

"They're fixing the chimes on Thursday," my mother said.

Skip and I suppressed grins. Several days earlier, after watching *Zorro*, we'd pulled the two doorbell chimes from their sockets and fenced with them. Now every time someone rang the front doorbell, we only heard a dull thunk. I was waiting to see if the repair cost would come from my allowance. (It didn't.)

That's how it went—small talk, precisely what my mother needed after the cold years. I gathered that's what Stan needed as well. He'd endured his own escape from the tantrums of an alcoholic wife, his own departure with a suitcase heaved into the car, his drive down a San Fernando Valley street, leaving behind two children, his dog Gamma, and his brown ranch house.

"Before I reached Ventura Boulevard," Stan told me once, "I was in tears." After he'd composed himself, he turned east, in search of a place to spend the night.

Tonight, when dinner was over and before Stan went into the living room, he folded his large arms around my mother and gave her a long kiss. "Mmmmm," he said as he nuzzled his head into her brown hair. "Mmmmm, I'm going to beat the hell out of you."

I did a double take. "What?"

"I'm just joshing," Stan said. He hugged my mother again, this time with a love pat to her rear. She kissed him again. Relieved, I went into the kitchen. In thirty-five years of marriage, he never hit her, but again, those words, so inconsistent with his actions. I never got used to them, no matter how much I realized they were part of Stan's sense of humor.

Skip washed; I dried. Then we marched upstairs to finish our homework. The duplex remained calm for the rest of the night. My mother and Stan talked or watched TV as Skip cursed his way through French and I tried to conjugate lie and lay.

Skip introduced me to the wonderful world of practical jokes—good-natured stuff like short-sheeting beds and balancing a dixie cup of water atop a door, poised to fall on whoever walked in, usually Leslie during her every-other-weekend visits. I dreamed up a number of stunts on my own, again with Leslie as the target—catching a dragonfly, tying it to a thread, and siccing it on her as she was falling asleep. Neither Stan nor my mother was exempt, and one night while they were out, I set up what I thought was a harmless prank. Just what, I don't remember.

Skip and I were in bed when Stan and my mother returned. Skip had already fallen asleep, but I heard the front door open, their normal, quiet conversation, and then it stopped. The silence continued longer than expected, followed by the thump thump of Stan's footfalls on the stairs, and still no voice.

Stan snapped on our light. He pulled the blanket and sheets from Skip's bed until they'd gathered on the floor. Then he snarled at his groggy son, "You happy with what you did down there?"

Dazed, squinting against the light, Skip said, "What are you—"

Stan cut him off. "Don't give me that."

Then he hit him. Somewhere on the side, maybe near his butt, just as Skip was sitting up. He hit Skip only once, but he hit him hard. He hit him probably before Skip's eyes had adjusted to the light. Skip fell backwards against the pillow.

"What did I do?" Skip managed to ask.

Stan told him.

"That was me," I said. I didn't want Stan to hit Skip again, even if he'd hit me next.

Stan didn't hit me. He left the room without a word until he was down the hall. That's when he said, in a tone resembling an afterthought, "Sorry I hit you, Skip."

Skip pulled the bedding back over himself and rolled over so that he faced the wall. He didn't call after his father, or to me. The light in the room went off—I don't remember who switched it off. Skip went back to sleep, but not before letting out an audible heave, followed by a sigh. At breakfast the following morning, nobody said anything about the incident.

A distant thunder roll of fear came in after that evening. Whatever joke I had pulled didn't qualify as serious misconduct, at least I didn't think so. Stan had overreacted, had struck out at Skip, and had offered nothing more than an offhand apology to his son. Stan hadn't hit me yet, at least as far as I recall, but he was capable of doing so. That in itself didn't shock me. My father could spank too. I recall nothing more than a close brush on a birthday, I think my sixth. Friends had arrived for a party, including Valory. She and I were playing in the driveway, maybe climbing on my father's new Ford. Out from his bedroom came my father, onto the balcony above the garage, and yelled for me to stop. Then he said,

"If you don't stop, you'll get a spanking, birthday party or not."

I stopped.

The punishment Stan had meted out to the wrong person did not fit the offense, not in the slightest.

⊙ ⊙ ⊙

They called Beverly Vista a grammar school, a British term. The phrase middle school had yet to enter the language, and it wasn't a junior high school because it contained grades Kindergarten through eighth. BV covered a long block in the middle of a neighborhood of tidy townhouse apartments. Most of the campus consisted of a playground. Its two-story building had a red tile roof and brick walls punctuated by ornaments, soffits, and double-hung windows. Lawns, not pavement, surrounded it.

They sent me to a classroom that appeared messy and dark. Some thirty-five boys and girls sat there under the tutelage of Mrs. Dunker, an old crone with a pinched face, white hair, and blue veins that crisscrossed the claws that passed for her hands. Moments after I walked in—it was in the middle of a lesson—she gestured me to a seat near the back and carried on.

Toward the end of the day, while everyone was supposed to write something, she said, "We're staying after school today because you didn't do your homework. Isn't that jolly?"

"Oh please, Mrs. Dunker," a girl said. "Some of us did—"

"You be quiet, or I'll keep you here longer."

Henry, a pudgy boy, blurted out, "This is asinine."

Mrs. Dunker wheeled and said, "Just for that, Henry, you will stay after school again tomorrow."

That was how my first day at school ended, by serving detention thanks to a teacher almost as mean as Miss Haber. Once it was over, Henry sidled up to me. He had a doughy face hidden behind thick black horn-rimmed glasses. His hair looked too slick and oily. The first thing Henry said to me was, "Now you know why we call her Dunker the Flunker."

Henry took me home to a cluttered apartment and a mother who mumbled a "Hi" as she dragged a hand through her washed-out curly hair. The expression on her plain face signaled, *lost*. Her voice sounded forlorn. She wandered into her bedroom. I quickly learned that Henry's parents were divorced.

Henry raided the refrigerator and wolfed down a piece of cake. I ate one bite.

The doorbell rang. Into the house lumbered Henry's father, a burly man with a thick neck and barely a hello for his son. He'd come to pick up something.

He sat down at the kitchen table until his ex-wife emerged from the bedroom and approached him mumbling, "Here's the envelope you wanted."

He nodded, then asked, "There any coffee?"

"There is," said Henry's mother.

"Let's have it."

Before Henry's mother could serve the cup, I said I had to leave; it was getting late. I'd had enough of broken homes.

◉ ◉ ◉

"Oh my goodness," Mrs. Dunker said a few days later. "It's time for physical education."

Unlike PS 6, Beverly Vista had no gymnasium, but then who needed one? Our playground covered the block, with no skyscrapers to block the sun.

They sent the girls to the far end of the playground. We boys trooped out to the middle and lined up. The student squad leader for the week barked the orders. "Form columns; dress right dress."

I watched the others measure out their distances from each other by extending their arms, and I tried to do the same thing.

"Jumping jacks," he bellowed. "Ready, begin."

Since I didn't know what he was talking about, I missed the first few before joining in. When we finished, my throat was starting to hurt. The air was laden with smog.

"Alternate toe-toucher. Position, take."

Again, I had to watch before swinging my outstretched hands as low as possible. I couldn't reach my toes.

"Washer woman. Ready, begin."

Knee, ankle, toe. For me, the exercise became knee, ankle, ankle.

"Six count burpees."

The group squatted, kicked back their legs, performed a single pushup, returned to a squat, and rose. Now my chest hurt from the smog.

Henry said something like this was "intolerable torture."

Coach Basham, a small man with marble eyes and a tight mouth, walked up to Henry and addressed him by his last name. "You want to run laps in the smog?"

I looked up at the muzzy yellow sky.

Henry said, "No." It was a very small no.

"Then shut up."

That was a feat which Henry was incapable of achieving. He may not have yelled it, but the stage whisper—something like, "This is a fascist dictatorship"—reached Coach Basham's ears.

"Two laps," Coach Basham said.

"I can't breathe," Henry said.

"Two laps. Get going."

Henry looked at his classmates, all of whom returned his gaze and some of whom chuckled.

Henry stammered something.

"Get going. Now," Coach Basham ordered.

Henry got going, a speedy sort of waddle along the perimeter of the playground.

"Faster," yelled Coach Basham.

"Go Tiger," one of the boys called out. That's how I learned Henry's schoolyard nickname.

Even from a distance, Henry's body projected a portrait of misery. Halfway through the first lap, he slowed to a walk.

"Push," Coach Basham called to him.

Henry pushed but moved no faster.

Someone started talking about the Dodgers. They'd win the pennant, he said. They had Roseboro. Hodges. Drysdale. Koufax. Labine. Snider. Moon. Neal. Wills.

"You sure about that?" Coach Basham asked him.

"You bet," another said.

Henry completed his first lap and slowed down again.

"Keep going," Coach Basham called to Henry. "I told you. Two laps." Then he turned to the rest of us and said, "I don't know. The Giants have Willie Mays, Orlando Cepeda, Willie McCovey . . ." Then back to Henry: "Come on. Run or you'll get a third lap."

Henry staggered through, and when he finished, his horn-rimmed glasses tilted at an angle and his shirt hung out of his pants. But his thick hair remained firm, not a strand out of place thanks to whatever goop he used. Henry's face remained red for the rest of the period during which, because the smog was intense, Coach Basham allowed us to pass the time playing catch. Several threw the ball in Henry's direction and laughed when he missed it.

Time with Henry showed me an alternative history, what my life could have become had Stan not entered in. Put simply, Henry was maladjusted, unable to edit his thoughts, a dangerous trait thanks to his astounding wit that wandered too often into nasty quips. On days that his attitude didn't get him in trouble with teachers, kids ignored him. If he raised his hand and a teacher called on him, off he went, nonstop chatter until the teacher managed to quiet him down. I saw him try to kick the strongest boy in the class, who to his credit did nothing more than grab Henry's leg, plant it back on the ground, and say, "Oh, Henry, come now." I knew I should have spent less time with Henry, whom so many labeled *a bad influence*. The reason I didn't? Henry was wickedly clever and funny. The real reason? I didn't figure it out for years. I couldn't pull away from the contrasting image of myself in the world of no fathers. Henry was a reminder. Henry made me grateful. Henry gave me survivor's guilt.

My time in Mrs. Dunker's hellhole was blessedly short. Reacting to the baby boom, the overcrowded Beverly Vista added a new sixth grade class. The twenty-one students they chose— included me. Our new teacher was a twenty-one-year-old former Rose Parade princess. Everybody loved Miss Nielsen. I found myself learning again.

CHAPTER TWELVE

Strictly Business

During the late 1950s, a subset of California men liked to putter and tinker in their garages, building Rube Goldbergs and what they hoped were better mouse traps. Many ended up in jobs with Lockheed, Hughes, and Rockwell, all of which were centered in LA then. Not my father. He was as dense as I with tools. Stan, however, tinkered, but not in a garage. He started on a larger scale, with business machines.

My first look at my new stepfather's business occurred one day after school, when my mother drove me to Dashew Business Machines. Stan's company, all his, filled a one-story building at 5886 Smiley Drive in Culver City, a bedroom community in 1959, not far from LAX (the airport's name then and its name now, may it never change). I wasn't surprised to find Stan wearing his suit jacket even though he was alone, seated behind his large wooden desk in a corner office with a couple of windows positioned near the ceiling. He looked large, imposing, the prototypical businessman— balding and heavy. A column of white smoke curled away from his pipe. On the desk was a picture of my mother. Mounted on the wall behind Stan's desk was the marlin she'd caught during their honeymoon in Baja California.

Stan was talking on the phone. Each time his side of the conversation became animated, he chopped at the air with his free hand. Since he showed no signs of hanging up, I wandered out to the secretarial bay and roamed among the gray institutional metal desks, each topped with Formica surfaces, each with an electric typewriter. Several executive offices beckoned, dark and empty. So this was what a business looked like. I spun in the swivel chairs, fiddled with one of the Dictaphones, slipped a thin brown dictabelt onto the spools, and poured out a story. No editing; I let go with whatever palaver entered my mind at the moment. When the belt ran out—ten or fifteen minutes later—I pocketed it, then wandered past the kitchen area with its small refrigerator next to a water cooler and a shelf stocked with sugar and non-dairy creamer and thin swivel sticks. I opened a door that led into the darkened factory area, its silent machinery resembling sleeping beasts whose oily smell blended with the odor of unfolded cardboard boxes stacked against the walls. I entered the stock room. On the shelves were plastic credit cards, easily over a thousand, arranged by companies. El Paso Natural Gas, Montgomery Ward, Chase Manhattan Bank, and at least nine more. One pile featured the Navy blue PMR (Pacific Missile Range, at Point Mugu) credit card, complete with a drawing of a guided missile. Then, on its own shelf, the BANKAMERICARD—*BANK* in blue, *AMERICARD* in gold, the rest of the card, white.

None of these plastics contained the customer's name and account number, which made them look as surreal as a clock without its hands. One of Stan's machines would emboss that information onto each of them. I was too young to appreciate the impact these items were having on the world, but *Mad Magazine* gave me a hint when they ran a satire showing a rich man, dressed in a suit and top hat resplendent of the gilded age, displaying a wad of cash to an admiring group of women. The next panel showed the same man flashing a handful of credit cards.

On the wall was a dispenser that contained little red tablets that looked like M&Ms. Out came a few when I pulled at the

[139]

bottom. They didn't taste sweet, which disappointed me. They didn't taste like anything, but that didn't stop me from swallowing a few more before returning to Stan, still on the phone, pipe still in his mouth.

Back in Stan's office, my mother sat on one of the chairs in front of his desk. She looked so prim, every brown hair in place, her skirt without a wrinkle, her high heels shining under the fluorescent light. The side wall behind her brimmed with photographs, almost all of them of some machine surrounded by portly men standing next to or huddling over the contraption. The men (and they were men; no women appeared in any of the pictures) were pale, bald, and stout. Each wore a gray suit, white shirt, and thin dark tie. Each was smiling. They looked nothing like the actors in the glossy prints that my father brought home from the studios. If a director called "Action," what would these businessmen do? The word *action* made my father laugh, hiss, or kiss the girl. As I'd learn when I started meeting them, Stan's underlings permitted themselves at most a muffled guffaw, sometimes covering their mouths as they did so, while their double chins wiggled.

Stan cupped the receiver and motioned to me. After I approached, he scribbled a phone number on a piece of paper and pressed it into my hand. "Skip, I mean Tony," he whispered, "get me Alan Beale in New York. Person-to-person."

Unsure what to do, I went to his secretary's desk and dialed *Operator* on the rotary. My mouth was starting to feel dry.

Fortunately, the operator was friendly and explained that Stan would not have to pay for a person-to-person call if Mr. Beale was not available. I gave her the number Stan had written on the paper. As the phone call traveled east from Culver City, from operator to operator across the Rockies and onward to New York, the static on the line grew. A few moments later, a distant ring tone sounded, followed by a woman's voice.

The operator said, "Mr. Alan Beale, please. Long distance is calling."

"He's not here right now. May I ask who's calling?"

My mouth was becoming very dry, very fast. In a raspy voice, I gave Stan's name.

Stan had just hung up when I walked back into his office to give him the news.

He looked at my mother and said, "Okay, sweetie, let's go home."

"Wait," I croaked. I needed water.

Alarmed, my mother asked what was wrong.

I didn't know why I was so thirsty. She asked if I'd eaten anything.

"Just some candy from the dispenser in the factory."

"Oh, for God's sake," Stan said.

Those tablets were not M&Ms. I'd eaten salt pills, there for the men who worked in the assembly area, which often became hot during the day. One or two tablets helped prevent dehydration, for sodium and chlorine were electrolytes. Take too many, as I had, and you become more dehydrated. It was as if I'd swallowed seawater.

On the way home, Stan and my mother talked about the company, which is to say Stan did most of the talking. They were close to a deal for the imprinters. They were close to a deal for several embossers. A new retail chain was negotiating an order for credit cards. Stan's former employer, Addressograph-Multigraph, was jealous of the success of Dashew Business Machines (he called it DBM). Mal, Stan's assistant, was doing a great job. So was Ace, one of his engineers, and Vi, the company publicist. But not Chuck. Chuck lacked drive. Chuck never came in early. Chuck never left late. Stan planned to let him go. Stan might have to go to New York in a week—some sort of meeting. Stan wallowed in work. His car talk never moved beyond business, concepts I didn't understand yet, and as we passed by a couple of pump jacks that extracted oil from the LA basin, I lost interest.

Stan said the company was going to get bigger. Move to a larger plant. Maybe go public and be listed on a stock exchange. Maybe he'd sell the business.

A brief lull ensued. Into it, I asked Stan, "Why do you want to sell the company?"

My mother steered around a cone that lay sideways on the road.

"Well, Tony," Stan said, "the name of the game is profit."

"Oh," I said, and filed his advice away, to do what F. Scott Fitzgerald's Nick Carraway did with his father's advice: turn it over in my mind ever since. But Stan never gave me the advice Nick's father gave him: "Whenever you feel like criticizing anyone," said Carraway's dad, "just remember that all the people in this world haven't had the advantages that you've had." My own father would tell me that shortly before I graduated from high school.

In the end, Stan didn't follow his advice. He didn't make a profit because he didn't sell DBM when he should have. He hoped the company would become a family business, with his son Skip at the helm and his daughter Leslie and me running whatever divisions suited our talents. The three of us would have other ideas, but that didn't stop Stan. Long before he'd married my mother, I'd soon learn, he'd recruited Skip and Leslie to spend their weekends at his office. Skip, then in his teens, could make himself useful. Since she was seven years younger than Skip, all Leslie did was sit on the floor and draw pictures.

My chores there began shortly after school let out for the summer. "Everybody's working," Stan said one morning, and since I had no other plans, I had no excuse not to ride with him to the plant and spend the day filing correspondence, invoices, and order forms. I wasn't sure how to handle them; Stan's instructions had been ambiguous.

Skip was "in the field," whatever that meant, so Leslie and I ate lunch alone. We didn't talk about the business. We both agreed we were bored.

"What'd you learn at the plant today?" Stan asked that evening as we drove home.

"I don't know," I said.

"I don't know," Leslie said. "Want to see a picture I drew?"

"Not while I'm driving," Stan said.

I looked at it. Leslie was a skilled artist and had portrayed the machine my mother had nicknamed Emma. It filled a small room. Leslie showed it clacking out credit cards on a metal belt that moved from one housing to another.

That night, our dinner talk remained stuck on business. The next night, too. And the next. Over pot roast, chicken, fish, steak, I kept hearing the same phrases. One evening, after telling my mother, "The steak is excellent," Stan said, "Skip, I mean Tony, how was school today?"

The telephone in the den rang.

Stan said, "Catch the phone, Tony. Go on, hurry up."

It was a command, not a request. I skittered into the den and made it to the phone before the caller gave up. The call was for Stan. That wasn't odd. Stan's evening business calls often ran long. He'd installed two phone lines into the house for that reason, not a common feature back then.

"Hi Bert," Stan said after I gave him the receiver. "Where you at?"

An easy thirty minutes later, after Stan hung up, he said another big order had come in. He needed help the next afternoon. The details were vague, but he said I was smart enough for the job.

The second and final subject of the family table talk centered on boats.

Stan wanted a catamaran, a big one, the largest on the West Coast. We heard about his plan during many meals, until one night, after we'd sat down, Stan said, "We shook hands on the catamaran today."

During the year it took to build the *Huka Makani* ("the wind whistles"), we continued to spend summer weekends at the house in Newport Beach. The environment called for relaxation, but Stan couldn't rest. Dashew Business Machines filled his mind. He had to keep racing, and he wanted everyone to rush with him, like the afternoon he, my mother, and I lazed at the end of the dock. I was gazing out at the sailboats that eased by on a gentle breeze. The salty air smelled sweet. Stan asked me to bring him something from the house. As I ambled down the dock, Stan called out, "Fast, Tony. Come on. Move fast."

I sped up, got whatever Stan wanted, and when I returned, he didn't say anything.

The incident hurt me. I saw no reason to be rushed, let alone snapped at, by someone who wasn't my dad. I never forgot what Stan said and the way he said it. I'd yet to read *Speak, Memory* by Vladimir Nabokov. Had I, I might have quoted him to Stan: "I appeal to parents: never, never say, 'Hurry up,' to a child."

CHAPTER THIRTEEN

Game of Hearts

By February 1959, with both my parents married to new people and with me three months shy of twelve, time with my father had settled into an every-other-weekend rhythm. One day that month, my father took me to a live Red Skelton broadcast. It was like a homecoming; I'd met Red as a much younger child. As before, he was charming, funny, witty. He took time to greet me and make me feel good by saying something amusing. His eyebrows hopscotched across his forehead. His face exploded into dimples when he gave me his rubber band smile. And there was his thick red hair that retreated on the sides. Within five minutes I felt as if he'd joined my family.

Red was already out of makeup. My father bantered with the woman who was applying his. The sound stage was a riot of activity. Cameras in position, cables, lights—all the good things I'd remembered from *Half Pint Panel*. Minutes before showtime, someone led me to the announcer's booth, where I sat on a stool next to a man with thick brown hair, combed straight back. His tan face looked as though it had been caked with makeup even though no camera would train an eye on him. He gave me a wink and signaled for quiet. A light went on, he faced the microphone and took a breath.

"Live from Hollywood," he said, with excitement worthy of an alien landing. "It's the *Red Skelton Show!*"

The story line ran like this: my father and Mary Beth Hughes played Philip and Velma, two crooks who ran a lonely-hearts racket which benefited from killing off clients. Red, otherwise known as the lovelorn hillbilly Clem Kadiddlehopper, played the pair's latest sucker.

The portion I remember best was the part where my father and Mary Beth Hughes toasted each other. She said something like, "Cheers." He said something like, "I've got to hand it to you, baby (or was it sweetheart or darling?) You've killed off three husbands and two insurance companies."

That's it. Nothing more. Sure, Red Skelton was the next victim, but by show's end Red was still standing, the sole lonely heart to survive the scheme. And my father? As usual, he played the bad guy. At least he didn't die in front of me on the sound stage.

◉ ◉ ◉

One day that same month, the corner of Charleville and Rodeo brimmed with reflectors, tripods, and cameras. Outdoor lights hung on large posts. Cables ran along the sidewalk and into trucks the size of moving vans. They blocked my view of Romanoff's, the upscale restaurant on Rodeo Drive across from our apartment. People in clothes that ranged from casual to downright sloppy milled about. Some picked at sandwiches that were stacked on a long table. A voice barked out orders. I didn't stop to watch. It was a shoot and I'd seen plenty of them. I never learned if they were filming a movie, a television show, or a commercial. It was a non-event, and I detoured around the jumble to cross the street and go home.

Skip arrived from high school a few minutes later. In the kitchen, he told my mother, "There's some guy with a bullhorn running around calling everybody a stupid imbecile."

My mother looked out the window and made a face. "He's probably the assistant director," she said. "They want everybody to think they have a lot of power."

"But why would he be calling everyone a stupid imbecile?" Skip's eyes narrowed. So did his mouth. I could have sworn he was preparing for a fistfight.

"That's the film industry," my mother said. Her voice executed a tonal shift as though she remembered something. Her new stepson's anger must have brought up memories she'd never shared with me. She flinched before she said, "It's a disgusting business." She'd never acted or even tried to, but she'd visited plenty of sets and must have seen her fair share of little dictators. I also imagine that despite what promised to be an excellent new marriage, much of her vehemence was due to her lasting anger at Mai and my father.

Skip wolfed down a bowl of Jell-O, which failed to calm him. I remained convinced he wanted to find the assistant director and beat him up. The man had offended his sense of justice. Skip had a protective streak, something I hadn't noticed until then.

"Do you have any homework?" my mother asked him.

Whatever he had, didn't prevent Skip from driving somewhere to get a part he needed for his 1946 Ford, which was parked across the street from the shoot. "I guess I better go before those bastards tow it," he said.

When my mother said that "bastard" was not a nice word, Skip apologized, but added that if the assistant director so much as looked his way, that's what he'd call him.

Skip didn't mention the incident over dinner, maybe because the meal was given over to one of Stan's lectures about Skip's Ford. The scolding came without warning. Once again, Stan claimed Skip was getting bad grades because of his car.

Skip looked bewildered. He hadn't brought home a bad grade

in a while, nor would he for another week or two, not until his French test.

This time Stan and Skip did not shift into the safe subject of sailing. Stan leaned his big head toward Skip and glared at him. Even when seated, Stan could intimidate me with his size. His harangue gathered strength as it proceeded. He berated Skip for grievances having nothing to do with his car, telling him he had to work harder, study harder, take life seriously. My mother remained quiet, as did I, afraid to put fork to mouth. By the time it ended, Stan forbade Skip from using the car for the rest of the week. "And Friday night, too, for your date."

Skip started to protest, but Stan waved the back of his hand at him. "I don't want to discuss it."

Skip got up from the table, his face red, his eyes moist. It was the first time I'd seen that emotion in him. He said something like, "Just because you're grumpy about the business doesn't mean you have to take it out on me." He barely succeeded in choking out the remark before running up the stairs, leaving the rest of us in a silence I had no intention of breaking.

Skip was right. Stan was grumpy, ready, I feared, to let fly in my direction with yet another lecture. This was the most unpredictable aspect of Stan's personality. He could cruise through a meal or a conversation even-keeled, and then for what seemed to be no reason at all, launch into a diatribe. Skip's car. My skipping a chore. Peccadillos in my mind, but sometimes something somewhere somehow roused the tyrant in him. I wanted to finish my meal and start my homework—fast, before Stan latched onto some fault of mine, of which there were plenty. The conversation returned to Stan's business. I listened, understanding little, retaining less, and thinking that what he'd done to Skip was uncalled -for.

◉ ◉ ◉

A month or so later, on a weekend night that I was spending with my father and Mai, they invited friends over to play Hearts, my father's favorite card game. From the living room couch where I lay trying to do my homework, I could see the five of them at the dining table. The group played round after round, and in between tricks, they drank coffee (no alcohol) and chomped on Fritos. "Goddamn it," my father yelled. "He shot the moon again."

It wasn't the first time someone at the table had raised a voice.

"Holy crap," said Gene. Using both hands, he pretended to pull out tufts of his dullish red hair. Gene O'Donnell was another struggling actor. He'd had bits parts on, among others, *Sergeant Preston of the Yukon*, *Death Valley Days*, and *The Lucy Show*. I'd met him and his wife Dolores a few years earlier, shortly before my parents' divorce.

"That's three times tonight, so far," said Bert, the winner, after gulping down the last of his coffee and stubbing out his cigarette. He pressed his thick lips together, a move that made him look dissatisfied despite his victory. He said something about how this victory would impress his new girlfriend, "an actress, of course."

"Is this one your age?" Mai asked as she gathered the cards and shuffled them.

Bert, in his forties like the rest of the group, said, "Are you kidding?" Then, with a grin, he asked, "Want to bet some money on the next hand?"

"What money?" Gene said, a little too loudly. "I need work."

So did my father. He often said, "Money's tight," and each time he did, I felt a mixture of pain and fear. He, Mai, and her two boys were still renting their modest house near the mid-Wilshire area of Los Angeles. The night would pass with nobody betting.

The cards flew to the middle of the table, to be scooped up by one of the five at the end of the hand. I got the impression that the longer they played and the louder they laughed, the easier it was for everyone to forget their finances. Mai won that round, but I don't think anyone wrote down the scores. As my father dealt the next hand, Gene mentioned a director he'd worked with, a man who cheated at Hearts. Bert called him an asshole.

"He can't direct his way out of a paper bag," my father said before lighting another cigarette.

They passed left. Mai picked up three cards from Gene, the singleton queen of spades I was sure, because she looked at Gene and said, "Oh, aren't you a sweetheart."

Off they went again, whooping through the night, cards winging into the pile and coffee cups rattling against saucers. Columns of cigarette smoke rose to the cottage cheese ceiling, where they mushroomed out and drifted toward where I lay with my geography textbook, trying to memorize Denmark's cash crops.

A few moments later, Bert called out, "The rest are mine."

Gene let out an "oh *shit*."

My father hollered, "He shot again." I could swear his voice made the bay window rattle.

Watching my father at the table, something appeared different from the way he acted when I was a child eavesdropping on my parents' Sherman Oaks parties. He was the Iron Duke of radio, back then, the most famous person in the room, dressed in a fashion forward sport coat, surrounded by industry friends who were optimistic and working and reveling in a lovely world. Not now. In clothes just this side of sloppy, he was playing cards with men fighting for their money, like him. My father may have sounded as though he was having as much fun as he used to, and he still may have been the most famous person at the table, but now I think, at least for one night, he was screening out the world.

They took a break. Mai went into the kitchen to make some more coffee, and Gene walked over to me. "How's your beautiful mother?" he asked.

"Fine," I said. While Gene and Dolores had remained friends

with my father after the divorce, they apparently harbored no ill will toward my mother. Since my parents' separation, none of the couples on my mother's side of the ledger had ever asked about my father.

I didn't know what else to say. I didn't think of my mother as beautiful, although she was. I thought of her as an extraordinary person, kinder and more empathetic than I'd ever be. But she never would have enjoyed this kind of an evening. She preferred quieter conversation, and she'd quit smoking after marrying Stan, a few months before Stan quit smoking pipes.

Gene leaned toward me, so close I could smell the coffee on his breath. "You know how gorgeous your mother is?" he asked. Before I could answer, he said that as a kid in Brooklyn, my mother had entered a beauty contest.

"She missed perfection by a quarter of an inch," he said.

I had no idea how he knew this and only a dim notion of what he was talking about.

Until then, nobody had told me my mother's measurements nor that she'd competed in a beauty contest, nor what Red Doff's publicist had told the moguls in town: that my mother was "pretty enough to be a glamour star herself, with an IQ to match." I looked across the room at Mai, still in the kitchen. Both women had sweet faces; my mother's, almost always. Mai, at times.

It was almost midnight. I alternated between Danish agriculture and watching my father and his friends. Out of work or not, actors knew how to have more fun than Stan. Stan never acted this frisky, but he made me feel safe. With that thought, I drifted off to sleep.

It was the sunlight through the window that woke me, not the voices from the dining table, where my father and his friends were still tossing cards and laughing. A crumpled Fritos bag lay on the floor. The room reeked of stale smoke and coffee, and as they kept playing, my father said something about the House of the Seven Toilets. "It's somewhere up in the Hollywood Hills," he said. A big place, home to an actor who'd scored a series and had an overheated sense of bathroom humor. Each of his throne rooms contained a gimmick. The proud owner threw a party one night, and before it got underway, he'd given my father a tour de toilette.

I strained to listen in. What grade-school boy didn't appreciate bathroom humor? I didn't pause to wonder whether all men in their late forties would find it funny. My father clearly did. Ensconced in his tale, his white teeth gleaming, he recounted how his friend had seated a half-dressed mannequin in the powder room. Whenever guests opened the door, they said, "Oh I'm sorry," shut the door, and waited outside. And waited. And fidgeted. And grew miserable.

"Oh Christ," Gene said.

Mai and Dolores remained silent.

My father puffed on his cigarette before moving to the next bathroom. "You sit down on the toilet, and hairy arms come out from behind and hug you around the chest."

Gene and Bert broke into laughter.

My father raced through the rest of the bathroom tricks: A recorded message that, when triggered by a bum on the commode, shouted out, "Not yet, we're still painting down here." A camera dropping from the ceiling. A Timpani that crashed the moment someone flushed. Two more I can't remember. I made a mental note to ask my father for this house's address, but never did.

After my father's story, Bert needed to use the bathroom.

Mai pointed down the hall and said, "There it is. We can't afford a lot of bathrooms."

I looked at my father, who grimaced.

Stan could afford a lot of bathrooms, but looking back, that's not what I thought about. It was the contrast between the two personalities, between Stan—serious—and my father—playful. I was oscillating between two worlds. At times I'd watch my father, tense next to Mai, and feel lucky I lived with my mother and Stan. Other times while enduring one of Stan's outbursts, I missed my father's frolics and detours. More and more, I thought of school, the center between two worlds and the source of good grades, which, if I could earn them, would bring accolades from both families.

⊙ ⊙ ⊙

My mother and Stan bought a two-story traditional on McCarty Drive, four blocks from Beverly Hills High School. My first trip there occurred with Stan, my mother, and her decorator, a vivacious lady with an engaging voice. En route, Stan and I remained quiet while my mother and the decorator traded ideas. Rarely had my mother sounded so cheerful.

We pulled into the driveway. A plane tree shaded the front yard. On the left, flanked by black shutters, was a beveled window. Looking at me, my mother said, "That's the maid's room." To the right was the garage and above it, an open space large enough, the decorator said, to add on another room. A brick walkway led between flower beds to the front door.

"I hope you like it," my mother said to me.

I already did.

Together, we walked into the foyer. To the right was the living room; to the left, a circular staircase; and—fifteen or so feet in front of us—the powder room.

Pointing straight ahead, my mother described the first change she planned to make in our new home. "We need a wall and a door there," she told the decorator, her voice full of gusto, "because otherwise when you come in, the first thing you see is a toilet."

Stan nodded in agreement.

Not long before, my father had riveted his friends with a story about an actor with seven toilets, all rigged as practical jokes. At the time, I was too self-absorbed to think about the contrast between him and my mother, but as I grew older and asked myself why I still recalled the seven toilets story and the exchange between my mother and her decorator in the entry of our new house, I realized the truth it exposed—that divorcing my father had been the best thing that could have happened to my mother.

My parents were opposite in so many ways. I never understood why they married. Sure, they were childhood sweethearts. Sure, my mother was beautiful and sweet. Sure, my father was dashing. He'd left Brooklyn for California and before long had called my mother.

"I have seven hundred and fifty dollars in the bank," he said, "Take the Super Chief out here. I want to marry you."

The Depression was on. My mother was working as a legal secretary in Manhattan. Her little salary helped her family pay the bills. At the lunch counter each day, like many others, she asked for a cup of hot water, added some ketchup, and drank the mixture as tomato soup. If she had an extra nickel, maybe my mother ordered a piece of buttered toast. Is that why she said yes? I should have asked her.

CHAPTER FOURTEEN

The Angry Red Planet

"I have to look good all the time," my father said when I asked why he got a haircut every week. "You never know when my agent will call."

His agent had not called in a long time.

My father was driving toward Drucker's, his favorite barbershop, on Wilshire Boulevard in Beverly Hills. I didn't care that it was a celebrity hangout; I didn't recognize George Raft or Lawrence Welk or anyone else who frequented the place. I was resolving myself to another morning of boredom.

A man in front of us failed to accelerate when the light turned green.

"Sometime today you going to move that car?" my father said under his breath. The motorist didn't move until my father blasted his horn.

As usual, at the barbershop I skimmed through the magazines in the waiting area. The articles were duller than usual, and within minutes I started wandering among the barber chairs, where a number of customers were talking on extension telephones the staff brought to them. I did something—what I don't recall, but probably I interrupted one of my father's phone calls.

He hung up. Then, glaring at me without budging from his

barber's chair, my father said, "The first thing you have to learn on the long road to becoming a gentleman is—"

My father paused, thanks, I believe, to his good peripheral vision. Two chairs away sat a boy roughly my age. He had a strong, square jawline. Eyes set far apart. Thick, dirty-blond hair.

My father said, "He's perfect for the camera."

If the boy heard my father, he didn't react. As a barber continued to shape the boy's curls, he remained placid, as though he was used to being admired.

"Yes, he's handsome," said my father's barber.

The boy's parents walked over to my father.

"Is he in pictures?" my father asked.

"Not yet," his mother said.

"He ought to be," my father said in a voice close to breathless. "He has such a *level look*." I didn't know what that meant, but figured it had something to do with stardom.

His parents said something like, "Coming from you, that's a compliment." Then they asked for my father's autograph.

My father didn't introduce them to me.

⊙ ⊙ ⊙

If my father had been a producer, the boy would have been discovered, that magical, heady event struggling actors lived for. Maybe the kid already had his SAG (Screen Actors Guild) card. Whatever his status, he never said a word as his barber kept snipping.

Enough of Hollywood was left in me to know that this boy had *the look*, and it made me sad. I wasn't ugly, but whatever gene turns you into a movie star had missed me.

Or maybe I didn't care to catch it. If I couldn't look as debonair as my father, I'd put on my glasses and reach for the high grades.

The first things to learn? Algebra, literature, history, French. Not how to become a gentleman.

My father didn't offer me a haircut that morning, nor did I care. I couldn't have sat through a two-hour marathon. Whenever my mother and stepfather gave me two dollars for a haircut, they sent me to a barber who whizzed through my thicket in twenty minutes, and even that I barely tolerated.

I may have been only twelve in 1959, but I was beginning to understand that my father's career was slipping. Too often he said, "money's tight." One Sunday morning, after looking through a stack of bills on the kitchen table, he whispered, "I need work." I doubt he knew I heard him. My mother told me he wasn't sending child support checks, although on one occasion, she said, sweetly, "Your daddy mailed a check this week." (A hundred dollars, I'd find out after decades had passed.) That followed, I also discovered, a lecture from a Superior Court judge "to meet the obligations under the order." The judge's warning made the papers. My mother never sought a contempt order. She didn't have to because Stan was taking care of me, which raised feelings of gratitude and guilt. I felt torn between my fathers. Protected by one, energized by the other, grateful that nobody was forcing me to choose.

To better his career, what should my father have done?

"Why doesn't he write?" my mother said one day. "He writes beautifully. Or he should try to direct. He shouldn't sleep so late."

The reasons for my father's problems mystified me. As far as I could tell, the public's taste in actors wasn't changing. But in fairness, those years were a tired era for show business, at least for movies. From 1950 through 1960, weekly admissions in movie theaters fell by more than half. Journalist Ronald Brownstein quotes a young Michael Medavoy saying that the Warner Bros. lot was deserted.

Looking back, however, there were personal reasons. My

father's slide began after he accepted the leading role in the third season of *Foreign Intrigue*, a dying TV series that took him to Sweden for a year. Once we returned, I imagine my father's agent spread a "Hey, I'm back" message around town, which didn't work. Leaving my mother didn't help either, not in the mid-fifties, when many thought divorce was immoral.

My father's downward slide was gentle. Out first went the big screen parts. They may not have been starring roles, but before his European detour, he'd appeared in movies with names like Dean Martin, Jerry Lewis, Humphrey Bogart, Rita Hayworth, Barbara Stanwyck, Kirk Douglas, and Rita Moreno. Once he returned to LA, he had to content himself with feature roles in TV Westerns. My father levelled with me about this slow-motion reversal of fortune. "I can't just take any role," he said over lunch. "If an actor does that, people start saying, 'He's slipping.'" He wanted to hold out for the leads and the series, but with bills to pay, he accepted starring roles in three B-flicks—*Terror in the Haunted House*; *Guns, Girls, and Gangsters*; and *Date With Death*. He took me to see the first one, but not the next two.

Were casting directors passing on him? I'm sure. Movie directors? Writers? They don't pick the players, although at times they make suggestions.

The producers, then. When I was twenty-three, two years after my father's death, my mother and I sat across from each other on the creamy white sofas in our living room, a coffee cup in her hand, orange juice in mine. "You know Gerry had a temper," she said.

"I know," I said. He'd shouted at me more than once. I still recalled him in our dinette, sometime during first grade, yelling at me not to "make a fuss" at dinner one night—something about my cherished hot biscuits: "And if you make a fuss tomorrow night, you'll get two biscuits. And if you make a fuss that night, you'll get one biscuit. And if you make a fuss again, you'll get no biscuit." There was a night in Stockholm when he boasted about how he'd scolded everyone on the set of *Foreign Intrigue*. On another occasion, with my mother and me in the car, my father almost had an accident. He hollered at the other driver, who didn't speak English, "I've never hit a woman, but I'll start with you."

"Oh dear," my mother had said, "Gerry needs some lunch."

Gerry didn't hit the driver, and after a decent lunch, he'd calmed down.

My mother put her cup on the coffee table and leaned toward me before speaking again. "I talked one time—with a producer, somebody well-known." She didn't name him; I should have asked her to. She continued, "And even though your daddy and I weren't married anymore, I asked what Gerry could do to get back on track."

I leaned toward her, saying nothing.

The producer had a part in a movie that was just right for my dad, she said, but the man went on to tell her, "'You know? Life's too short.'"

It hurt to hear that, but my father's worth as a parent didn't change—or maybe it did. Children can sense a parent's bad behavior. I wondered if my father ever suspected what was holding him back. Sitting on that couch with my mother, I realized that after my father moved out, he never yelled at me again. Not once. The times he was upset with me, he let me know it in a calm, measured voice.

⊙ ⊙ ⊙

Finally, in 1959, my father scored a mild victory—the lead in *The Angry Red Planet*.

It was at most ten days' work, but the part excited my father, which in turn excited me. It wasn't a Western. It was a science fiction/horror movie, and best of all, it was the second time I could watch him play the good guy. I wouldn't have to see him die on the screen. I'd only have to watch him *almost* die. Thanks to an amoeba, my father lay in a hospital bed, motionless, unable to speak, his face a web of agony with protozoan green slime all over his forearm, "Literally eating his tissue," the doctor said.

⊙ ⊙ ⊙

Naturally Stan was on the telephone when my mother and I arrived at the plant before closing time the week before Thanksgiving, 1959. It was the first time I'd seen his domain fully populated— women in nylons, puffed hair, and high heels. Men with narrow ties and shirts as white as their complexions. They raced about, moving fast, the way Stan liked it, shuttling from accounts payable to shipping to accounts receivable to the coffee pot. In the shop, men worked with the embossing and imprinting machines, testing them, oiling them, adjusting them. Farther back near the loading dock, other men packed the merchandise.

Stan cupped the receiver. "Skip—I mean Tony—I have a job for you," he said. A pile of materials lay on one of the secretarial desks, next to an equally high pile of envelopes. "These need to go out."

They were copies of *Data Digest*, DBM's house organ, each month's issue featuring "monthly facts and figures for industry." As a present, Stan would give me a copy of Volume 1 number 1, which he'd published in 1954. As I stuffed, I glanced at some of the story headlines:

DASHASTRIPPER USERS SING PRAISES

COLOR CODING AIDS PROCESSING
(DBM DASHAPLATES, LIGHTWEIGHT METAL
PLATES FOR ADDRESSING MACHINE AND
IDENTIFICATION USE, ARE NOW AVAILABLE IN
NINE COLORS)

POSITIVE IDENTIFICATION CONTROL
SCORES SUCCESSES
DBM DEVELOPS AUTOMATIC NUMBER
-DATA POSTING UNIT

PRECISION MARKS DB PRODUCTS

DASHAPLATES ARE 1/3 AS HEAVY AS OTHER TYPES OF
ADDRESSING MACHINE PLATES. WITH THIS TREMENDOUS
SAVING IN WEIGHT, ADDRESSING-MACHINE OPERATORS,
FEMALE, HAVE ENOUGH RESERVE ENERGY AT THE END OF
A WORKING DAY TO LICK THEIR WEIGHT IN WILD-CATS,
PROVIDED WILD-CATS CAN BE FOUND.

I finished and returned to Stan's office in time to see him hang up the phone. I could have sworn that his balding head was glowing.

"Honey," he said to my mother, "next week Dashew Business Machines will become a publicly-owned company."

Sensational news, I began to realize. Every morning I could open up the business section of the *Los Angeles Times* and read Stan's surname in the stock listings. For days, the family was excited, especially Skip, who understood the significance better than I. Stan talked shop through breakfast. My mother zipped through the women's section of the *Los Angeles Times*, with more delight than usual it seemed. Men with suits and ties showed up more often for dinner. There was something about these businessmen. They had complexions no camera would care for. They talked in ways no screenwriter would dream of penning. Their foreheads glistened despite the absence of spotlights. Many had jowls and yellow teeth. Their jokes weren't funny. They talked of FIFO and LIFO, rates of return, cash and graphs, gross and net. All new terms for me.

⊙ ⊙ ⊙

Like Stan, my father felt upbeat during the fall of 1959. He'd finished filming *The Angry Red Planet* and with the space race reaching its heights, he was sure the story—man's first trip to Mars—would become a hit.

The events would fall within the same November week, the release of *The Angry Red Planet* and the public offering of Dashew Business Machines. It was going to be a stellar Thanksgiving weekend.

I say that with no memory of what was supposed to happen, whether one set of parents or the other would have a party, whether people would gather at Stan's house or my father's house or both. Nobody talked about celebrations, which is most likely why I didn't feel disappointed when nothing happened. My mother and Stan had me for the holiday weekend. I did my homework. Stan talked on the phone. My mother saw her friends. Skip probably took Eve to a movie (not my father's). I doubt I mentioned *The Angry Red Planet* to any of them. The event passed so quietly that I forgot that DBM had gone public. Stan had to remind me to look up DBM in the morning paper, which I did. His name was there all right, among the "over the counter" listings. *Dashew*. How could I not be impressed?

⊙ ⊙ ⊙

One week later. Saturday, December 5, 1959, at breakfast to be precise—my father finished his eggs and started in on his burned bacon and toast. I was spending one of my every-other weekends with him and Mai. She finished her coffee. Her two sons, Tommy and Timmy, fidgeted and ate their buttered toast. I used my fork to push a sausage around my plate. Outside, the sky was gray. I know I didn't say that Stan's company had gone public.

My father already had combed his hair, combed it just so, as always. He wore one of his jumpsuits. He was the only one of us five who didn't look like they'd just woken up.

Dad said to us, "And tonight, we're all going to see," he dropped his voice an octave, "*The Angry Red Planet.*"

He looked at Tommy and Timmy. "You'll like the monsters." His voice deepened with the word *monsters*.

His stepsons perked up.

"Like the giant *rat-bat.*" He pronounced the trochee name of the beast in quick staccato and with a wicked grin.

Tommy squealed. In his disheveled clothes, he looked like the eight-year-old he was. Timmy asked if rat-bats could fly. He may have been six, but he acted calmer, more composed than his older brother.

Mai had yet to put on any makeup or comb her hair. She said, "I hope this movie makes us some money. We could use it."

Her words shot the smile out of Dad's mouth, and his countenance returned to what I'd become used to over the past year: tight mouth, creased forehead, sad eyes. The poignant look of an actor struggling for roles that had flowed his way once, but not now.

His expression didn't change until Timmy asked what other monsters lived on Mars.

Dad said, "Wait until you see the giant amoeba."

"What's that?"

"A big slimy cell," Dad said. "It slithers up and *gets* ya."

Timmy flinched and then laughed. Dad finished his breakfast and lit a cigarette.

I was happy for another reason. A year earlier I'd sat beside my father in a theater and watched him star in *Terror in the Haunted House* (also called *My World Dies Screaming*) while we shared a bag of popcorn. I'd looked at his forty-foot face on the screen, then at his real face next to me, then back to him on the screen. I felt special. How many kids could do that? Not many, even in LA. That film had been a campy flop, but I didn't care. Dad and I had been together, and—a bonus for me—he'd played the hero; he didn't die. Now we'd share another movie, with him as the good guy. I spread a dollop of jelly onto my toast and ate it slowly to savor the taste.

◉ ◉ ◉

"I can't wait for the rat-bat," Tommy said from the backseat of Dad's car.

Timmy didn't say anything as we drove through the evening drizzle.

I wondered out loud if there was life on Mars.

"I don't know," Mai said.

"I'll bet there is," Tommy said.

"Let's hope we get up there before the Russians do," my father said.

Two months earlier, the Soviet Union had launched the first rocket to the moon, and last month, they'd taken the first pictures of the far side of the moon.

My father drove us into a section of Hollywood where the local chamber of commerce hadn't bothered to put up Christmas decorations. The pedestrians on the wet sidewalk looked as drab as the one-and two-story buildings that lined the street. Many of the billboards above them read, *This space for rent.* The theater (a single screen, as most were then) was so nondescript we almost missed it. On the marquee was the movie's title, in plain black letters. A freestanding kiosk in the middle of the entrance served as the box office. The bored-looking man didn't recognize my father as he took his money, a sure sign that he hadn't cared to see the movie. The empty lobby felt musty and smelled of popcorn. One of the lights was out. Near the candy counter, torn sections of dull red carpet peeled off the floor.

My seat squeaked as I settled into it, and the cushion was so thin I could feel the metal underneath. We sat halfway back, toward house left. Next to us was nobody. Dad said it was still early. Tommy asked for popcorn, and Dad went out to buy some.

"Now share it," he said when he returned with the little bag.

A few patrons shuffled down the aisle, removed their raincoats, and dropped themselves into seats on the other side of the theater. Maybe fifteen people had joined us by the time the lights dimmed. I took a handful of popcorn when Tommy passed the bag.

The moment my father appeared on the screen, I clapped—twice, I think, before realizing that I was clapping alone. Embarrassed, I looked about to see if anyone was glaring at me. This wasn't a private screening or a premiere, where friends applauded the moment a colleague entered a scene or appeared in the credits. Nobody seemed to have heard me, perhaps because on the other side of the theater, someone was coughing.

The rat-bat made its appearance, all right, complete with fangs, claws, and drool, but rather than terrorizing, the creature looked as if it belonged in a cartoon drawn by an earthling of limited talent. The fact that the exteriors had been filmed through a red-tinted lens didn't help either; it robbed the scenes of realism.

Next, as my father and his crew rowed an inflatable raft across a lake, the giant blob of an amoeba surfaced. What passed for its skin looked like a blend of bubble bath and Jell-O. I would have laughed, except that by then I was engaged in the story. I leaned forward and waited to see how my father would handle this crisis.

The amoeba didn't stop at the shore. It was amphibious and it moved fast, forcing the group to run for their rocket, but as it gained on them, a wavy line materialized at the top of the screen. For a long moment it hung there, and then it began to jerk back and forth like a worm on a fishhook. Somehow a thread had become attached to the projector lens.

It wouldn't let go. The theater remained quiet while the thread oscillated and wriggled, faster, slower, then faster again until it became impossible to ignore, no matter what the amoeba was about to do to my father. The thread upstaged man and monster. Upset that nobody did anything about it, I looked away and focused on the dust motes that filled the projector beam. A second or two later, my father started to fidget, and I sensed his anger building. Finally, Dad summoned an usher. "Go up there," he whispered, "and tell them to get rid of that thread." The man hurried off but at least another couple of minutes passed before the thread went away. By then, Dad and his crew had made it back to their rocket, but not before the amoeba had caught up to them and, moments after the hatch closed, enveloped the ship and started dissolving the metal.

I offered Dad the popcorn bag. He gestured it away.

When the film ended, the few in the audience donned their coats. Even the catchy instrumental that played under the credits failed to hold them. One by one, they filed out to the street.

The car was quiet as Dad drove us home. We didn't stop for ice cream. At one point during the ride, Mai let out a sigh. I grew nervous. I wanted my father to say something.

Into the silence, either Tommy or Timmy said, "The rat-bat was neat."

My father's reply, "That's nice," came out like a growl.

No one spoke after that. The silence unnerved me more than the movie had. I sat as still as possible, trying not to breathe the smoke from my father's cigarette, and I listened to the steady *thunk* of the windshield wipers as the car skimmed through puddles in the street. At the time, I was sure my father was seething, ready to explode. Now I'm sure he was sad, ready to cry.

After Tommy and Timmy went to the bedroom they shared, Dad converted the living room couch into a bed. That's where I slept during weekends with him. Something was wrong with the heating, and a chill from the rain had forced its way into the house.

"Here," he said, and draped his heavy gray trench coat over my pudgy body. It was the coat he'd worn while filming *Foreign Intrigue.* "It still has my good lining in it," he said. I wasn't sure what he meant by the word *lining,* but didn't ask for a definition. I was just happy his mood had improved. With a few deft moves of his arms, he tucked me in and hugged me good night.

Once the light was out, I pulled his trench coat more tightly around me and replayed his movie through my mind, lingering over the amoeba with its single cyclopean eye that spun round and round, this time without a thread to interfere as it glided out of the lake and—ever so lightly touched my father's arm.

CHAPTER FIFTEEN

The Verdict is Yours

My father and I were spending the day in my grandmother's studio apartment. It was too cold to swim in the building's pool, so we sat in her room; my father drinking coffee, and me eating an oversized piece of my grandmother's bundt kuchen. I was four months into my freshman year at Beverly Hills High School.

My father couldn't stop talking about *The Verdict Is Yours*, a television series in which actual lawyers played the TV lawyers and the judges were men—*only* men back then—who'd actually sat on the bench. Professional actors played the defendants and witnesses. They received a general outline and had to ad lib the dialogue and joust with the lawyers the same as a defendant or witness might do in a real courtroom.

"You see how lousy a court can be," said my father, "and how lawyers treat you?"

A day or two before, one of his friends, an attorney who'd recently appeared on the show, had described the experience.

"Oh, Gerry," my grandmother said while I listened.

"They twist the truth," my father said. "They turn everything you say against you."

My grandmother said, "How horrible."

My father put down his coffee and described how quickly and

how deeply you "get into it. And pretty soon, *you're fighting for your life."*

As he spoke, my father's attitude shifted. I could tell he was imagining himself in a more realistic situation than the scripted part he'd played the year before, in *Perry Mason*. This might have been the first time I'd seen him fearful of something besides his shaky finances. I was facing a father intimidated by the concept of a courtroom full of clever bullies.

My father paused to light another cigarette before adding that he'd asked his friend, the lawyer, how he'd handle a witness who had absolute, mathematical proof to support his testimony.

The lawyer said, "I'd mock you. I'd say, 'Oh, you know so much. Where'd you go to school? You're so good at math? What's the product of forty-seven times thirty-two? What's the square root of nineteen?'"

This wasn't right, I thought. Trials were supposed to be fair fights. What my father described was a match where the truth didn't matter at all. I didn't consider how a judge should handle bad behavior, but I did realize the safest place to be in a courtroom was on the judge's bench, the highest perch in every way. All a judge had to do, it seemed, was watch the fight and make some rulings, a process, I found out, that also defined justice at Beverly Hills High School.

⊙ ⊙ ⊙

Student Court was Beverly High's own judiciary. I learned about it from our student manual whose title reflected our mascot, the *Norman Guide*. Because it aroused my curiosity, one winter day after school let out, I walked to the business education center, a one-story slab of a building where the court was located. There, in the front of a classroom, at long tables lined together in an attempt to simulate a bench, sat nine boys, all juniors and seniors. None of them smiled.

They called them *justices*. I guess the title *judge* was too commonplace for Beverly Hills High School. The only law book they needed was the *Norman Guide.* Its statutes were clear and succinct, unlike many California laws, as I discovered after I became a judge for real. Here were some:

> It's taboo to . . . sleep in class, or seem to . . .

> Examples of unsuitable dress (for boys): blue jeans, T-shirts, round shirttails worn outside pants.

> Appropriate appearance for girls: skirts must come to the middle of the knee and hang freely.

> Examples of unsuitable hairdress: curler devices in hair, head scarf . . . or bangs or hair falling over eyes or in such a way that it distracts from studies.

Smoking, gambling, causing class disturbances—such were the offenses that filled the docket, along with any behavior the administration chose to label *conduct unbecoming a Norman.* We were too innocent for crimes involving weapons and drugs. No one worried about pesky details like the Constitution.

In Student Court, you were guilty until proven guilty. The court's only purpose was to "determine the disciplinary action for Normans who have broken school rules." And unlike the intricate sentencing guidelines California judges must follow, the *Norman Guide* made punishment easy. Everyone started a semester with forty *Norman points.* The justices simply deducted a certain number for each offense. Lose twenty points and you joined the *lost privilege list*; ten more put you on the *restricted list.* Lose all forty and they suspended you.

The girls' vice principal rose to present the first case. No longer did she evoke the day in September when, in a sweet, throaty voice suggestive of a loving grandmother, she'd welcomed us ninth graders. Now Mrs. Pauley sounded ruthless as she called out a boy's name. A prosecutor's scowl took over her normally pleasant face even though Mrs. Pauley wasn't prosecuting anybody. The boy who shambled forward had already been convicted.

"Conduct unbecoming a Norman," Mrs. Pauley said. He'd been caught out of bounds, wherever that was. No one identified the forbidden location, and none of the justices cared to learn the details. The boy stood there and said nothing.

The chief justice looked to his right and then to his left while his associate jurists jotted down something and, without a word, passed their slips of paper to the center, where the chief uncapped his pen. I realized he was calculating, not writing, when, a few moments later, he announced the punishment: detention and the loss of ten Norman points.

So that was it. The court's ruling consisted of an integer, and the chief justice's sole function was to sum up the digits and divide by nine.

If any of the justices noticed me in the back of the classroom, they would have seen a nervous little freshman with horn-rimmed glasses and curly hair, not well-combed. My rotund body remained still, fearful that if I attracted attention, they'd make me a defendant on the spot. I almost scooted out the door, but I wanted to witness another case.

The next victim was a tall girl with trendy white lipstick and ratted brown hair. As she stood at a table that served as the dock, Mrs. Pauley consulted a manila folder and gave the number of the girl's locker. "When opened," Mrs. Pauley recited, "student's locker was found to contain cigarettes." Years would pass before I'd learn that at faculty meetings, Mrs. Pauley lit up cigarillos.

My eighth-grade teacher taught us that the Fourth Amendment kept Americans "secure in their . . . papers, and effects, against unreasonable searches and seizures." But despite a combination lock, the papers and effects in this girl's locker were not secure at all. Someone—no one told the justices who—had opened it. Mrs. Pauley never told the court why, and nobody bothered to ask.

Once again, the chief gestured, his colleagues submitted their numbers, he did the math and fixed the girl with a stare meant to convey rectitude beyond his age. He must have practiced the expression in front of his bathroom mirror.

"Twenty Norman points," he said. The maximum penalty. And detention.

In *Great Expectations*, Charles Dickens wrote, "In the little world in which children have their existence . . . there is nothing so finely perceived and so finely felt as injustice." And in the Beverly Hills of the early 1960s, sixteen was closer to childhood than to maturity.

Over dinner, I told Stan and my mother what I'd witnessed.

"What are you going to do about that?" Stan asked.

I ate another forkful of my mother's chicken casserole. I had no answer to his question.

"I want you to think of something," Stan said.

If I did, I don't remember, but I didn't think about a career on the bench. I wondered, however, what it took to become a justice on Student Court. The answer was obvious: become friends with the student body president.

The phone rang. For Stan. One of his executives. Something about a "big order." Stan and I would never talk about Student Court again. A quarter of a century on the bench would elapse before I'd devote a kernel of thought to that travesty.

⊙ ⊙ ⊙

During my first year in high school, I wanted to excel at

everything, to be what some called *a great*. I wanted to win speech tournaments, win chess tournaments, win a class office, win a Boys' League office, win a student body office, and pass algebra. But that night, trying to fall asleep, I didn't think about winning a Student Court judgeship. Or a real judgeship.

My father never appeared on *The Verdict Is Yours*. Why? I don't know. Did the producers know my dad's career was slipping? Was it because they filmed their episodes in New York and wouldn't pay my father's travel costs? Or did my father fear matching wits with real lawyers? Maybe the reason was simpler, that by the time my father learned about the show, it was headed off the air. In 1961–2, *The Verdict Is Yours* had entered its fifth and final year, the sole season it received a nomination for a Daytime Emmy Award.

CHAPTER SIXTEEN

Santa Claus Lane Parade

Chucko the clown burst through a bass drum, bowed at the TV camera, and saluted all of Southern California. "And now," said the announcer, "from Hollywood, the Santa Claus Lane Parade." This event signaled the opening of the holiday season in the Southland. Sponsored by the Hollywood Chamber of Commerce, it featured, along with floats and bands, a cavalcade of television and movie stars, most of them from the B list.

It was late November 1962, and my father took me there. Better, he brought me to the party the Hollywood Chamber of Commerce put on for the stars who rode in the parade. Well, maybe not for the stars so much as for the merchants. The Chamber had started the parade in the late 1920s in order to encourage shopping on Hollywood Boulevard.

The event grew; the number of celebrities grew; and by the time I went, the Chamber was holding its party in a large auto repair shop at 6161 Hollywood Boulevard. Although no amount of streamers and candy canes could make it cozy, the facility became a festive banquet hall that night. The Chamber used the place because it was big enough to accommodate all the TV personalities and their families who rode in the parade. Volunteers set up long tables, covered them with colorful vinyl, and surrounded them with a haphazard collection of wooden chairs. A buffet of sandwiches, doughnuts, and coffee urns lined the walls. In the corners, television sets played for anyone who wanted to monitor the procession. And of course, Santa showed up.

For me, the night was charmed. As they waited their turn to join the parade, the guests kidded and mingled and caught up on industry news. I could meet any of them and did. Chucko clowned with me. KFWB disc jockey Bill Ballance schmoozed with everyone. Buster Keaton deadpanned for my Brownie camera. Jimmie Dodd, the *Mickey Mouse Club*'s adult emcee, still looked as though he he had his twenty-four Mouseketeers in tow. Soupy Sales joked with me. Soupy! Half my class revered him, as did I. On Beverly Hills High School's front lawn, the camera club had built a makeshift shell of a television set with a sign reading, "Soupy Sales Show." They'd invited everyone to pose inside and be photographed in Soupy's costume—large black hat, oversized white collar, oversized white bow tie full of red spots. I stood in line through the noon hour in order to mug for the camera.

Shelley Fabares took the time to talk with me. So did her friend Paul Petersen. Both appeared on *The Donna Reed Show* and embodied America's perfect teenagers. These kids were having too much fun to act like the stars they were. As Paul would tell me years later, we "ate far too many doughnuts and got to visit with (Hollywood's honorary mayor) Johnny Grant, then off we went down the route, waving and smiling and having a ball."

My father steered Mai, Tommy, Timmy, and me into the buffet line. Somewhere between the bread and the meat, a brown-eyed blonde with an endless smile greeted my father.

"Tony," he said, "meet Evelyn Rudie."

She beamed at me. "How do you do?"

Her face, her smile, the pitch of her four words—how could a girl my age be so charming? I was about to say something to Evelyn—God knows what—but one of the volunteers called to her.

The parade calls started at 7:05 p.m. Once it was our turn

to ride, they announced my father's name over the PA system. "Gerald Mohr. Please proceed to your car in the parking lot and prepare to enter the line of march."

We moved there immediately, lest we hold up the parade. The car was easy to find. Taped to both passenger doors were white sheets of poster paper with my father's name emblazoned on them. As the Chamber of Commerce's guidelines explained, the signs would "identify the participants by name only, and all other dates regarding TV or picture credits will be on the announcer's script."

At that moment, a bottle in his hand, Broderick Crawford (Chief Dan Mathews on *Highway Patrol*) walked up. "Gerry, I haven't seen you all night."

My father asked how he was.

Crawford took a swallow and said he'd just completed his ride through the parade. Another swallow. Then he said, "Let's talk, Gerry. I'll ride with you if that's okay."

"Sure," my father said in a welcoming tone.

Libation still in hand, Brod hoisted himself into the backseat, then raised himself to the top next to my father.

The two of them gossiped atop the open car while, slowly, our driver steered us into the line of march. Within seconds we were drifting past the fans. They flanked us on both sides, human levees stretching down Hollywood Boulevard, some waving and clapping, all bundled and huddled against the late November night.

Before long, we neared the bleachers, where Bill Welsh, the emcee, gave each celebrity a minute or two on the air. I could hear him over the loudspeakers as he interviewed the actors whose cars were just ahead of ours.

"Here's Whatshisface," Welsh gushed, "who had a feature role in"—pick a series—*Mister Ed*, *Peter Gunn*, *McHale's Navy*. The lights glared, cameras rolled, and the bleachers whistled. The star of the moment delivered some comments, and they were routinely gracious.

As our car approached the stands, Brod said, "Gerry, I'm not going to hog your time." He climbed into the front, where Tommy and I sat together, and then Brod dropped to the floor so Bill Welsh wouldn't see him. There he hid, scrunched down, gripping his bottle. Moments later, Welsh was upon us, dressed in his conservative suit and tie, his microphone in my father's face.

My father lit up. What a thrill it was, he said, to ride in the parade. Welsh said he loved his feature roles in all those westerns—*The Rifleman* (his episode "Squeeze Play" was about to air), *Bronco*, *Outlaw*—and then Welsh reached the moment when, normally, he'd turn to members of the family. We had to get away before he asked Tommy or me anything, because if Welsh and his camera looked at us, they, as well as everyone out there in Televisionland, would see Broderick Crawford in repose, below.

My father gave a flourish of his arm and a "Thanks a million" to his audience.

Welsh took the hint. If he saw Brod, he was too professional to say anything.

Back in the auto repair garage, Soupy Sales continued to frolic. Bill Ballance had left, but Chucko remained, dressed in his red-and-white costume with Elizabethan collars and cuffs. And there were still plenty of doughnuts.

I walked over to one of the television monitors and watched Evelyn Rudie express the hope that everybody "gets what they want" for Christmas. I wanted the station to replay that snip, replay it a hundred times. For a moment, I remained at the TV, where nothing seemed to be happening. At least five seconds passed with no other star appearing, and that's when the emcee said, into the dead air, "There are a lot of pretty girls here, but I don't know their names."

Until that night, I didn't know that Gene Autry wrote "Here Comes Santa Claus (Right Down Santa Claus Lane)" specifically about this parade, a night when the stars acted like plain folks. The Chamber of Commerce had included the following remark in their guidelines: "Unfortunately, we are unable to secure volunteers who are familiar with all our famous friends, so you will save embarrassment if you identify yourself."

I moved toward the entrance, waiting for Evelyn to reappear. Not far away were my father and Mai. I couldn't hear what they said to each other, but their gestures didn't look carefree. My father's pointing finger, a severe nod of Mai's head, my father's furrowed eyebrows. Before Evelyn returned, my father strode toward me and said, in a voice that brooked no nonsense, that it was time to go.

Later, under the covers, I reviewed the artifacts of the evening that my father let me keep. The map of the line of march. The police pass to park in the restricted area. Our personal pass to cross the police lines. Instructions such as, "If you are riding a horse, your wrangler should follow the instructions for equestrians."

I never learned what my father and Mai had argued about.

⊙ ⊙ ⊙

One year later, the eve of Thanksgiving recess, it was time again for the Santa Claus Lane Parade.

As before, the auto garage teemed with B-list personalities. While I scanned the place for Evelyn, Jimmie Dodd, the adult host of the *Mickey Mouse Club*, materialized, still with the boyish face I'd admired on the black-and-white Philco, but in person and in color, he looked juvenile. There was something odd about his appearance, as if his youthful look came from a disease. I asked if he still was in touch with Annette, Karen, Cheryl, and Darlene, all of whom I'd had childhood crushes on though we'd never met.

Jimmie said they were all "fine. I wish they were here." His smile appeared to be glued onto his face.

I asked about Roy Williams, the "Big Mooseketeer," a gifted artist with a voice gruff but friendly. We'd met several years earlier in his cluttered office at the Disney studio, where he'd asked me to make a squiggle and then turned it into a professional-looking drawing.

Again, no details other than "fine." Jimmie's smile remained unchanged, and his eyes seemed a little too open. Had I met Jimmie when I was eight, I'd have run down Dopey Drive with excitement, but that night my feelings verged on pity. So ironic: The only Mouseketeers I ever met were the show's two adults: Jimmie and Roy.

Over Jimmie's shoulder was Bill Ballance, back this time with—I excused myself and moved closer to be sure—a girl who'd edited my high school newspaper. Apparently, she'd sought him out for an interview, and now here they were. The age difference astounded me. Bill Ballance was some twenty-eight years older than this former editor. I was afraid to ask out a freshman I'd recently met. I too would edit Beverly High's paper but would remain too shy to call Shelley Fabares or Evelyn Rudie for an interview. The only person I'd reach out to was the student body president at UCLA, hoping he'd make a plug for participating in student government. (He did: "Student government from grade school up helps to build the foundation for a democratic system.")

Then I spotted Evelyn, back from the line of march and now at one of the long tables, eating dinner with her parents. I'd watched her on the TV monitor, saying as she had the year before, that for Christmas she hoped "everybody gets what they want." I breathed hard and forced myself toward them.

Evelyn invited me to sit down. Thrilled, I ran out of words after she introduced me to her parents. Casting about for something to say, I asked how she liked the car she'd ridden in.

"It's a good car," she said. A comfortable car. She added something, but I was too busy looking at her, trying to figure out what to say next, to recall what it was.

An announcement came over the speakers. "Santa Claus, please report to your float and prepare to enter the line of march."

Evelyn's father asked where I went to high school. He said Evelyn attended Hollywood High.

I almost choked on my hamburger as I told him. He and his wife looked exotic, learned, wise. And they were quite a bit shorter than I.

Before Evelyn's father could react, the PA system crackled back to life. "Santa Claus! Report at once to your float!" Evelyn and I looked about. Santa was in a far corner flirting with a group of women dressed in white-colored Indian costumes, costumes that displayed their tan, well-shaped legs. On the wall above them hung the red profile of a Native American with the name Mohawk on it. It would take America several more years before it would drop the word *Injun* from its lexicon, stop turning songs like "Indian Giver" into Top 40 hits, and stop dressing white actors in Hollywood's versions of Native American clothes.

Santa did not report at once to his float. It took another minute or two for him to disengage, and as he stumbled toward the door, he kept turning back to the girls and waving. I should have said something about this to Evelyn. I'm sure the two of us would have shared a laugh, but I didn't. Instead, I asked her a question about her classes at Hollywood High School.

The PA system called out my father's name. Our car was waiting. I remained seated, asking Evelyn more lame questions until my father came by and greeted us.

"So good to see you again, Gerry," Evelyn said, such charm in her voice.

As I stood up, I asked my father if we could stay a moment longer.

My father leaned down toward my ear. Quietly but sternly, he said, "Just get her phone number and let's go."

My father might as well have told me to proposition her. I froze, but I didn't want to hear a loud, commanding PA announcement to my father like what Santa Claus had received, nor did I want to go through another year before seeing Evelyn again.

She actually wrote it down, HOllywood 4-3748, and put the piece of paper into my shaking hand.

I'd succeeded, in front of her parents. It would take the length of the parade route to calm me down.

⊙ ⊙ ⊙

It was cold along the line of march. Mai and her sons huddled under a blanket, while my father rode on top. As before, I sat in front, feeling ebullient with Evelyn's phone number warming my pocket, and so, like my father, I waved to the crowd and even blew a kiss to a bunch of girls who huddled on the curb. From the other side of the street, a voice called out, "Look over here."

I turned in that direction and kept waving until, from the crowd, a voice shot at me. "No, not you."

Before I could recover from the sting of that rejection, we approached the bleachers, where like last year, Bill Welsh emceed. The lights hit the car, the cameras pushed in close, and Welsh said, "Here's Gerald Mohr."

The interview tumbled into platitudes like "How are you" and "Merry Christmas" before—too soon I thought—Welsh turned his chiseled face into the cameras and said something like, "Gerald Mohr"—pause—"has appeared on TV"—pause—"and"—pause; I can't forget his last line—"done some very fine work." Bill Welsh was too professional to make it obvious, but anyone back at the garage who was watching the monitors must have winced if they heard those final five words, a clear signal that my father was not working. Bill Welsh failed to name one show. Smiling as if nothing was wrong, my father endured the last hundred or so yards of the parade route before our driver returned us to the party. I didn't see Evelyn after the parade, or ever again. I wasn't hungry for doughnuts, and my father said he was tired. He wanted to go home.

CHAPTER SEVENTEEN

Blue Eyes at the Wheel

We were aboard Stan's catamaran, the start of a weekend trip to Catalina. Stan was steering. DBM's stock was rising. Litton Industries had asked about a merger. Stan was unsure. He wanted Dashew Business Machines in the family, but Litton was the new decade's go-go company. It may have been July, but the headwind carried a chill that, combined with the ocean swells, made me queasy.

"Here, Tony," Stan said, "Take the wheel. The course is one fifty."

I did so and hoped looking at the compass wouldn't make my seasickness worse.

"Say it back, Tony," Stan said. "Always repeat the course."

The boat dipped between two swells as I parroted the number.

A small wave whumped between the Huka Makani's two hulls, followed by another that sounded like the crump of artillery. My one goal was not to throw up. An hour remained before we'd reach Catalina. Maybe Leslie would awaken from her nap and relieve me at the wheel.

"There's a good story behind DBM," Stan said. "I'm sure they want to make a deal."

"Make a deal"—the remark sounded so much like what my father had said over the dinner table after filming a pilot for the failed series *Rough Sketch*.

I can't recall my answer to Stan. I knew little about business and had trouble learning the basics, but business made up the bulk of Stan's conversational repertoire. My father was more erudite, especially about topics that I understood better, and he craved banter, a quality absent from Stan's playbook. Dinner talk revolved around his business, his boat, and politics during election years. Never Shakespeare, psychology, the occult, the Dodgers, or any other of my father's favorite conversation topics. Stan was quick to lecture and needed no cue to do so. (One night, out of the blue: "You know, Tony, your contributions to this household are very minor.")

But my father's career was stumbling while Stan's was rising.

⊙ ⊙ ⊙

We stopped at Two Harbors, Catalina Island. Teenagers dove off a boat moored near Cherry Cove, where we'd anchored. On the deck of a nearby sloop, a couple baked in the sun as they read. Stan and my mother took the dinghy, which doubled as our lifeboat, for a slow ride along the rocks and cliffs that bordered the anchorage, where they could look through the clear water and spot starfish and sea urchins and saltwater goldfish. Stan adored Two Harbors—its almost pristine inlets, its one restaurant, and the handful of small wooden buildings ashore. Palm trees shaded the beach; many had been planted during the 1930s when the area had become a set for *Mutiny on the Bounty*. During the winter, the ground turned almost as green as Hawaii. In summer the scrub brush ranged from brown to gold. After they returned to the boat, my mother and I sat in the cockpit, she in the shade, me in the sunlight. Stan went below to take a nap.

During their ride, my mother said that Stan had asked, in a plaintive tone, "Why must people kill each other when there's so much beauty in the world?"

I had no answer to the question, but it made me realize that Stan had never ruminated like that with me. Did he reserve reflection for romantic moments with his wife? To be left out of that aspect of him made me sad.

I don't recall how I answered my mother, but my reaction must have cued her to my need. My mother was perspicacious. Maybe she told Stan to wax philosophical with me, because two weeks later, back in Newport Beach he did, sort of.

That Saturday broke sunny and warm. Stan and I were sailing in Leslie's sabot, *Glub Glub*, tacking up Newport Bay. Somehow Stan's large frame fit inside the eight-foot boat and left room for me to scrunch near the bow. We lowered our heads each time the little boom swung from one side to the other. Stan appeared pensive, almost content. He drew in a breath and looked up at the sky.

Stan said, "Man has a subconscious desire to get out and battle the elements."

I didn't stop to think this may have been the first time Stan had ventured with me into a philosophical topic. I took what he said at face value. I didn't ask myself whether this was why he relished sailing. The implication seemed clear. I probably said something like "Really?"

Stan continued. "Some want to hike, or camp, or climb mountains."

He went on to describe a storm he'd sailed through during the year and a half he and his first wife had spent in the Caribbean. The tempest came on fast. If they couldn't bring down the sails, they might lose their gear, they might lose their mast, they might lose their boat. "I thought we were licked," he said, "but we had to get those sails down." They'd managed, and they saved their ship.

We sailed to the top of Newport Bay, where tied to docks were fishing boats laden with local catches. Next to them was Western Canners Company, a two-story facility with a steep outside conveyor belt that whined and clanked as it raised the fishermen's catches from the holds into a part of the building that overhung the docks. The hot wind warmed my face, pleasant even with the odor of fish blended in. When Stan saw me paying attention to the men loading their hauls onto the conveyor, he headed into the wind to prevent us from sailing away.

After two fishing boats offloaded their catches, Stan trimmed the mainsail (the only sail on a sabot). We were running downwind now, back to the house. The breeze freshened maybe half a knot. I let my fingers drag through the water.

Where was Stan going with this? Was I supposed to solo from LA to San Francisco? Start racing, like Skip? I was indolent, and Stan knew it. The subject passed, and we continued our harbor tour in silence until Stan said something about his company. "It's really doing well." He almost, but not quite, looked relaxed, and I almost, but not quite, felt comfortable. I guess it took longer than I expected to accept a new parent.

Later that summer, we sailed north to Santa Cruz Island and, for one day, to Santa Barbara, where Stan rented a car. My mother took the passenger seat; Leslie and I, the back. I didn't know where Stan wanted to take us but didn't care. I never got carsick. While he drove, Leslie and I played geography. Stan navigated into the hills, past the San Ysidro Ranch, where Jack and Jackie Kennedy had honeymooned. Stan didn't like the Kennedys; my father did, and so did my mother. Thanks to Stan, I no longer was sure how I felt about them.

Down from the hills Stan drove, then through downtown Santa Barbara, along State Street, past the courthouse that, with its Spanish colonial architecture, resembled one of California's Franciscan missions. We turned west along the coastline. To our left, twenty miles across the water, lay Santa Cruz Island. It appeared closer than usual that day. So did the Santa Ynez Mountains, which reared up on our right, two miles away, their ridges brown with green and gold flecks in the chaparral.

We started to get hungry. We were supposed to be near the University of California at Santa Barbara, but the only thing that surrounded us was citrus trees. I rolled down the back window as far as it could go, stuck my head out, and breathed the fruity air with its hint of salt from the sea. We were the sole car in sight. The fields came up to the road. Stan drove slowly, which delighted my nervous mother and started to make me impatient. I felt we were meandering to nowhere. I was too young to realize that was the point.

Ahead and slightly to the right was an on-ramp to a highway that had yet to open. A sign said, *Do Not Enter*. This was not a unique sight in the California of the early 1960s, when the state was building freeways to everywhere, even to the orange groves we'd just passed.

The barriers did not completely block the entrance.

Stan turned to me. "Let's see where it goes," he said. His eyes danced with life, brighter than I'd ever noticed before. His face, normally impassive, acquired a hint of a grin.

"Stanley," my mother said in her nervous voice I knew so well. Disobeying that sign frightened her. She and Stan were Depression-era kids, but while Stan had emerged an optimist, my mother continued to fear bad consequences around every corner and down every straightaway, avoidable only by clinging to the rules.

Stan's grin widened as he said, "Relax. This'll be fun."

I agreed and shouted out a "Yes!" as he weaved around the cones and we ascended to the freeway.

Stan almost, but not quite, floored it. The entrance felt like a ramp to a Valhalla in the distance, where the mountains cut the summer sky. We were zooming over new pavement, maybe the first private car on that stretch, a concrete ribbon that was wholly ours. There were no oil stains, no tread marks, and no police cars.

We cruised above the fields, howling toward the hills at a speed that made me feel as though we were about to take flight and made my mother yelp that we'd drive off a ledge. She was sure the road wasn't finished. But Stan relaxed into the ride. "Sweetie, it's fine," he said. And the tone of his voice made me believe him and made me giddy.

My mother was wrong. Our slice of new highway fed us into US-101 where, on prominent display, was a sign for food. Stan drove down an off-ramp and within moments found his daughter's favorite type of restaurant—a "nineteen-cent hamburger pad." I'm sure I ate two of them, covered with pickles and a bun soaked with ketchup, and I know all four of us shared the French fries.

Suddenly Stan was no longer a businessman who fought his weight, paid his bills on time, and boasted that he'd lost an account because he refused to pay a bribe. He'd slipped the envelope in order to celebrate a few moments of evanescent freedom and, incidentally, display another dimension of fatherhood. Over a decade had passed since he'd chucked his career and spent eighteen months on a boat with his family, including an infant. That Caribbean voyage had been a calculated risk. On a much smaller scale, so had this road trip.

CHAPTER EIGHTEEN

Every Other Weekend

"Well. Filet mignon," my father said as he took a seat at the end of the dinner table. He seemed buoyant.

Mai sat to my right, at the other end of the table. Across from me were Tommy and Timmy.

Mai said in her Scandinavian clip, "You know how much these cost? A dollar fifty each." She fixed her anxious face on my father.

Without a word, my father put fork to meat and started eating. If there were vegetables on his plate, which I doubt, he ignored them. Tommy, Timmy, and I stayed quiet.

The price of food was never a talking point in my mother's house. The one price she and Stan discussed—at least in front of me—was the rising value of Dashew Business Machines' stock. Mai announced the cost of everything and added the tag line, "We can't afford it." She said it so often that it became one of the few sentences she pronounced without a Swedish accent. It was as if the word *afford* had dropped out of my mother's vocabulary, migrated across town to my father's rented house, and into Mai's mouth.

The next morning, my father took me to the Sportsmen's Lodge, a six-acre combination of hotel, restaurant, and gardens in the San Fernando Valley, where the management stocked a pond with trout. From the shore or a small wooden bridge, patrons could fish for a meal.

"We're going to be moving," my father said as I jiggled the pole. He added that I'd like the new place.

I did. They'd rented a white Spanish style stucco that over-looked the empty back lot of Universal Studios. Stairways filled this home—the entry, the basement (which Tommy converted into a lab for his chemistry set), the bedrooms. Tommy, Timmy, and I began playing hide-and-go seek and other games throughout the place.

It seemed grander than their last house, but Mai kept complaining about money. My father was getting parts—appearances on westerns like *Lawman, Overland Trail, Stagecoach West, Cheyenne, Maverick, Bat Masterson*, as well as in series like *The Aquanauts, Harrigan and Son*, and *The Barbara Stanwyck Show*. Trouble was, these were guest roles that offered modest pay and work for no more than a few days. Residuals were rare, almost non-existent. He didn't talk with me about these shows. He never called to say, "Hey Tony, turn on your TV next Wednesday." He even failed to tell me when he appeared on *Men Into Space*, an episode involving the moon.

My father wanted another series, and there were no prospects.

◎ ◎ ◎

On several Saturdays, my father took me to "The Club," California's Department of Employment, affectionately known as *unemployment*. If these visits embarrassed him, my father never showed it, the mark of a good actor.

"I see all my friends there," he said, an easy grin on his face, the way he often looked before the divorce.

Located in a middling section of town, The Club was a massive building with a low ceiling whose rows of lights failed to brighten the drab faded yellow—or was it brown?—interior. Lines of people stretched across the room. My father took his place in one of the queues, where I tried to ignore the patient murmurs of the out-of-works waiting for their money.

"Gerry," a voice called out from one line over, a man in a baseball cap.

He was another actor. I forgot his name after my father introduced us. The man looked jaunty and relaxed, as though he were about to buy a Dodger Dog at a double-header.

"My agent called. I may have work next week," he said. Two scenes in a Western I never watched.

My father said the star of that Western was a "nice guy."

"Fingers crossed," the man said, shifting from one foot to the other. He didn't look so relaxed any more. His complexion, clear as a ten-year-old's at first, began to turn red.

The place made me uncomfortable. Most of the people appeared grim. I didn't want to think of my father among these men (I recall few women) in need. This was not a club I cared to join.

As the lines shuffled a couple of steps toward the counter, the actor said, after mentioning a name, that "He's been written off the show."

"I heard," my father said.

A short woman, pen and small notebook in hand, left whatever line she was in and approached my father. "Please? Can I have your autograph?" she said in a hoarse voice.

My father signed with a flourish and a smile, as always. He never took his fans for granted. She rasped a thank you at him.

"Good luck, baby," he said, sincerity in his voice.

We reached the counter, a wall punctuated by brass metal bars with enough of an opening to allow hands to pass through. The stout woman on the other side wore a plain three-quarter sleeve blouse. She had a face full of folds and wrinkles. She didn't gush at my father—she'd probably seen too many actors—but she was polite. My father pushed a piece of paper through the gap. She read it, opened a drawer, counted out several greenbacks, and slid them toward my father. In a graceful move, he transferred the currency into his billfold and thanked her.

The woman wished us both luck.

Outside, my father withdrew a Virginia Rounds and lit it before we got in the car. We returned to Beverly Hills for lunch at the Konditori, a Scandinavian cafe on Camden Drive, which we frequented often, thanks to Mai. I didn't care for the kruppkakor, fruit soups, fruit cake, blood dumplings, mashed rutabaga, lutfiske, or ground veal patties—and their finger sandwiches were not filling. The place lacked color and charm. You picked your meal, such as it was, off a metal counter and took it to one of their nondescript tables full of Mai's Swedish friends. My father didn't seem happy there. He didn't fit in the way he did at our coffee shops, where he loved to go and so did I, or at the Brown Derby, where he and his buddies joked through the night. It felt as though Mai had snapped me back to Sweden, snowy and dark. Had my father and Mai reached a compromise of sorts with this place as a deal point?

We sat alone at the table with what passed for our meals. Across the room, Mai talked with a plump, middle-aged couple.

My father asked how school had been that week. I told him a teacher had been fired for dating a high school student. They saw each other until, overwhelmed I assume by his conscience, the teacher had written the girl a letter, saying he adored her but couldn't go on. The girl sobbed until her mother asked what was wrong.

Of course, the girl's family had connections; they lived in Beverly Hills. The parents presented their non-negotiable demand to the superintendent of schools: either the teacher goes—as in right now—or the father goes to the newspapers. The district fired the man immediately, but as a sop, they shoehorned him into a teaching position at the Los Angeles City schools.

My father nodded as I spoke, and when I finished, he said it wasn't that teacher's fault. "Some of these teenage girls ought to be locked up." He speculated that the girl was "a tease."

"A what?" (I'm sure now that she wasn't.)

This was not our first conversation about sex or women; my father had raised the subject before. In 1960, when I was twelve, a seventh-grade girl had worn a sundress to school. The principal sent her home, her mother complained, and the incident made page one of the metropolitan section of the *Los Angeles Times*. My father laughed as I described the incident.

"She's probably too well-developed for a girl her age," he said, a remark that made me uncomfortable; I didn't want to discuss her body.

But now that I was passing through age fifteen, my father was boring deeper into the subject of sex. Mai returned to the table. My father asked if he could be excused for a few minutes to "go look at something at Martindale's," a bookstore up the street. He motioned to me and we left.

Outside, my father said that I should never tolerate any girl who tried to tease me and then refuse to have sex. Next, he said, "No girl will tease if you show her that you don't need her."

"Huh?" This was getting confusing.

"I know a young actor," my father said. "A good-looking guy. We worked together on a Western. He started showing up on the set looking miserable."

Because of a girl, of course. The actor was dying for her. At the end of their date, she led him into her bedroom, they started to undress, then she stopped him. He asked why. She laughed. He was throbbing. She put on her clothes. He begged. She mussed his hair. He got blue balls.

"What's that?" I asked. I looked up at the sky, yellow with smog.

My father explained and as he did, mine started to hurt.

We reached the corner of Santa Monica Boulevard. Martindale's was a block away, near Rodeo Drive. A car pulled into a parking space near us.

My father said that he'd sat down with the actor and said, "You don't need her. You may want her, but you don't need her."

"What do you mean?" I asked.

"Just listen," he said. "They returned to her apartment after the next date, they undressed again, and she lay naked on the bed." My father stared at me. "She started undulating, and then she said, 'Does it hurt, baby, does it hurt? You're not going to fuck me. You're not going to fuck me.' And he said, 'Who needs you?' Then he rolled over on his back and jerked off."

My throat caught. A horn sounded down the street before I asked what happened next.

"She hit the ceiling. She yelled; she sucked him, pulled it, did everything she could to get him up again, and when nothing worked, he told her,"—borrowing from one of my father's Philip Marlowe lines—"'Get this and get it straight: I don't need you.'"

"And?" I asked. I felt confused and nervous as I tried to absorb this lesson.

"The next time she fucked him senseless."

I couldn't imagine myself in such a situation. My goal remained getting a date with someone who'd let me kiss her goodnight. I felt as though my father was teaching calculus to a student who still couldn't multiply.

Every time I recall this conversation, I cringe. My father was endorsing, if not misogyny, then at least the careless and carefree use of women. I'd never feel comfortable talking to any child of my own in such stark, sexual terms, especially during their early teens. His attitude frightened me away from the girls I knew and made me reluctant to ask anyone out, let alone find a girlfriend. Despite my father's detailed instructions and my awards in impromptu speaking, I didn't know what to say around girls. His advice didn't help me understand them. If anything, it made me fear them.

Although Stan and I didn't discuss women until my father died, I began to understand romance by watching how he treated my mother. Simply put, Stan made my mother feel loved, starting with the endearing nickname "Sweetie." (My father did nothing more than shorten my mother's name from Rita to Rit—pronounced "Reet." He reserved the word *darling* for waitresses.) With Stan, every birthday and anniversary called for bespoke jewelry as well as a party. One involved a bus ride, thirty of us to a movie premiere and then to Chinatown for dinner. Because the heeling action of sailboats frightened my mother, Stan had built a catamaran, which was more stable. Periodically he sent her flowers, just because. He hugged her. He held her hand. And my mother reciprocated. She tended to him and supported Stan's career. She dove into animated conversation with his business associates, no matter who or how boring they were. And yes, she obeyed the advice in the lyrics of a song of that era, "Wives and Lovers." She never saw him off with curlers in her hair.

Women were not a topic between Stan and me, not because they made him uncomfortable. Looking back, we didn't talk about them because, well, I had access to what I thought was the Grand Master. But my father seduced—womanized some might say. He seldom romanced, a distinction I wouldn't perceive until adulthood. My father's brashness overpowered Stan's modesty.

"Cultivate the woman in her," my father said.

What the hell did that mean?

"You want to get her into bed? Lead her into a discussion about sex."

I was only fifteen.

"Here's how to handle a tease: show her you don't need her."

Huh?

"Go ahead and say 'fuck' during intercourse. Women love to hear it."

Really? Beverly High's *Norman Guide* barred "profanity and vulgarity."

"Here's how to avoid getting the clap."

Instructions too lengthy to recount here.

And above all: "Don't fall in love with the first girl you sleep with," a warning my father delivered at least ten times.

I didn't ask if it was okay to fall in love with the first girl I kissed.

"We couldn't find the book," my father told Mai after we returned to the Konditori and sat down at her table.

My father lost his virginity when he was twelve. He probably couldn't imagine having such a naïve son.

☉ ☉ ☉

That night, as Mai, her two sons, my father, and I ate dinner, the conversation rambled across trivial subjects before migrating into what we should do on Sunday.

I suggested renting horses at the top of Beechwood Canyon and heading across Griffith Park. On the valley side was a Mexican restaurant where riders hitched their horses while they ate.

That drew a twin "Let's go" from Tommy and Timmy and a grin from my father.

Mai shook her head.

I mentioned Nu-Pike, an amusement park in Long Beach. Then I suggested Pacific Ocean Park. My father had taken me there many years earlier, to a private party that was "limited," he said, "to the stars," and I wanted to go back.

ANTHONY J. MOHR

Mai glared across the dinner table and said, "Tony, don't you realize that *we're poor*?"

Her question—more like a statement—rang like a carillon through the room and didn't fade away. It wasn't the first time she'd yelled at me.

I wasn't prepared to believe my father was poor. Money may have been "tight," but the word "poor" dropped him into a category that didn't ring true. After all, there was food on the table and a roof over his head. I didn't know what to say, nor did my father, who looked down at the remains of his meal.

I still have some of my father's tax returns. He made $7,481 in 1963 and $8,501 in 1964. Just under $2,000 of his 1963 income was due to Mai working as a script supervisor. Not wealthy, but not poor either, compared to salaries at that time.

Later from their bedroom, I heard flashes of an argument between my father and Mai. They kept it low, but the word *money* was clear enough for me to hear. The noun sounded nastier each time Mai used it until, finally, my father said, "That's enough." A silence followed, punctuated by running water from the bathroom and then the sounds of them getting into bed. I didn't hear either one say good night.

Sunday, my father took me to play miniature golf at the Gittleson Brothers course on Hollywood Boulevard, near Silver Lake. At the entrance—a quaint white wood shack with a shake roof—a small pang of guilt hit me as I watched my father hand over two of the precious dollar bills he'd received at unemployment. He knew this was my favorite place to play. The holes were either intricate, difficult, or both. One of them, the Volcano, featured a four-foot-high mountain with a caldera at the top. Another ran over a hundred feet in a gentle curve along the back wall. A third featured three drawbridges, only one of which led to the hole.

I sank the longest hole in two strokes and played the

drawbridge and the volcano under par. After my ball dropped down the eighteenth hole, I didn't ask to play again. I didn't want to see two more dollar bills vanish from my father's wallet. We sat at a round wooden table where he smoked a cigarette, I drank an Orange Julius, and our conversation alighted on politics.

"America's prestige in the world," he said, "was at an all-time low when Eisenhower left." Not now, he said. "We're respected abroad."

A nod of the head from me. I didn't say that Stan disagreed.

"We were five years behind the Russians in space when Kennedy became president," he said. "Now we're catching up."

I asked what he thought Richard Nixon was going to do next. He'd lost his campaign to become governor of California.

"You heard Tricky Dick's last press conference? He's through, thank God."

I'd seen a replay on television: "You won't have Nixon to kick around anymore."

My father piled on the nasty labels. Jackal. Bastard. Liar. As he spoke, I sipped my Orange Julius. I wanted the sweet concoction to last.

My father leaned toward me. He hadn't been working, he said, "So Christmas is going to be a little lean from this end." He must have struggled to present those words to his son, who lived in a house with a full-time maid and spent every other weekend on a yacht.

I'm sure I said something like "I understand" or "That's okay," and I meant it.

My father hugged me. I hugged him back. The sun was still out. I trailed alongside him to the parking lot. He looked special in his tan jumpsuit. His easy stride and perfect posture set him apart. We got into his car and drove along Santa Monica Boulevard, then a crowded two-lane mess with abandoned trolley tracks down the middle, which made the ride rough and bumpy. Mass transit in the form of the red cars had disappeared years before.

"Sometime today you going to move that car?" my father snarled under his breath at a motorist who'd blocked the intersection. Good, I thought. My father was acting like himself again. I scrunched deeper into the seat, comfortable once more.

CHAPTER NINETEEN

A Bowl of Jell-O

It was sports night in Beverly High's swim-gym, with its retractable basketball court built over a swimming pool, showcasing professional ping-pong players, a basketball demonstration by the Harlem Stars, tug-of-wars, and relay races in the pool, all topped off by a dance. At the end, several friends and I lingered on the lawn outside. The November 1962 chill, the play of the night lights on the grass, and the lingering laughter from the evening filled me with cheer.

"Call me in the morning," one of the guys said. "Maybe we'll do something."

I scooted across the four blocks to home where, as usual, I ate a bowl of Jell-O in my mother's immaculate kitchen. Into the sink went the spoon and bowl; I ran some water over them and trotted upstairs.

Back from college for a few days, Skip was already asleep in his room, but my parents' bedroom door was open, with the light on.

I sat on their bed, on my mother's side, which was closer to the door. The wallpaper was a light, gentle blue, her favorite color, the color of her eyes. So were the patterns of the bedspread and the window curtains.

My mother put down her book. "So how was it?" she asked.

"Neat," I said. Even some of our teachers had joined in the games.

There was a tender scent in the bedroom air, the slightest tinge of something sweet. The blanket I was sitting on felt cozy.

I launched into more details, and as I did, Stan managed a quick grin while my mother laughed. "I'm so glad you had a good time," she said.

The moment I finished, Stan said, "Well, I'm a teacher, too."

I didn't understand what he meant, and judging from her expression, neither did my mother, until Stan ordered me to go clean up the kitchen. He said it was "filthy."

I asked how he knew that. He hadn't been down there since I'd come home.

"I know," Stan said. "Go down and clean up that kitchen."

Save for one bowl and one spoon in the sink, the kitchen was as spotless as it had been before I came home.

Stan's voice hardened. "You go down and clean up that kitchen."

"It's clean," I said. "Why do you think it's dirty?"

Stan lunged for my arm. As I tried to pull away, he said it again. "You go down and clean up that kitchen."

"It's clean," I gasped. He'd seized my arm.

Stan was hurting me. Then, with his free hand, he smacked me. I was shocked, unable at the time to ponder how a gentle bedtime talk could snap into violence.

My mother yelled at Stan to stop. He didn't. He struck me again. He said it again, "You go down and clean up that kitchen." He wound up for another blow.

I struck back. I did so without thinking. The next thing I remember, we were rolling on the soft off-white carpet that was thick enough to suppress the sounds of a fight. I think, but am not sure, that my mother screamed again.

"You go down and clean up that kitchen," Stan raged.

"No," I said.

The issue had shot beyond a bowl of Jell-O. The blue left Stan's eyes. He was no longer a parent—real, substitute, or anything else. He was a bully. I wanted to hurt Stan. I tried to hit him hard, but at six-foot-two, he was bigger than I, and while he was overweight, years of sailing had given him more strength than my flabby body could muster. I swung, and I know I connected, but it was as if he felt nothing. I grabbed his forearm and tried to stop him but couldn't. He hit me again.

"You go down and clean up that kitchen."

How long this ruction lasted, I can't say. At some point I relented. In tears, red from pain, I stumbled downstairs and washed the one spoon and the one bowl in the sink. My time in the kitchen could not have exceeded four minutes.

Stan remained upstairs. I would have thought he'd check to see if I'd obeyed his orders, but instead the house grew quiet. When I returned upstairs, their bedroom door was shut. There was no sound from Skip's room either. I didn't brush my teeth. I didn't put on my pajamas. I was hurting. Somehow, I fell asleep.

I awoke the next morning to voices in the hall, Stan's and Skip's. They must have thought I was still asleep.

"You hear it last night, Skip?"

"Yeah, that was really a go-ad."

Stan said, "He has to justify everything."

I couldn't hear Skip's reply.

Then from Stan: "Well, it's a problem, Skip. I'm not sure what to do about it. Maybe we should send him to a psychologist."

I shivered under the sheets. The prospect of a psychologist unnerved me. In the early 1960s, there was a stigma about needing one. The sole boy in my class who admitted to seeing a psychologist would soon be arrested in a Beverly Hills public toilet. (He'd become a National Merit Scholar, matriculate to Harvard, and fifteen years later, die of AIDS.) To see a psychologist meant that you were mentally ill. The school kept one on staff, a dour-looking man in spectacles whom everyone avoided because should you break a rule, Dr. Morgenstern's job was to prove you were a disturbed child.

I wish I could remember what I did for the rest of that Saturday. The day became a blur until the evening, when my mother said that Stan wanted to take us out to dinner. I had no excuse that would help me back out.

Stan picked a dark, quiet restaurant. My mother and I met him there; he'd come from work. We slipped into a banquette toward the rear, a space big enough for five. Once I settled in, both my mother and Stan seemed far away. For what felt like an hour, but was most likely a minute, we sat in silence. My mother looked as though someone had tightened a vice across her chest.

My mother said, "Do either of you want to say anything to each other?"

I wanted this chapter to end, though I knew I'd never forget it. No matter how close Stan and I would draw in the years ahead, no matter how completely he'd support me—which he did—the episode would remain a scar. While future gestures of genuine love would help obscure it, I'd never forget this beating. Stan's fury would forever stay lodged in my head.

Having said that, I understand that memory can morph into little more than creative thinking. Was my recall of that night inaccurate? Stan and I had an argument. He got angry. It turned physical. I thought he was unfair. Of all that, I'm sure. But have I exaggerated? Have I understated? Did I leave a sink full of pots and pans instead of a bowl and spoon, lightly rinsed? Did Stan strike me only once, like the night he struck Skip? And after she yelled once or twice, what did my mother do? I can't remember; whatever she did is a blank.

I shifted my weight in the banquette, looked at Stan and said, "I'm willing to admit that I'm wrong if you'll admit you're wrong."

Without a word, he nodded, then opened his hand and reached across the table. I took it. He offered a thin smile, the best he could do, and even under the dim light, his eyes flickered back to life. It wasn't the straight-on apology he'd offered Skip the night he'd hit him in bed, but he had not spoken in an offhand tone, as he had with Skip. He didn't say anything to me. His open hand was enough. But when I look back on it, I wonder why Stan couldn't have said he was wrong, too. And said it before my mother prompted him. My father had let my mother tell me about his marriage to Mai. Now Stan let my mother broach the matter of an apology.

Stan changed the subject. He said, almost in a whisper, "I understand you want to spend the summer at a debate program at USC."

I did—the Western Forensics Institute, a boot camp for high school kids who liked public speaking.

"I think you should," he said with a slight nod of his big head.

Stan was inconsistent, a word I didn't think to use back then, but the trait had a lasting impact. Not knowing what to expect, a scolding or a beating without warning—how could I feel completely comfortable around such a parent? I didn't deserve Stan's reaction, which, incidentally, was the first and last time he ever hit me. Did my mother warn him never to do that again?

Decades later, when, without prompting from me, he recalled that night, Stan said that while "we were wrestling" on the floor, my mother "jumped around like a wet hen." He was in a good mood, trying to make the incident sound funny. His version made me sad. He still couldn't acknowledge what had happened and face it with candor.

I said something innocuous like "really" and eased us into another memory, one that wouldn't sting. Wrestling? Wrestlers don't hit each other. But from time to time, Stan and Skip enjoyed a good-natured father-son wrestling match—an activity I had no desire to engage in. Finally, during a match, Stan hurt a tendon or a ligament and could never wrestle with Skip again. Maybe Stan's mind had conflated our night into such a contest. I never did. It wasn't sport and I doubt he thought so either.

During my next weekend with him, I told my father what happened. Naturally, he sided with me; he had only my version. When I told my father about Stan's idea of a psychologist, he laughed. I didn't end up seeing one. Before the weekend ended, Mai snapped at me, for what I don't recall.

I'd like to say that the incident with Stan launched me onto my path to the bench, that he so battered my sense of justice that I resolved to don a robe, always listen to both sides, and never treat people unfairly. But that wouldn't be true. Like the day I watched Student Court, I didn't devote any thought to becoming a judge, nor would I for years. Nevertheless, maybe that night added another element to my judicial temperament, making me ponder the proper way to do justice between the parties, regardless of their standing or strength.

Rainy Day Schedule

It was February 1963. Beverly Hills High School's morning bulletin read *RAINY DAY SCHEDULE TODAY*, and I was not thinking about my father, who was missing. I was thinking about Mr. Occhipinti's class, where I felt calm and safe. Along with twenty-three other sophomores at the door to Room 121, I was waiting for him to arrive.

He taught modern history, my favorite subject that year, and he was my favorite teacher. Mr. Occhipinti was a small man who wore black suits and black-rimmed glasses and something slick in his thick black hair. His head was a little too narrow. His smooth tenor voice was ideal for formal lectures, which he tape-recorded in order to make sure that each of his classes heard the same material, delivered in prose that verged on the lyrical. ("And they drank the intoxicating wine of Renaissance culture that suffused their continent.") He drove an Edsel. Every summer he visited Europe's museums and brought home postcards with which he festooned the classroom walls. Wherever we looked, we saw little pictures of battles, landscapes, saints, and monarchs.

He also served as the faculty sponsor of the Squires, Beverly High's honors service club for freshmen and sophomore boys, who'd voted me in a week earlier.

I was in Mr. Occhipinti's honors section (the school adored

the word *honors*), with the type of kids who remained in their car outside a party until the symphony on KFAC finished, in order to learn if they'd correctly guessed its composer and number. My closest friends—Bobby and Larry—were among them. So were some of the brightest girls, a couple of whom had invited me to their parties, even though I was a newcomer who had only lived in Beverly Hills since the sixth grade. They'd known each other since kindergarten. Their families defined the ethos of Beverly Hills, then a small town despite its wealth, a Mayberry in the middle of Los Angeles.

We dressed in accordance with the school manual: the boys, clean slacks or tan Levi's; the girls, tailored dresses, skirts that reached below the knees, oxfords or flats, socks or hose. At least half the class wore Honor Club sweaters: blue pullovers for the boys, red cardigans for the girls. Hardly anyone had acne, but I kept Clearasil in business. Our hair was combed just so, except for mine, forever a dark thicket of messy black curls. Being with these kids made me happy, and Room 121 felt like the stable center of my world, a place where I didn't have to balance loyalties between fathers.

As I waited for class to start, I thought about Evelyn, the actress my father had introduced to me at the Santa Claus Lane Parade and whom I lacked the nerve to call. Then Mr. Occhipinti arrived and began his lesson.

Mr. Occhipinti's reel-to-reel tape recorder was out of sight that morning, along with his solemn demeanor. Our lesson about Louis XVI and the French Revolution called for ironic humor. I leaned forward. It was clear from the mischievous expression on Mr. Occhipinti's face that we were about to hear another one of his good stories.

The Tuileries had been Louis XVI's palace in the heart of Paris. During the French Revolution he had decamped from there and fled to Versailles, a secure place far from the mob. Yet he came back. He didn't have to, Mr. Occhipinti said, but he did, and that triggered the events that lead to Louis XVI's imprisonment and execution.

A titter escaped from a boy one row over. Behind him a girl with a sweet face perked up.

Mr. Occhipinti ignored the lectern and moved about like a windup doll. He circled back to Marie Antoinette and her "Let them eat cake" comment. He lingered over the wealth on display in the Louis XVI court. I knew he was building to something.

Rainwater poured into the bushes outside. I wished that on rainy days, the school didn't send us home ten minutes early. I wanted modern history to go on forever.

"And why," Mr. Occhipinti asked, "did Louis XVI return to the Tuileries?"

Either the answer itself—"The king was *stupid*"—or the tone in which Mr. Occhipinti delivered the answer turned us into a collection of hysterical teens. I hooted and howled, and Bobby laughed so hard he nearly fell out of his seat. He had the face of a lovable genius and a voice that, the following year, would make him California's speech champion.

Mr. Occhipinti didn't resume his lesson until we calmed down and one of us—me, I think—let out the final whoop. At least precipitation did not shorten modern history, but it made me wonder whether it had rained when Louis XVI had traveled to Versailles or when he'd returned. Our history textbook ignored the weather.

⊙ ⊙ ⊙

By the time school let out, the rain was pounding down, and someone who had just obtained his driver's license offered me a ride home. I chose to walk, which meant jumping over puddles because the runoff overloaded first the drains and then the streets. Water flowed over the curbs, a frequent problem in the Los Angeles basin despite flood control channels that had been built a decade earlier. During the four blocks between Beverly High and my house, I stopped thinking about Louis XVI.

That's because my father had been missing for three days.

Mai must have been frantic. She'd called my mother to ask if she or I had heard from my father. We hadn't. I guess Dad hadn't warned his bride that whenever his life faltered, he disappeared for a while. Dad had vanished a few months before he left my mother, but just for a day. He'd come home before I awoke the following morning. I had no idea where he had gone or why. After all, I was eight, too young to understand, but now I'm sure he had driven to Mai's apartment on Barham Boulevard, near Universal Studios.

Apropos of Mai's apartment, here's an aside and a reminder of 1950s culture. After my father moved out but before the divorce was final, my mother's attorney wrote my father's agent to the effect that my mother was "distressed" to learn that my father was living with Mai. The agent lobbed back an "unequivocal denial" calling the accusation "vicious rumors . . . which are not uncommon in marital proceedings" and describing my father's "initial outrage and shock at the terrible information."

So, unlike Mai, I wasn't panicked. I was more concerned about what my honors class would say if the newspapers learned of my father's latest absence. My group of friends came from two-parent families who, at least on the surface, seemed happy. They only knew my mother and Stan. I don't think any had met my father.

I pulled a bowl of red Jell-O from the fridge, leaned against the door, and started to devour it. My mother walked into the kitchen and put a bag of groceries on the counter.

"You shouldn't eat so fast," she said gently, and then she hugged me. Her eyes were full of love. Her white blouse was spotless, like her kitchen. I picked up the spoon, continued eating, and listened to the rain.

"I know Daddy will come back," she said in a soft tone. As usual she was trying to be sympathetic, but she probably felt relieved that my father was no longer her problem and that Stan loved her without letup. I'm sure Mom would have hugged me again if I had moved even slightly in her direction. I should have. She would have said more soothing things to me, had I given her the opening.

But I didn't. All I said was, "I guess so," and neutralized my feelings by swallowing quivering dollops of Jell-O.

We walked into the den. On the small off-white sofa sandwiched between two built-in counters, Stan was talking on "CRestview 18835," the telephone line we reserved for his work calls. He looked nothing like my dashing father. All they had in common was their height. My father could seduce with his mellifluous baritone. Stan tended to mumble, which I heard him do now, into the receiver: "If Mr. Hughes is listening, tell him to go to hell." Hughes, as in Howard Hughes. One of his enterprises was negotiating to buy Dashew Business Machines. Stan waved as he continued to talk, and I went upstairs to study.

Shortly after 8 p.m., the phone rang. I answered it before the second ring. It was my father. His voice sounded tinny against background noise that resembled rushing water, typical for long-distance calls in 1963. I sat on the edge of my bed, and as we talked, one of my fingers drifted from hole to hole along the rotary dial, moving it slightly but not enough to make it click.

"I want you to know I'm all right," he said.

I said, "Good." I didn't feel relieved. I didn't feel anything.

"Everything is okay," he said.

I asked, "Where are you?"

"Up the coast." That probably meant San Luis Obispo, the town where he and my mother had honeymooned. I pictured him there, alone, calling from a phone booth at the entrance to a motor court near the beach. Was he looking at the ground as he pressed the receiver to his ear, or was he peering through the glass door—closed against the rain—at his 1952 Jaguar, parked in the gravel next to a faded bungalow where he was staying? Ensconced at Versailles, pondering his future, did Louis XVI stare—in the rain?—at one of his ornate coaches? Didn't my father have a phone in his room? While tracing calls was difficult then, it could be arranged, especially when a person went missing. Maybe that's why he was calling from outside.

I asked when he was coming back.

"I can't say." The interference on the line, probably due to the rain, rose until it almost drowned him out.

I asked what he planned to do the next day. He didn't know. I think I asked again how he was, and I think he said "Fine."

With exchanges like this we consumed almost three minutes, the time after which the cost of a long-distance call mounted furiously.

He said, "We're still pals, right?"

"Yeah."

"Great," he said before he hung up.

I didn't ask why he'd vanished. His marriage to Mai had to be the reason. It was failing. The first fight I witnessed between them had occurred at least three years earlier—over what, I don't remember. Soon, almost any peccadillo triggered a quarrel, scenes that at times I'd had to watch or at least hear, because their house—no longer the one near Universal; they'd rented another place—was small, and they were loud. That had to be the reason my father had decamped. Alcohol was never involved. During one of my every-other-weekend stays, a month or so earlier, Mai had ordered me to put their parakeet back in his cage. We were in a little room that served as a den.

"Why?" I asked. Trixie appeared happy perched on my shoulder.

"Those are the rules," she snapped. Her eyebrows furrowed

and her lips tightened. "You only get ten minutes with the bird."

She and my father had initiated that protocol when, once, Tommy, Timmy, and I had wanted to play with Trixie at the same time. But today Tommy and Timmy were away.

My father looked up from his script. "What are we doing? Timing this with a stopwatch?"

Mai stormed from the den and left the house.

"Oh, shit," my father said. He tried to follow her, but she slammed the front door before he could catch up. When my father came back into the room, I said nothing. Neither did he, but Trixie remained on my shoulder.

◉ ◉ ◉

Shortly before 8:30 p.m., Stan appeared at my bedroom door. "How's school?"

This was not his normal opening. Usually Stan would ask, "What did you learn today?" He sounded tired thanks, I'm sure, to his sessions with Hughes.

"Okay," I said. Rain played across the roof and plinked through the downspouts.

For a few seconds Stan said nothing, which made me uncomfortable. While I still felt grateful that he'd freed my mother and me from the scary backwash of a divorce, I was not entirely used to him yet, nor willing to share thoughts about my father. Despite having lived with Stan for over four years, I was not perceptive enough to read many of his signals. I looked down at my history book and wished one of his business associates would telephone.

He said, "Want to come sailing this weekend?" Sailing was the only way he could relax.

"Can I see how homework goes?" I had a test the following

week and had to write a paper for Mr. Occhipinti. Also, my tendency to get seasick had not let up.

He lingered. "We're going Sunday too." He'd take his boat out even if it rained.

The salon was meeting Sunday. I knew he'd approve of that excuse. The salon was Bobby's brainchild, typical of his brilliance. Every few weeks he gathered our friends and invited an expert in some field to meet with us for a discussion, followed by dinner. Finding speakers was easy; most of our fathers were authorities on something. I hoped Stan didn't expect an invitation, because I'd have to introduce him and didn't want to use the word *stepfather* in front of twenty kids from solid homes. If he asked (he never did), I'd say that Bobby and I had passed on our own fathers. Like mine, Bobby's dad worked in the film industry, not a unique topic at Beverly High. For this coming Sunday Bobby's uncle, the editor of an essay collection titled *The Meaning of Death*, would ask us to answer a "death questionnaire" he had written to gauge people's attitudes on his favorite subject.

Stan nodded. After a pause he said, "Looks like we're going to sell the company."

I said, "Good," and I meant it. But all I wanted to do at that moment was study.

"I think we'll make a deal."

Months earlier my father's agent had said that a "deal" to cast him as the lead in a new series was "ninety-nine percent done." The final percent had never materialized. I didn't say that to Stan.

Stan must have been concerned about me, his chubby stepson who preferred lectures on death to sailing, but he seemed unsure how to pull us closer, and I was too withdrawn to help. I wonder how I would have acted if Stan had sat on my bed and asked, "Tell me how you're feeling. You're worried about your father, aren't you?" Suppose he'd said, "I love your mother so much; I promise

I'll never run away." Would I have felt less hollow? Would I have shared whatever hurt—or simply cried?

I glanced at my history text, open to the Napoleonic Wars, tonight's soothing balm.

Stan said softly, "When we close the deal, I think I should get your mother a mink coat."

"She'll like that," I said, and kept listening to the rain.

⊙ ⊙ ⊙

"Get a hundred. Make a million," my mother said the next morning before Stan and I left the house. Normally I walked to school, but the rain had not stopped, and Stan wanted to drive me.

I asked him if there was a chance he'd meet Howard Hughes. I wondered how many eighteenth-century French kids asked their fathers, "Will you ever meet the king?"

"He's an odd man," Stan said. How many had said that about Louis XVI? Stan and Hughes never would meet. He'd been dealing with Hughes's underlings.

Stan got in line with the Falcons, Mercurys, Tempests, and Thunderbirds that were entering the student parking lot, and then he pulled as close to the main entrance as possible. After a quick embrace, he told me to have a good day. I neglected to thank him for the ride.

I burst through the double doors like an animal returned to its habitat. A girl yelled to a boy that his Sting Ray "looked sharp." Under their raincoats a couple held hands. From a record player in a room near the auditorium came the rollicking final fugue of Benjamin Britten's *Young Person's Guide to the Orchestra*, loud enough to compete with the slamming of locker doors. Somebody dropped a copy of *Ivanhoe*. A fellow Squire said something about our upcoming picnic with the Adelphians, the lower division girls' honor club. As he walked, a boy lobbed a tennis ball in the air. Another kid bellowed, "Party at 980 Roxbury Friday." I felt a lift each time someone said "Hi" and a locker door banged.

⊙ ⊙ ⊙

I want to say that I remember what I was doing when my father called to say, "Hi, pal. I'm home now." I don't, other than it was still raining. I want to say that despite having a mere learner's permit, I hijacked one of the family cars and drove into Hollywood to see him and that, after a long hug, he said his agent had called with a script.

But that's not what happened.

All I know is that he showed up at the end of the week at the house he shared with Mai, and another week passed before I saw him. I spent Sunday as planned, in Bobby's living room with my friends, bantering until his uncle handed out his death questionnaire. The booklet had the heft of an aptitude test. One question required a choice among similes: *To me, death is like (a) a beach at sunset, (b) the end of a song, (c) a curtain coming down in a theater.* With my No. 2 pencil, I filled in the oval next to the curtain. The room grew quiet as we worked, save for the rustle of pages and some nervous giggles.

My father picked me up the following Saturday morning. We drove east out of Beverly Hills and along the Sunset Strip. The sun hovered between two massive cumulus clouds. The smog was gone, washed away by the rain. We didn't talk. He didn't tell me how he and Mai had greeted each other after his absence— whether with yells, tears, or silence—and I didn't ask.

We passed a modern building of mostly glass that housed Scandia, an elegant Scandinavian restaurant where Dad could not afford to take Mai. We drove by Ciro's, an iconic nightclub, and kept going until the buildings became more ordinary and we reached Carolina Pines Jr., one of my father's favorite coffee shops, a Googie-style structure with a wavy roof at the intersection of Sunset Boulevard and La Brea Avenue.

As usual we sat in a booth next to one of the bay windows. After ordering scrambled eggs and onions with burnt bacon on the side, Dad said to the waitress—a plump woman with frosted hair and puffy cheeks who looked as though she'd worked there for years—"Darling, can I have coffee while I wait?" And then, as always, he lit a cigarette. His hair was turning gray. His face sagged.

He didn't say where he'd been. I didn't wonder whether he had been wise to leave. Or return. But I was glad we were together. I still felt more at ease with him than with Stan, and part of me felt guilty about that.

"Is school okay?" he asked.

I described our lesson about the French Revolution, beginning with Mr. Occhipinti pacing in front of us with his crescent-moon grin. My dad nodded and sipped his coffee.

I took my time. There was a lot to say before I reached Mr. Occhipinti's question: "And why did Louis XVI return to the Tuileries?" I wanted to put it in context, build to it, and then imitate Mr. Occhipinti's tone of voice, which I think I did fairly well.

My father nodded at me.

I told him the reasons my classmates had offered for the king's decision to return there. Then I shook my head, the way Mr. Occhipinti had shaken his when he said they were wrong.

"So what's the answer?" my father asked with a tinge of impatience.

In slow but cheery singsong, I tried to mimic Mr. Occhipinti. "The king was—*stupid.*"

Then I laughed, exactly as I—as the entire class—had: so loudly that a couple across the aisle turned and watched me almost spill my glass of skim milk. I was laughing too hard to tell my father what had occurred next: that Larry had stretched out his arms as he repeated the answer, and since Larry was tall and sat in the front row, his arms had framed the scene of our classroom roaring into bedlam, hooting the word "stupid" while Mr. Occhipinti beamed at us. Nor did I tell my father that each day since then, when Larry and I had seen each other, we'd said, in synchrony, "The king was *stupid.*"

Dad smiled. A courteous grin to humor his son. He lit another cigarette and sipped his coffee before he asked if I liked any girls.

I looked down at my napkin. I took a breath. I said, "Evelyn." Evelyn Rudie, from the Santa Claus Lane Parade.

My excuse for not calling was that Evelyn lived too far away for a boy without a driver's license.

"Call her. I'll arrange something," my father said. He added that she was a good actress. She and Mamie Eisenhower had posed together once to promote United States savings bonds.

I nodded and didn't say anything.

"You still have her phone number?" he asked.

"Yes." I should have asked my father to feed me some opening lines—he knew them all—but I didn't.

He leaned back and puffed on his cigarette. When Evelyn was nine, he said, she had wanted to see Mamie Eisenhower again, and to do so, she'd sneaked out of her house and flown alone across the country. The event made the newspapers.

I asked, "How could a nine-year-old manage such a thing?"

The check arrived and my father put down three or four one-dollar bills plus a silver half-dollar. Then he said, "She emptied her piggy bank, called a cab to the airport, and bought a ticket."

The way my father told the story made it clear that he admired her confidence and derring-do, qualities we both knew I lacked.

"Wow," was all I could say. I wondered if she would tolerate a timid boy like me.

My father got up from the table and I followed him outside. The clouds had departed, leaving behind a sky about as blue as it could be in Los Angeles.

As soon as we left the parking lot, Dad said, "Look. Before we see Mai, I want you to know that Trixie flew away."

The parakeet had escaped through a door she'd left open.

"Please don't get upset with her over that," he said.

I promised not to say anything.

He turned onto Santa Monica Boulevard. The afternoon traffic was wretched.

◉ ◉ ◉

In April 1963, Stan sold his business to the Hughes Tool Company. By then he'd developed a thorough dislike of Mr. Hughes' minions. Once over breakfast, he called them stupid, punctuating the word hard. I broke out laughing and didn't say why.

The night after the closing, several of Stan's friends came for dinner, close friends who knew how badly he'd needed to make the sale. Stan said his company had been bleeding money, a fact he wanted to keep secret, "but the Hughes people probably knew. I wouldn't be surprised if our phones were bugged."

I'd sensed Stan's tension over the past weeks, but tapping telephones? Like Stan, I believed Hughes had done so. Suddenly the son in me worried about him. Then the teenager in me took over and wished that I'd called Evelyn. What would we have talked about—schoolwork? Whether she had enjoyed playing Eloise on TV's *Playhouse 90* or any of her other twenty-two roles?—while an eavesdropping Howard Hughes licked his lips? I'd even been hesitant to name her in response to one of the questions Bobby's uncle had included in his survey: "When you die, whom would you like to be buried with?" I thought of her; then I looked about the room, searching for the right honors class girl and, too embarrassed to pick any of them, wrote down *my mother*.

After dessert, I excused myself to finish a paper for Mr. Occhipinti. He was guiding us through the nineteenth century, a calmer time thanks in part to kings who were less stupid than Louis XVI. While Mr. Occhipinti focused on the treaties and diplomacy that kept Europe peaceful, one of his quick asides—another factoid not in our textbook—grabbed at me.

In 1816, a year after the Congress of Vienna, the summer turned wintry, cold, overcast, and rainy to the point that crops failed in several countries, including France. The season was so miserable that, confined to a house in Switzerland, several writers challenged themselves to create dark stories. One member of the group, Mary Shelley, ended up with *Frankenstein*. Predictably, that made the class laugh, almost as much as we had over Louis XVI, and while we did, I looked out the window at a day of brilliant sunshine and wondered if it had been the rain that had driven my father to flee from Mai—or return to her.

⊙ ⊙ ⊙

Before he said good night, Stan offered to give me a ride on Saturday to the Squire-Adelphian picnic. I said, "Sure." The annual event took place in Coldwater Park, an isolated sward on the northern edge of Beverly Hills, at the foot of the mountains that bisected the LA area. No buses ran near it, and many of us, me included, had yet to turn sixteen and get our driver's licenses. Coldwater Park was no Versailles, but with clipped hedges along the perimeter, walkways across the lawn, and an ornamental stone fountain in the middle, it offered hints of a French baroque garden: not too shady, not too exposed, a place to feel as though we'd escaped the world without actually quitting Beverly Hills. Sitting on blankets, eating sandwiches the Adelphians would prepare, I'd feel like a character from one of the paintings by Fragonard and Watteau that Mr. Occhipinti had shown us in class, royals at play in their woods. I envisioned all of us imitating them, albeit dressed in shorts. I hoped it wouldn't rain.

CHAPTER TWENTY-ONE

Real Hearts

It was a Saturday in March 1963. My father and I were having lunch at the Rendezvous Room in the Beverly Hilton Hotel. Somewhere during the meal, I told him that I'd been accepted to the Western Forensics Institute, a summer program at USC for high school debaters.

"You speak well," he said. Dad saw in me the same traits that had led him into acting. "And now you'll learn to think your way through difficult situations. I always want you to have a plan."

I was about to say something about free trade, that year's debate topic, but didn't, for behind my father and closing on us fast was a tan woman with flaming red hair.

"Gerry," she said in a theatrical voice. I thought she wanted his autograph, but then she sat down, and Dad introduced Miriam to me. A necklace settled into her cleavage.

Had I not been a naive high school sophomore, I would have recognized Miriam as a threat to Mai—your quintessential homewrecker. Instead, I considered her just another friend of my father's who'd chanced by. Had I known she and he were lovers, I would have applauded them both. I was still upset about what Mai had done to my parents' marriage and would have hoped Miriam would return the favor. To do so wouldn't be hard, I thought. My father's second marriage to Mai was crumbling. Two weeks earlier, he'd said something so harmless I no longer recall what it was.

Mai said, "I resent that."

"Oh, come on," said my father.

"How dare you," Mai yelled, followed by a lunge for the car keys and the announcement, "Come on, Tommy and Timmy, we're going *out.*"

Mai and her sons drove off, and with no car for the rest of the day, my father and I couldn't play miniature golf, which had been our plan.

While Miriam prattled on about—I don't know what—and my father asked for more coffee, I started to say something about the Soviet Union's recent lunar failure. The topic didn't stick, and so I retreated into thoughts about Jo Anne, a serene little pixie with the most angelic voice on Beverly High's speech team. At the end of a recent tournament, I'd started to suggest that we should see a movie together—*Son of Flubber* or *To Kill a Mockingbird*—but before my question was out, she said her parents wanted her to sit for a portrait that night—a Saturday night—and I'd believed her. As she glided away, I recalled the lyrics from Steve Lawrence's song "Portrait of My Love," how painting his beloved was impossible because nobody could paint a dream.

I fidgeted in my seat after finishing my sandwich. Eventually Miriam left, and my father and I played miniature golf, only one round though, because Miriam had stayed for so long.

I forgot about her until two Saturdays later when, during another lunch at the Beverly Hilton, Miriam reappeared, this time in a sleeveless sundress. Her red hair looked wilder than before; her cleavage, a deeper canyon. While they chattered on for at least an hour, I slipped into daydreams of Jo Anne. I still had not asked her for another date.

Two weeks later Miriam materialized again and flopped her breasts on the table. This time she asked how I liked school. I said I liked it fine and took another bite of my club sandwich. She wanted to know my favorite classes.

"French, modern history, English, geometry," I said and then bit into my pickle.

My father sat quietly, smoking a cigarette. A waitress refilled his cup of coffee. "Thank you, darling," he said.

"My daughter is your age," Miriam said to me. She also had a son, George, who was a couple of years older.

"Oh," I said.

"You'd like Nancy."

"Oh."

"Gerry," Miriam said, "let's get Nancy and Tony together for dinner one night."

I didn't say anything. I couldn't imagine the four of us joining Mai and her two sons around the dining room table at my father's latest rented house atop Kings Road with its view of the Los Angeles basin, all of us looking out at the lights, saying little to each other. I couldn't imagine Miriam or Mai holding their own as my father and I discussed the Civil Rights Movement.

After Miriam left—hours later, it felt like—my father maneuvered his Jaguar out of the parking lot between the Beverly Hilton and Robinson's Department Store and headed north toward Sunset Boulevard. The marine layer had turned the sky gray, the air chilly.

I asked if we could still play miniature golf.

"It's getting late," he said in his that's-the-way-it-goes tone of voice. Miriam had ruined my day again.

I didn't call Jo Anne that weekend. I decided to ask her in person, in forensics the following week. But she arrived moments before the bell rang and zipped out of the room right after class.

I turned sixteen in May, and to celebrate, my father and I played miniature golf and then planned to have dinner at my grandmother's. We were halfway through our game at, naturally, the Gittleson Brothers and I was scoring par or below on the holes, my only sports triumph that year. That's when my father flicked the remains of his cigarette into the trash before saying, "Is it okay if Miriam and her daughter come tonight?"

Something told me my answer would make no difference. I should have said I didn't want to share my birthday with strangers, even if one of them was a girl my age. Instead I mumbled "okay" and shot over par on the following hole.

⊙ ⊙ ⊙

The card table my grandmother set up almost filled her studio apartment. She'd draped it with a white cloth. The olive-colored folding metal chairs, in which her friends—"the girls" as she called them—sat for their weekly game of canasta, surrounded the table. The smell of cooking meat floated in from her little kitchen. I sat on one of the two identical sofas that were built into the wall, and I rested an arm on the faux wooden credenza between them. While we were alone, I thought about asking my father for advice about Jo Anne but hesitated. I remained as shy about discussing her as I'd been about calling her, and before I could rev up the courage to say anything, there were several staccato knocks on the door.

Nancy, Miriam's daughter, had a pleasant smile, a pleasant tan, and a pleasant voice along with pleasant dark hair, straight to her shoulders, where it ended in pleasant curls. And this pleasant girl appeared as uncomfortable as I felt.

I know that my grandmother served meat because my father wouldn't eat anything else. She cooked it until it surpassed tender and turned mushy. Then she added plenty of gravy, which she knew I liked. I ladled it on thick, over the potatoes as well as the peas, which were faded and runny, because they most likely came from a can. To me, the combination tasted soft and good.

I ate quietly, as did the others, while odors from the kitchen lingered inside, because the windows (which overlooked a back alley) were closed with the curtains drawn.

Midway through dinner Miriam said, "Tony, aren't you getting A's in school?"

Why did she say it that way? Embarrassed, I stammered, "Not really," which was the truth. My sophomore grades were salted with plenty of B's. No one asked Nancy for her marks. Jo Anne, I knew, was earning straight A's. By now I was sure that Nancy, like me, was trying to devise a method to speed up time.

Miriam said, "Tony, are you winning lots of debate tournaments?"

I looked at the curtains behind her and said I'd won one or two, which was true. The words came out slurred, lacking the timbre becoming a member of a speech team. Nancy kept on eating. I wished someone would shift the conversation to Red China.

From Miriam again: "Tony, what are you doing this summer?"

"How wonderful," she said when I mentioned the Western Forensics Institute, and then after a pause, "Nancy, isn't that wonderful?"

I'm sure Nancy said it was wonderful.

On it went. Nothing about the Civil Rights movement, the space race, or the slow cooker that was Vietnam, topics that, whenever my father and I were alone, we dissected while my grandmother beamed at us with pride. Miriam kept lobbing softballs. What's the year's debate topic? What clubs are you in? Is Beverly High's golf team winning? How about its tennis team? At least she didn't inject a comment about my father not having any money as Mai always did. I had yet to understand that she and my father were having an affair.

Toward dessert I asked Nancy about Palisades High, her campus of modern buildings with flat roofs a short distance up a hill from the beach. You could spend lunch surfing and return to class before the tardy bell rang. When I mentioned that, Nancy smiled, if for real, I couldn't tell.

Out came the birthday cake, a bundt kuchen with a golden-brown exterior and a soft yellow interior that I knew would taste moist and sweet. Sixteen candles ringed the top. After the group sang "Happy Birthday," I mouthed a fast thank-you before launching into the cake. Then everything fell still, as if singing had drained the room of energy.

⊙ ⊙ ⊙

My father and I didn't talk about Miriam during the ride home. I'm sure I thanked him for whatever birthday present he gave me, an item long since forgotten. I may have mentioned an upcoming test. I should have mentioned Jo Anne. I should have mentioned Miriam. I should have said a lot of things but was too confused to frame the words. When he dropped me off, we hugged each other.

Decades later I'd learn that the evening was far from Miriam's first visit to 1211 North Detroit Street. I wonder if I should have appreciated my grandmother, the enabler. She despised Mai. While my grandmother played canasta with "the girls" at her friend Flossie's house, her studio apartment on North Detroit Street became a paradise for my father and his lady. I never learned which of the two sofas that pulled out into single beds my father and Miriam chose. My guess is the one closer to the kitchen, because whenever I stayed over, my grandmother slept in the farther bed. But maybe they tried out both.

At school the following week, Jo Anne and I passed each other on the second-story breezeway between the foreign language wing and the main building. I paused to say hi.

"Oh, hello," Jo Anne said without slowing down.

At least she'd said something to me, and so, buoyed, I made a decision. As hard as it would be, I planned to ask my father for lessons on how to win Jo Anne. If anyone could teach me, Dad could. Some, including the lady who wrote the Hollywood mogul letter, had compared him to Humphrey Bogart. "The only thing is," she added, "he has more and better of the same." I saw women stare at my father each time we entered a restaurant, exactly what they did two Sundays later, when we returned to the Rendezvous Room.

My father asked for eggs and onions with burnt toast on the side. I ordered a hamburger.

"Darling, can I have coffee while I wait," he asked the waitress.

I took a breath and started to frame my opening sentence. "There's this girl in school, and I'm thinking, I mean, uh, well, I don't know . . ."

Miriam approached from behind me this time. When she left—two? three hours later?—my courage had dissipated and wouldn't return until the end of the weekend. And my father didn't revive the subject.

He dropped me off Sunday evening, early enough to do my homework.

I opened a textbook—*Modern Chemistry*—read the same sentence six times and still didn't know what titration meant. I switched to French but couldn't conjugate a single verb, even in the easy future tense. The same with geometry: the side-angle-side theorem felt inscrutable. I scratched my cheeks and pursed my lips. I ran my fingers over the burlap cover of my three-ring notebook and opened it to one of the tabs. My eyes blinked until they closed. I wanted to stand; I wanted to sit. That's when, dressed in a white robe, my mother came into my bedroom to say good night. It was getting late. She and Stan were going to bed.

My mother said, "You look as though you're ready to cry."

All I said, as I started to cry, was that for the past couple of months, a "friend" of my father's kept popping up and preventing us from spending time alone.

"Now who again is this woman?" my mother asked as Stan walked into the room.

"A friend of his."

I might as well have said "his bedmate." My mother's body stiffened. Her face assumed a look of disgust.

"I'm calling him," she said. "Gerry can do whatever he wants with his marriage, but I will not let him drag my son into it."

Each word came out with an increasingly stronger punch. She seethed in a manner I'd never seen from her, and now I felt guilty. Although my father had not asked me to keep Miriam a secret, I felt as though I'd breached his trust.

Stan shook his head. "Your father should never have done this," he said, just above a whisper.

I sensed him tiptoeing through the subject, unsure how deeply to plunge into his stepson's relationship with his father, and I couldn't provide any guidance. I felt bewildered. I wanted the pain to go away. Even now that it was obvious my father was having an affair, I was reluctant to criticize him to Stan. I'd never done so. Between Stan and me, my father was no-man's-land.

Perhaps I should have felt hopeful. Perhaps I didn't want to admit to myself that I was rooting for another divorce. If Miriam could give my father comfort and solace, who was I—who was my mother—to stop them? If anything, I could have hastened my father's split from Mai, especially if I'd feigned interest in Nancy. I didn't think of it then, me with the daughter of the mistress, a wicked combination that, on some level, might have excited me as well as Nancy if she knew—did she know?—that my father was married. I never tried to imagine Nancy, her mother, my father, and me watching movies together at the Egyptian Theater, riding into the tunnel of love at Nu-Pike, or trotting horses through Griffith Park. Half a century later I learned that Miriam was a widow. Had I known, maybe I would have felt sorry for her. Maybe she was feeling sorry for me.

I didn't hear what my mother said to my father, but the next time I saw him, Miriam did not materialize. We played miniature golf, again at the Gittleson Brothers, and as we walked among the trees from one hole to the next, we discussed Vietnam. My father's birthday had just passed, and on that day, a monk had burned himself to death on a Saigon boulevard in order to protest the government's treatment of Buddhists. Not a word about Miriam passed between us. I managed the volcano in one stroke, the drawbridge in two, and finished under par. My success steeled me, as we got in the car, to mention Jo Anne. I tried to think of an opening as we eased along Hollywood Boulevard, dropped down to Santa Monica Boulevard, and then stopped at a car wash. As his Jaguar rolled through, I was still crafting my topic sentence about Jo Anne.

About thirty feet away, also awaiting her car, stood a woman in a sleeveless dress. Her hair was thicker than Miriam's, if that was possible, and while she was not as buxom, her figure kept me looking. Even from our distance I could sense moisture on her full lips. She glanced at my dad, longer than she had to, which gave me time to study her elegant, steamy quality. My father offered her a return look before slowly withdrawing a cigarette from its pack.

She watched my father tap a finger against his Virginia Rounds, as he always did to make sure the tobacco was firmly packed. Dad's lips remained together; she left hers slightly parted. From the car wash tunnel behind her, lights started to flash, as they always did when a customer wanted his car waxed. Then the letters lit up: "Hot Carnauba Wax is being applied here." The whine of the dryers drowned out the traffic noise from Santa Monica Boulevard. My father used his silver lighter to fire up his cigarette. He bowed his head to the flame and made sure the cigarette tip was red before returning his gaze to the woman.

My father took a puff. The smoke lingered above him, his expression unchanged, nonchalant like hers, yet like hers, burning with potential. At most she tilted her head. I never realized how nonchalance could seduce. I thought about trying it out on Jo Anne, but neither of us smoked.

One of the workers signaled my father; they'd completed drying off his car. He nodded and we got in.

"Did you notice that lady?" I asked, master of the obvious.

"What do *you* think?" my father said a little too quickly. "She has a mouth made for a cock."

I didn't reply. I didn't know what to say. It would take time for me to appreciate how inappropriate it was for him to make that remark, even if I were his pal instead of his son. Maybe I'd have had a rejoinder if one of my high school buddies said it, but none of my close friends was that crass.

For a moment I wondered if, but for me, my father would have met her and spent a pleasant afternoon. Now, I'd separated him from two women.

⊙ ⊙ ⊙

I don't care how magnificent a second father turns out to be. It's damned hard to replace the first, especially when the original father lives nearby and keeps in touch. From the day my father left my mother, he told me he wanted to be my pal, a goal he achieved, not just by opening every phone call with "Hi, pal," but with the actions of a good chum albeit thirty years older, a playmate as fun-loving as the Swinging Gentlemen on KFWB. And like radio deejays, my father craved practical jokes. One morning, he conjured up an art hoax with him impersonating a hot new avant-garde painter and me in the backyard slopping paint onto canvases he'd display. (We abandoned the project when Skip and Stan warned me away, saying we were "perpetrating a fraud.")

Stan never became my pal. He maintained the distance of a parent with the willingness to discipline and correct. That said, he rescued me. Without him I'd have come of age with only my mother, both of us lonely and scared. I'm sure there would have been no return to LA, no chance to view once more the film industry from a close-in vantage point. Visits with my father would have been confined to a two or three-week period in the summer. Fewer outstanding teachers like Mr. Occhipinti would have entered my life because Beverly Hills High School paid its teachers the highest salary in California, and one of the highest in the nation, causing the best to flock there.

Slowly, Stan and I grew close. He used business analogies to teach me about the world.

"Tony," he growled, "life is like a bank account. You get out of it what you put into it." We were en route home from a sail after I'd failed to help out as much as he'd expected.

"This boy is going to get initiated into sex properly," my father told my mother shortly after I was born and then told me later. "At the right time"—I never learned when that was—"I'm going to get him a call girl."

My mother blanched but, as things turned out, she didn't need to worry. Somewhere between age fifteen and eighteen, when the right time ostensibly arrived, my father couldn't afford the price. During my senior year in high school, I squirmed when he revealed his original plan. At the time my father said this, all I craved was the courage to kiss one of my straight-A crushes good night.

☉ ☉ ☉

Stan had other plans for his Beverly Hills brat. During the eighth grade, he arranged for me to spend a weekend with Bill, the man he'd hired to maintain and crew on his fifty-eight-foot catamaran.

"Skip—I mean Tony," Stan said, "Bill can teach you a lot about boats, and maybe after you two have dinner, he'll show you how to tie some knots."

I'm sure Bill considered me the last person he wanted to spend thirty-six hours with, and the feeling was mutual. Bill reminded me of Popeye, stocky with a voice that blended gruff and reedy. He lumbered along on bowed legs and salted his language with nautical slang. On the boat, we barely spoke. I struggled to think of something I had to do for the next twenty weekends, but when Stan hatched an idea, he became the immovable object. Often my mother could run interference when Stan planned something disagreeable for his kids. This time she couldn't stop him. He was convinced the experience would be good for me.

The weekend with Bill was interminable. I would have felt more at ease with a Martian. Perhaps if Stan had presented the experience as a chance to learn about others in order to prepare me for a career in law or politics, I might have displayed more enthusiasm. Instead, I thought Stan wanted to humble me. His behavior reminded me of what my sixth-grade teacher said about the Red Chinese—that they were sending intellectuals to work in communes in order to chasten them. Was that what Stan had in mind?

I wondered if Stan paid Bill to take care of me from Saturday to Sunday. If he did, maybe he got a refund because Bill never taught me how to tie knots. I didn't care, but if that knowledge was so important, why didn't Stan take the time to teach me?

There was quite a difference between the two men—Stan ordering me to forfeit the beach in order to spend time with an old salt, my father eager to deposit me into the bed of a call girl.

CHAPTER TWENTY-TWO

Broken Hearts

In late June I arrived at USC for the debate program and checked into Trojan Hall, a three-story dormitory near the edge of the campus. Its reception area was ordinary, with flyers taped to a bulletin board along with a set of house rules. No girls in the room. No alcohol in the room. The usual. A slender woman behind the counter handed me a key and a card that gave the names of my roommate and dorm counselor.

Despite the smog, the ensuing days were bright for us thirty or so rising juniors. The faculty walked us through the upcoming year's debate topic. (Resolved: That Social Security benefits should be extended to include complete medical care.) They drilled us in dramatic interpretation ("Read the poem. Don't play to the ceiling. Just read the poem.") and impromptu speaking ("The only way to learn impromptu is to speak impromptu.").

Toward the end of our first week, Ruth, another high school participant, walked up to me. She had tender eyes and a crack-the-whip debate style.

"There's the guy with the good-looking legs," she said as she ran a hand through her hair. Her voice was steady and pleasant. (Of course it was; we all belonged to speech teams.) She brimmed with life, a California teenager in the summer of '63 who knew, without being told, that her future lay open, boundless, and bright.

Unsure what to say, I managed an innocuous answer and regretted that I had yet to have an occasion to wear Bermuda shorts around Jo Anne. Then Ruth and I slipped into a conversation about the cold war. She was as interested in current events as I was.

That night my mother called. An invitation from a Beverly High classmate had arrived. Two Fridays from now, July 12, 1963. Dinner on the backyard lawn, with a live band. Emboldened by Ruth's flattery, I slipped down to the payphone on our floor to call Jo Anne. Halfway through her number I almost hung up but kept going because someone warned me that the phone never returned our dimes.

She wasn't home. I asked her mother to leave a message about the party. She sounded friendly, which made me feel hopeful, but moments after I hung up, I flogged myself for not telling Jo Anne's mother that she knew my mother from the PTA. It was an opportunity missed; she might have told Jo Anne that my mother was nice and added something like: "I want you to get to know this Tony. Say yes and go to the party."

The faculty organized a picnic for us in a shady section of the campus. It was hot, even for July. Twelve miles west my Beverly High friends probably were playing Marco Polo in one of their swimming pools.

The griddles hissed with frying hamburgers. A tin of potato salad appeared on the table, next to the coleslaw. My roommate scooped up a handful of potato chips.

Ben, the most overweight boy in the speech institute, waddled over to us. "Okay, I wrote it," he said. A parody of "Surf City." The night before, several of us in the dorm had been listening to Jan and Dean's song.

He moved under a tree to get out of the sun. "Here we go," Ben said, and then he sang, louder than he needed to.

Ruth walked up. She wore light, long pants and a thin top.

"Wow," she said for the third time, or perhaps the fifth. "There's the guy with the good-looking legs."

I guess I should have felt grateful that her gaze didn't migrate up to my not-so-good-looking stomach or higher still to my not-so-good-looking acne.

Ben kept going. "Oh, I'm goin' to Surf City, gonna dress real tough. Oh, I'm goin' to Surf City, gonna act real rough . . ."

It never dawned on me to ask Ruth to the party. I had yet to hear from Jo Anne, and foolish optimist that I was, I thought I'd given her enough notice so that nothing would conflict with her schedule. She'd say yes. It didn't matter that part of me knew I'd have more fun with Ruth. I remained faithful to Jo Anne.

Ben belted out the line he'd worked up to. "Twelve boys for every boooaarrrd."

My roommate whooped a salute to him. Our little group of speakers didn't miss the beach. Let the July sun bake. We—future champs who came from the best schools in the Southland: Arcadia, Mark Keppel, Grossmont, Saint Monica's, and of course Beverly—had chosen to spend the summer where we were, twelve miles inland, south of downtown Los Angeles. Surf City. What crap. I reached for a hot dog and smeared it with mustard and relish.

That evening our dorm counselor knocked on the door. He was a twenty-five-year-old USC graduate, a wannabe politician whom I found hard to take. He had pronounced eyebrows and a shaved head, and he kept warning us to obey the rules. With a touch of suspicion in his voice, he said that "some girl" was on the hall phone.

It had to be Jo Anne. My roommate gave me the kind of look sixteen-year-olds assumed when a guy was poised to "get a little action." I walked to the black pay phone on the wall, hoping she'd say we had a date.

It was Miriam.

"Tony. Can you help me get my Gerry back?"

"What?" I was so gobsmacked to hear her voice that I didn't wonder how Miriam had tracked me down.

"Help me get Gerry back. I love him."

Miriam kept saying that. I kept stammering that I didn't know what to say, much less do, until she finally let me go.

She called again the following night. "I love your father," she said, "and I know he loves me." Unable to make her stop, I clung to the receiver and faced the gray cinder block wall. She kept beseeching me for answers as her voice rose.

A fellow debater walked by, and while he may not have understood her babble, Miriam was yelling loudly enough that he had to hear her.

"That's a helluva girlfriend," he said later.

"She's not a girlfriend," I said.

"Sure. Who's next? Ruth?"

It was ironic that my prestige in the dorm soared because everyone thought I was a heartbreaker. But I didn't want to talk about it.

Jo Anne never called back. But Miriam did, the third night. She was in full sobbing mode the moment I picked up the receiver.

"Miriam, I don't know what to—"

"My Gerry loves me. You have to get him back."

"Miriam, I—"

She was screaming now. "My Gerry means everything! My Gerry! He's my *life*!"

"Miriam—"

And then she said it.

"I got a bottle of pills over here that would kill a horse, and I'm going to take them if I can't have my Gerry back."

I don't recall what I said in reply. I was too stunned. Whatever it was, I was stalling for time.

Miriam said, "My life's not worth living. I won't go on. I can't."

I'm sure I responded with every useless trite phrase I could muster in order to keep her alive.

When we hung up, I said nothing to my roommate and didn't call anybody. I couldn't think clearly enough to do anything.

Miriam's next call came on Friday afternoon, July 12, moments after I returned to the dorm from class. I wondered if she had contacted USC and learned that they were letting us out early for the weekend. As she screamed and sobbed and talked again of suicide, an idea hatched.

I told her I had to catch the bus home for the weekend and asked if we could talk later.

"You promise?"

I promised.

"Really, Tony? You really, really promise?"

I said I'd call in an hour and a half.

☉ ☉ ☉

I took the bus west on Olympic Boulevard to its stop near my street. The house was empty. I was lucky that Stan and my mother had taken the catamaran to Catalina Island for the weekend. I could work alone. But first I called Jo Anne.

"Hello?" She answered on the first ring.

"Is Jo Anne Gardner there?" (What an idiot. I actually said her last name.)

"This is she." Correct grammar. No hint that she knew who it was.

"This is Tony Mohr."

No delay in the comeback. "Hi." That sliver of a word conveyed the image of her face with its adorable mouth, large eyes, dark and set far apart, straight black hair worn short with bangs that didn't quite reach her thin eyebrows, a larger-than-normal nose that somehow added to her beauty.

My house was still, the only sound, an air-conditioning unit in one of my bedroom windows.

I asked how she was.

"I'm fine, thank you." Silence again.

"There's a party. Would you like to go with me?"

Before I realized that I had yet to say the date, she said she was busy, something to do with her parents, their anniversary, or was it her grandparents' anniversary? It didn't matter; she was busy and in a "terrific hurry."

She pretended never to have received my message. "I'm sorry," she said. Even in its clipped no-time-for-you mode, she sounded irresistible. "I hope you enjoy your party," she added. Then, "I have to go now."

There was no time to mourn. I'd promised to call Miriam. The party would start in an hour. I had to keep moving. And I had a plan.

I sat on the floor between the two beds, phone at my side, receiver in one hand, microphone in the other, so I could bring the two instruments as close together as possible. In front of me was my Recordio reel-to-reel tape recorder, a Christmas gift from my mother and Stan, spools threaded and at the ready. I hoped Miriam wouldn't hear me press the record button.

"Now, Miriam," I said, "I'd like you to tell me everything about you and Dad."

I wonder if she noticed my tone shift; I could. A trace of the debater had come in, poised to question someone about whether socialized medicine was necessary.

"You know Gerry wants me so much. He never left me."

Odd. My father told me that he and Mai had stopped fighting, and Mai had grown friendlier around me.

She described the party where she'd met my father—the home of some actor they both knew. She narrated their furtive first date over coffee, then the second date, which had lasted and lasted, leaving them sated, yet famished for more.

"I just don't understand," Miriam said through her tears, "how your father could turn off his love so fast."

My question popped out immediately. "Did he ever turn it on?"

Yes, she answered. Yes, at least four times. She described how his face lit up each time they met. How tenderly he held her hand. I guess as a concession to my age, she didn't tell me how he purred in bed—my grandmother's bed among them?—smoking cigarettes after they'd made love, her naked body pressed against his.

Months earlier, during one of our lunches before Miriam had started invading them, my father had guided me into one of his lessons about women, rhapsodizing about mutual orgasms, "that moment when you and your lover fly to the moon." I imagined him and Miriam on that journey, something I couldn't envision with my father and Mai.

The spools rotated slowly. The red light on the recording head flickered.

"Tony. Please. You've got to help me."

I told the truth. I had no advice for her.

"I love your father. You have to speak with him for me. You like me, Tony. Don't you?"

"Sure," I said quickly, and then—because I wanted it on tape— "I hope you're not serious about killing yourself."

"I am, Tony. I'll take those pills. I swear I will."

The tape was running out. The party would begin soon. Somehow, I managed to free myself from the conversation. Dazed, upset, guilty about what I'd done, I took a shower. My bar of soap slipped and hit my foot. For a moment, I recalled the "slippery soapy" game my father and I had played. I thought of erasing the tape but needed it as a weapon to stop Miriam from calling me.

I staggered through the party like a zombie. The steak tasted like sawdust, the petits fours like library paste. The band's music became a mash of notes. The spotlights didn't turn the lawn blue or bring up its green; they washed away all color, leaving bright swaths of nothing before my eyes. Ruth was lucky I hadn't asked her to go. She would have passed the evening alone. I didn't realize, then, that Miriam had done me a favor: I had no emotional room left to lament Jo Anne. I was disassociating from my father's failing relationships. It seemed the only way to cope. As for Jo Anne, my mind shut her down. Her nose seemed too big, her lips too thin, and I remembered a comment by someone who had danced with her once: she smelled.

I circled the swimming pool and wandered toward the outer fringe of the lawn, a glass of gooey red punch in my hand. I looked at the backyard wall, covered with flowers, and remembered Miriam's ponderous breasts lying on that restaurant table like two beached whales. I thought of my father's face buried between them, be it in the morning when he needed a shave or during the afternoon, fresh from the unemployment line, cash in hand but still in need of relief.

Once I was home and looked at the door to the master bed-room, I realized that my mother had married a faithful man. In the silence of the house, I felt grateful. Had they not been in Catalina that night, I might have walked in and thanked Stan. Another six years would pass before I did so, at my college graduation. Their marriage would last three more decades.

My father and Mai arrived Saturday morning to collect me for the rest of the weekend. I broke the rules: instead of running out to the street with my overnight bag in tow, I invited them into the house.

They looked surprised. It would be the first time either

had stepped foot inside where Mom and Stan lived. Now I was committing a boundary crossing but felt it necessary. They hesitated to walk into the foyer.

"I want you to hear something."

Mai trailed in behind my father. She looked to the right to catch a glimpse of the living room with its two creamy white sofas, an antique coffee table between them, the baby grand piano at the far wall, the Welsh cupboard at the near wall, paintings and serigraphs on the walls, and an antique game table next to the bay window. I led them left, up the circular staircase, then down the hall, past the guest room and into my bedroom. The door to the master bedroom was closed.

My recorder still lay on the floor. "Listen to this," I said. The brown tape hissed across the heads until they heard me: "Now, Miriam, I'd like you to . . ."

From the built-in speaker came Miriam's voice. "He always tells me he loves me, that he would be happy with me . . ."

Mai's hands whipped to her mouth. She gasped and her body drifted, slowly, to the floor. She uttered something in Swedish.

My father stood by, impassive.

"I know he wants to marry me. He says that every night . . ."

Mai suppressed a sob. My father didn't move.

The tape reached the point where I'd asked, "Did he ever turn it on?"

"What a good question," my father said.

"That's so brilliant of you," Mai said. I was surprised—and still am—that she didn't seem wounded. Or if she had been moments before, how quickly she'd changed. And if she'd changed, why?

I didn't expect their admiration. Part of me had feared what would happen if they heard the tape—would Mai take a swing at me? Would my father yell for me to turn it off? But I had to shock him into action. I couldn't take Miriam's phone calls anymore.

They frightened me. Making the tape would make her stop. I guess I was capable of showing my father what was troubling me, but incapable of verbalizing it.

After the tape ran out, my father picked up my telephone. He knew the number by heart. "Goddamn it, Miriam, I'm warning you. Stop calling my boy." He sounded savage, devoid of sympathy.

Miriam hollered something, too fast to understand, followed by hysterical sobs.

"Let me tell you something, Miriam. Tony made a *tape* of your call last night. I have it and I promise you I'll use it if I have to. Now leave him alone."

Another scream.

"I said don't call him anymore. Is that clear?"

A volley of words piling on top of each other.

"*Is that clear?*"

A meek sound from the receiver, then my father slammed it down. Mai clapped her hands, just once, as I exhaled.

I didn't feel satisfied or smug or victorious. Part of me regretted recording Miriam. Part of me wondered if what I'd done was legal. (Not in California, I'd learn in law school.) Part of me, I'm sure now, wanted Mai to wince at Miriam's voice as well as envy the beautiful house my mother and I lived in, thanks to Stan. The rest of me felt exhausted.

My father took the tape, which concerned me. I would have duplicated it had I the equipment to do so. He never returned it and I never asked for it back. I don't remember what we did for the rest of the day, only that the mood was low key and gentle. I got the feeling that Mai had forgiven him. They even held hands.

Sunday night, when I returned to Trojan Hall, the payphone remained silent, a silence that continued until, by Wednesday, one of my dormmates asked, "I assume it's over with your girlfriend?"

"It's over," I said, the easy answer.

"I'm sorry."

My mother and Stan never learned of the tape or that Mai had been in our house. My father and I never talked about Miriam again. She dropped from my mind like a stone into a dark sea, down to wherever Jo Anne was.

CHAPTER TWENTY-THREE

Reel Lives

One morning during my junior year at Beverly Hills High School, the clock radio snapped me awake with the Trashmen's "Surfin' Bird." As in, "Suuurrrrfin' biiirrrd," followed by a slew of nonsense syllables that sounded like the clatter of Skip's old Ford each time its engine died.

I donned the Pendleton shirt my mother bought for me and wore it as proudly as the Mickey Mouse Club ears she'd given me eight years earlier. "Surfin' Bird" made me bounce through the day, starting with first-period forensics, where, after an articulate rebuttal speech, I felt so intellectually superior to the Trashmen's brainless lyrics.

"Don't just quote the *Statistical Abstract*. Use logic," my debate coach always said, and that morning I'd done so. I'd taken his advice and convinced him why social security benefits should *not* be extended to include complete medical care.

"Hang five," a teammate said to me when our forensics class was over. Neither of us surfed, but from time to time, we borrowed the lingo.

◉ ◉ ◉

I arrived home that afternoon to hear my mother upstairs talking on the phone. She sat on her bed, because the extension cord didn't reach across the room to her desk. Instead of smiling when I came through the door, she waved me away. Her face—usually serene and content since marrying Stan—looked drawn.

"Beulah," she said into the receiver with obvious concern. Beulah was my mother's oldest friend.

I went into my bedroom and sat at my desk. For some time, no sound came from the other side of the wall. Then I heard my mother say something like, "That must be rough for Sumner."

They had to be discussing Beulah's second husband, Sumner Arthur Long, author of forty-six *Lassie* scripts and the play, *Never Too Late*, which had entered its second year on Broadway, soon to become one of New York's longest running hits.

Again, silence from the bedroom, while, I'm sure, Beulah spoke. As I debated between studying English or French, my mother asked, "Is there a chance he could become violent?"

My throat caught. Sumner was a big man with a moustache and a raspy voice. He was in his early forties. Beulah's first husband, also a writer, had died at forty-two, leaving behind my friend Robbie. He was two grades ahead of me at Beverly High. We'd known each other since our toddler years, and now I was frightened for him. Robbie had been four when his dad died, and I saw how devastated he'd been.

"What's wrong with Sumner?" I asked after my mother hung up.

My mother looked at me quizzically, as in "Where did that come from?" The moment I mentioned the phone call, she waved her hand, a dismissive, backhanded gesture.

"Oh that," she said. "We were talking about a script. Sumner's having trouble with one of his characters."

Looking back on it, I doubt it was a script. I think my mother invoked a Southland fantasy in order to comfort me. Beulah and Sumner drank a lot, I know now, and maybe that's what Beulah and my mother were talking about. In a town full of stars, fact and fiction blended seamlessly, making LA, at times, a confusing mix of the two. Beverly High's swim gym was featured in *It's a Wonderful Life*. Every time the school held a dance there, someone wondered if the floor would slide open and dump the student body into the pool, as it had in the movie. (It never did.) I couldn't visit the Griffith Observatory without recalling *Rebel Without a Cause*. My father's mentor, Orson Welles, used Venice Beach as a sleazy border town in *Touch of Evil*.

I'd heard stories of actors who became their characters. A classmate told me that once, Buddy Hackett drove by her house in his converted custom El Dorado station wagon, waving as though he were in a parade. Was he daydreaming? Unable to shed his public persona? When we reconnected as adults, my childhood neighbor Valory told me that she grew suspicious if a person had a one-syllable surname, because many such monikers were stage names. (Mohr was not.)

Even normal people could morph into fiction. My pediatrician became a character on *I Love Lucy* when, in the "Nursery School" episode, Lucy picked up the phone. "Dr. Gettelman. This is Lucy Ricardo. Something is wrong with our baby. Can you come over right away?" (Dr. Eugene Gettelman's patients included not only Lucille Ball's kid, but the children of Marlon Brando, Danny Kaye, and Dinah Shore. I have no idea if I met any of them in his waiting room.)

In *West of Eden*, Jean Stein related a story about someone recoiling when she saw a Nazi rally, not realizing they'd staged it for a movie. "Our object was to escape reality," director George Cukor told Stein. "We were quite conscious of all that."

Stein went on to describe Southern California as "a never-never land, a construct. These immigrants, these Jews from Eastern Europe, had developed this dream that had blond hair, blue eyes, and a straight nose. It all had to be beautiful. This was a fairy tale . . ." The book fed into the impressions and sensations I'd had as a teen. They floated below the surface, thoughts I'd never tried to articulate.

Even Stan joined the make-believe world with Sumner inserting him, as well as their mutual friend, film editor Harold Kress, into *Never Too Late.* The two became offstage characters as Paul Ford said to his costar Maureen O'Sullivan:

"Fun is tending to business down at the yard . . . Fun is when I go through that front gate and the men say 'Morning, sir,' and I say 'Morning, men.' Then I sit down in my office, look over the stacks of invoices, bills, and contracts—*that's* fun. . . . Then I get on the phone and tell Harold Kress he'd better pay the balance of his bill—or else! Then I drive a hard bargain with Stan Dashew for a load of first-grade lumber! That's what you call *fun* . . . I'm going down to the lumberyard and have some fun!"

⊙ ⊙ ⊙

The 1964 Academy Awards took place on April 13, a couple of weeks after Beulah's call to my mother. Harold Kress was up for best editing for *How the West Was Won.*

Stan made no business calls that evening. He, my mother, and I sat in the den, the television set recessed into the light tan wall, bookshelves surrounding it. When the host, Jack Lemmon, brought Sidney Poitier on stage to announce the Oscar for film editing, I could feel Mom and Stan tense up.

Poitier deadpanned the camera with his bright eyes and, without a single preliminary, got to the point. "Those nominated for the best achievement in film editing are—"

We strained forward as he reeled off the nominees. "Louis R. Loeffler for *The Cardinal.*"

"Turn up the volume," Stan said. I sprang across the room to the TV set and did so.

"Dorothy Spencer for *Cleopatra,*" Poitier said in his no-

nonsense voice. Even Stan appeared riveted, something television never did to him.

"Ferris Webster for *The Great Escape.*"

We remained quiet when he named Harold and, finally, a team of three editors for *It's a Mad, Mad, Mad, Mad World.* The moment Sidney Poitier finished, Lemmon handed him the envelope.

Mr. Poitier extracted the contents and said, "The winner is—"

A half-second pause.

"Harold F. Kress, for *How the West Was Won.*"

Sidney Poitier offered a brief smile, my mother emitted a shriek, and Stan said, "Oh, that's wonderful." I raised my arms, the gesture of a champion, and said, "All right."

Harold all but sprinted down a perimeter aisle and pulled at his right sleeve as he mounted the stage, his euphoria beaming out of the TV screen. His acceptance speech lasted twenty-one seconds: "The words 'thank you' can hardly express my feelings at this moment. I want to express my gratitude to all the young men and the women that helped me very much on this picture. And to stand here and," he paused a beat, "accept this from such a fine, fine actor is a great privilege and a great honor. Thank you." As the orchestra launched into the theme song from his movie, Harold and Sidney Poitier left the stage together, Harold's head no higher than Mr. Poitier's shoulder.

Not more than an hour passed before Harold and his wife Zelda glided through our front door. They weren't the type to go to whatever boozy after-parties took place that year. His bald head glowed like a lightbulb. His tuxedo appeared as unruffled as it had on television; even the pocket handkerchief seemed untouched. Harold hadn't smiled during his acceptance speech, but now a grin was in full bloom as he and Stan clapped each other on the shoulders. Zelda's white hair remained in perfect order as she threw her arms around my mother.

Harold's Oscar felt heavy in my hand; its surface, cool and smooth. I was surprised at the lack of expression on Oscar's flat face, more fitting for a bodyguard than a movie icon. Standing next to one of its winners buoyed me to the point that I didn't consider the irony of handling my first Oscar while standing next to Stan instead of my father. But gradually, I made the connection: Stan's industry friends had succeeded in this town. Melville Shavelson, president of the Writers Guild. Sumner, with his *Lassie* scripts and *Never Too Late*. Reece and Dorris Halsey, literary agents who represented, among others, Aldous Huxley and Ring Lardner. And Harold Kress. They'd all been my parents' friends, but following the divorce, they sided with my mother, leaving my father with the lesser-knowns.

In a tone as sweet as he'd used on television, Harold said, "Thank you," after I congratulated him.

I didn't wonder what my father was doing the night Harold won his Oscar. My father was in Sweden with his wife, Mai, and her two sons where he'd recently filmed a flop and now was in search of work. Released two months earlier, *Wild West Story*, a two-language cowboy film, had not, as they say in the trade, done good business. The concept must have sounded appealing at the time. The good guys spoke Swedish; the bad guys, English. Naturally, my father had played a bad guy.

Mai's sons, Tommy and Timmy, had appeared as extras. A slight roll of envy rippled through me when I found out. Flop or no flop, I was sure they'd had fun. I contrasted their time on the set with my jobs at Stan's office, filing purchase orders and running the Ozalid, a copy machine that glowed purple and gave off ammonia vapors.

I didn't resent Tommy and Timmy then, nor even five years later, when they played tennis with Lorne Greene and, during the filming of *Funny Girl*, lazed in the living room while Omar Sharif and my father played bridge and talked trash. But I felt ejected from the magic world, the exact sensation that had descended following my parents' divorce.

That's one of the few times, back then, that I reflected on my father's life with Tommy and Timmy. Only recently did that thought resurface thanks to an email I received from a Beverly High student who'd known them and wanted to learn how to get back in touch. He'd lived nearby during the time my father rented a house in Beverly Hills. "It was always such a thrill," he wrote, "for me and my pals to come to your dad's home, especially when he came into the room and showed us a nice friendly smile."

His email gnawed at me. Until reading it, I'd never imagined such a scene, my father at ease with his stepsons and their friends, a normal day without me. Shouldn't I have been in the room as well? Stan copied this scene countless times, entering our den and offering a cordial greeting to my friends, who waved back and asked how he was. But for my friends, it couldn't have been a thrill; just pleasant. Stan was not a Hollywood star.

⊙ ⊙ ⊙

And on the night of April 13, I stood next to a steeple of industry success. To hold an Oscar in my hands—I felt special. But I said nothing about it in school the next day. Somewhere close to my subconscious, I knew that many Beverly High families possessed Academy Awards, like the father of a girl with whom I worked on the school newspaper (best screenplay) and the father of that year's student body president (best director). Someone told me one Oscar winner used his as a doorstop. Margaret Herrick, the aunt of one of my classmates, had given the award its nickname, chosen, she said, because the statuette "looks like an Oscar." Despite the moniker, many at the Motion Picture Academy, as well as a number of students, referred to an Oscar back then as *the statue*.

Without makeup, most stars looked like anyone, at least to

me, rarely observant enough to recognize them. They shopped where we shopped, ate where we ate. Breakfast at Nate 'n Al's, the deli that catered the Oscars rehearsals. Dinner at Chasen's, whose chili was as renowned as the patrons. They walked their dogs and handed out Halloween candy. As we and they aged together in our small town, celebrities made whimsy real, turning the film industry into just another job, like Stan's business machines. Several reunions would have to pass before I'd hear the stories—about three classmates sitting in a bedroom, planning a campaign for a student office, hearing a noise, and then walking downstairs to see Joey Bishop and Don Rickles throwing lines back and forth. About an eighth-grade sleepover during which, clad in short tops, two girls came downstairs to find Marlon Brando in the living room, talking to the then general counsel of MGM. Brando nodded at the girls and said, "I wish I were twenty years younger."

With a handful of exceptions, I didn't know whose parents were famous, and that includes Danny Kaye's daughter, even when she ran for student body vice president. (She lost to a person whose parents, I believe, had nothing to do with film.) They acted like real people, and we kids didn't talk about them.

Though not entirely, it turned out. Take our surfers. One summer day in 1961, a photographer for *LIFE* magazine spotted Mike Nader, another Beverly High student, in the waves. He got Nader to don a tuxedo and then took pictures of him surfing in it. *LIFE* published the shot and, according to the conventional wisdom, the image drew national attention to the sport, which already was on the teenage radar screen thanks to the movie *Gidget.* Nine months later—that is to say, in June of my freshman year—Beverly High's yearbook, *The Watchtower,* reprinted the Nader photo.

It was a unique gesture by the school. We had no surfing club, yet the yearbook devoted two pages to surfing—more space than it allotted to our approved extracurricular activities. Even the honor clubs were rationed to, at most, a page while Mike Nader and his fellow surfer dudes rated individual photos of themselves nose riding and catching the hard ones at Malibu. I could see why. None of the Beverly High's "approved extracurricular activities" challenged us to balance on a fiberglass plank in a frothy body of water that curved from Malibu toward Asia.

I never met Nader. When we passed each other in the halls, we passed each other in the halls. Some called them dunces, but they were *our* dunces, sturdy mermen who added a layer of fantasy to the school's reputation, especially after American International Pictures cast Nader, his buddies, and his sister in the Frankie and Annette movies like *Beach Party*, *Bikini Beach,* and *Beach Blanket Bingo*. Their parts would be small but all-important, because it was the kids in the background—*the scene*—who made audiences fantasize about life in the Southland. The scene was everything in these films, and it took Nader et al to create it. They shimmied, they tossed beach balls, and they smooched while Annette Funicello and Frankie Avalon sang to each other. "Bonehead's really left the scene," Annette said of one *Beach Blanket Bingo* boy who chose to spend some time alone, and she was worried sick about him.

In one scene that takes place in a rather fancy beach hut, the group is making dinner while Ned Wynn, son of actor and comedian Ed Wynn, plays the guitar and Donna Loren sings as she roasts a hot dog in the fireplace. "It Only Hurts When I Cry" is her song, and before it ends, Mike Nader starts to cry, but then he's cutting up onions. After Donna finishes, the group applauds, she smiles, starts to laugh, and waggles her hot dog before eating it. Everyone is safe and happy in the Malibu pad where they live, rent-free I assume, since none of them has a summer job. On the screen, these kids look as joyful as the Mouseketeers.

◉ ◉ ◉

They weren't. In an article she wrote for *Vanity Fair* forty-five years later, journalist Sheila Weller labeled Mike Nader and his merry men "Malibu's Lost Boys." Weller—who during her years at Beverly High had served as "Commissioner of Spirit" and formed a pep club—said that Nader and his friends day-tripped to Malibu in order to get away from parents who ranged from violent to "perpetually inebriated," and the beach offered freedom as well as girls.

Life by the sea also, apparently, offered drugs. In his memoir, *We Will Always Live in Beverly Hills*, Ned Wynn described his days on the beach party sets. "Each morning, a dozen fresh joints rolled and stashed in my bag, we'd head out for either the studio for interiors, the beach, or someplace like the drag strip where the non-sand action sequences would be filmed." Then Wynn quoted the notorious surfer and party crasher Miki Dora. "We were in a bus going to location. We always sat in the back and got high so that by eight o'clock we were ready for the day." In other words, I realized, while making movies about their make-believe lives on the beach, at least some actors in *the scene* were avoiding their real lives.

So, things were not what they seemed. My childhood playmate, Valory, had figured that out by age five. It took me longer. In high school, I never saw any of these beach party movies. I guess I was too busy typing up debate cards and attending noontime classical (and sometimes jazz) music programs with their own whimsical titles like *Noctambulous* (relating to sleepwalking) and *Whigmaleerie*, a Scottish term for a fanciful contrivance. I had no desire to get up on a surfboard. I'd fall and crack my head and forget how to conjugate French verbs. Instead of surfer girls, I wanted someone within reach of my daydreams, a girl who wouldn't break out laughing if I asked her to the Pigskin Prom.

⊙ ⊙ ⊙

One winter four decades later, I came down with the flu.

It took a low-grade fever for me to watch *Beach Blanket Bingo*. I may have been an adult, but that night I needed fluff, and the film happened to be on cable.

Frankie and Annette did not take me back. It was the kids in the background; they're the ones who monkeyed with my memory. They frolicked in the waves. They raced cars. They danced on nightclub patios. And they were perfect specimens all. In school Mike Nader and I had been a species apart, the Greek god and the geek. He had a chiseled face, a square jaw, and a level look. I had none of the above but took comfort in the fact that Nader couldn't debate, and I doubt he spoke French.

CHAPTER TWENTY-FOUR

The Red Tide

Big Louie yelled as he pointed out to sea. "Outside! My God, outside! It's so big. Look at that thing form." The wave swelled and then piped, emitting a throaty rumble lasting almost fifteen seconds before turning into foam and crashing onto the beach. *Outside* referred to waves we could bodysurf. You swam in sync with the crest, then held yourself rigid, arms straight ahead for a ride on the inbound tide. Big Louie ran for the sea and the next wave. So did we all.

We were the products of a brilliant time, the Southern California of July 1964, the month that Gary, Brian, Joe, Eric, Big Louie, Rich, and I gave ourselves up to the water. Six weeks from the start of our senior year, we seven were poised to run our high school before heading east to college. We deserved these dreamy days on the sand. Lying on our blankets, talking about student government and the Johnson-Goldwater matchup as if they were equally important (which to us that summer, they were), we were stoked on teenage success and confident of a future even more brilliant. Even better, I'd learn to balance my two households, to toggle back and forth between the fathers with alacrity, buoyed by campus life and now the beach.

A wave was about to break. Joe caught it. I missed and dove under it. When I surfaced and looked back, Joe was rollicking through the foam to the shoreline. In control to the end, he let out a victory yell—"Team!" is what he hollered—as he flailed his arms and raced to our beach blankets.

That summer felt magical at the beach, then a teenage Eden stretching from Point Conception, fifty miles west of Santa Barbara, to the Mexican border. Gary, Brian, Joe, Eric, Big Louie, Rich, and I baked on our towels, sunscreen-free, radios going, reveling in gossip. No other place made me feel as good as that sandy ribbon. Burgers and fries were cheap, parking cost a dollar, adults were scarce, and the waves were free. I craved it—the sound of the surf, warm silicon granules against my fingers, and the sun, of course the sun, in the words of Eugene Burdick, "a kind sun . . . a sun designed for Utopia."

On one of those days, Joe rolled onto his back. "What's next year's debate topic?" he asked.

Before I could say "nuclear disarmament," a new song, "House of the Rising Sun," came over the transistor. "Hey, The Animals," Eric said. He sounded half asleep.

Someone mentioned lunch, so we traipsed to the food stand, a hut with sand for a floor and Top 40 songs piped through a speaker on its rickety roof. The melody blended with female voices nearby. One of those voices belonged to a blonde who didn't return my gaze as she paid for a Pepsi. It didn't matter. I'd land a beach babe someday. It would just happen, the way California teenagers used to believe good things would come their way.

After we finished our hamburgers, Gary, Brian, Joe, Eric, Big Louie, Rich, and I fell back to sleep until the afternoon marine layer moistened the air. Then we gathered our blankets and tramped through the sand to our cars. The radio blasted all the way to our houses, where we ran upstairs to shower before dinner.

The nights were like velvet. Our bodies became little ovens, giving off the heat we'd absorbed without sunscreen. We saw *Viva Las Vegas* at the drive-in. The Beatles made us smile and groove.

"A Hard Day's Night" reached Number One on the Fabulous Forty Survey. Their first movie by the same name was due out on August 11. We searched the beaches for grunion runs. We took turns driving there. Our grades were high. We flew east to look at schools. The Democrats were the party of peace and paychecks. Our swimming pools were heated so we could play Marco Polo in them until bedtime. We worried about nothing. Stan's new company was about to win a contract. My father was about to embark on a publicity tour to Indiana and Kentucky, paid for by a local who wanted to support a pilot that my father was sure would become his new TV series—*Holiday for Hire*: the story of a travel agent who catered to the very rich. He'd shot the pilot over a year before—in the fall of 1962—and was still trying to get it on television. He never could.

⊙ ⊙ ⊙

The red tide arrived in August. Most likely it was an algae bloom, probably nontoxic because none of us got sick. The diatoms made the water glow whenever something—like a swimmer or a wave—stirred them. And since breaking waves stirred them plenty, the surf line became a band of light.

Surfing that band of light sounded like a grand adventure, and on the night of August 4, we decided to try. Everyone gathered at my house. We'd just finished piling blankets and snacks in the car when Stan and my mother said the president was about to give a speech. At 8:36 Pacific Daylight Time, Lyndon Johnson's face appeared on the television.

He opened with the phrase "As president and commander in chief . . ." The group stiffened. Most of us had taken civics in summer school. We knew that when the president invoked that second title, a military response was coming.

Johnson continued: "[R]enewed hostile actions against United States ships on the high seas in the Gulf of Tonkin have today required me to order the military forces of the United States to take action in reply."

"It's about time," muttered Stan.

"That reply is being given as I speak to you tonight. Air action is now in execution against gunboats and certain supporting facilities in North Vietnam which have been used in these hostile operations."

We were bombing North Vietnam. Everyone in my den supported this long overdue move. So did LBJ's opponent. Looking straight into the TV camera, the president informed us, "I was able to reach Senator Goldwater and I am glad to say that he has expressed his support of the statement that I am making to you tonight."

Certain moments rate as a steeple in a life, the apex of a season. Tuesday night, August 4, 1964, offered such a moment. My friends and I whooped through the twenty-minute drive from my house to the sea. The deejay on KRLA said it best: "Finally, we're showing those communists what for." He sounded as ebullient as we felt, racing west toward the red tide. Even better, President Johnson promised that he would get Congress "to pass a resolution making it clear that our government is united in its determination to take all necessary measures in support of freedom and in defense of peace in Southeast Asia."

Surely, we'd win there. My friends and I saw no risk in ratcheting up the war. Neither did Stan. Neither did my father. Beating the communists in Vietnam and everywhere else on the planet had become one of the few subjects about which both of my fathers agreed. They as well as I looked forward to enjoying Walter Cronkite's coverage of a victory march through Hanoi followed by a free Vietnam joining Thailand, Pakistan, and the Philippines in SEATO, the Southeast Asia Treaty Organization. The country would become, as a journalist had written of South

Korea, "a worthy ally of the United States." One of my friends said that with long stretches of beach and perfect waves all year, Da Nang offered great surfing. Maybe one day I'd bicycle through the rice paddies. Could anybody have been so dumb about the war? West LA brimmed with American naïfs. We little princes were as stupid as Louie XVI.

We barreled down the California Incline, "The best on-ramp in the world" as author Deanne Stillman labeled it, for the road dropped us from the top of Santa Monica's cliffs to the Pacific Coast Highway. A quick left and we arrived at Tee's Beach.

Brian was the first into the sea. Gary joined him and they swam toward an oncoming shadow of water the top of which was a strip of lit algae. Before diving under the wave, I saw Brian's head sticking out from the vertical water, his mouth an oval, eyes glaring. For an instant a corona surrounded him; then the wave crashed. Brian scored a perfect ride to the beach. "All right, all right," he shouted. Next came Gary. Emerging from the glowing froth, he threw back his head and hollered, "Hey Bamboola!"

We drove home at midnight. En route, Eric voiced an idea for Student Council. Gary invited us to a swimming party on Saturday. And I decided to ask out Margie, a vivacious girl who believed in student government as fervently as I. Braving the red tide gave me the courage to call her. The Pigskin Prom was set for September 26. If I reached her in the morning, Margie would have enough notice. She'd say yes. It was going to be a sensational senior year. A year full of parties and fun. A carefree year, with splendid years to come, especially now that Vietnam was taken care of.

Vietnam took care of us, it turned out. But good. The war divided and crippled my generation. But thanks to Beverly Hills privilege, not one of my close high school friends had to fight there. To escape the draft, some joined the national guard. The lucky ones drew high lottery numbers. Not I; I placed thirty-five.

But thanks to my double vision and a beautiful pilonidal cyst, the Selective Service System awarded me a 4F, their coveted label that marked you medically unfit to serve.

I visited Vietnam in 2006. The instant our plane touched down at Tan Son Nhat International Airport, like some veterans who were aboard, I burst into tears.

CHAPTER TWENTY-FIVE

Come Blow Your Horn

My father never told me why he wore jumpsuits. They seemed to be a popular attire for actors back then, so was it his desire to be viewed as one of Southern California's select? Years later, someone told me that when celebrities weren't in front of a camera, they liked to slum in jumpsuits. Or maybe my father knew he looked good in them. I do know that he never bought me one. Jumpsuits required slim bodies.

One Saturday afternoon—after another ordeal at Drucker's barbershop—my father took me to Sy Devore, a fashion-forward men's clothing store on Vine Street in Hollywood, in the same building as ABC Television, where I'd been years before to appear on *Half Pint Panel*.

I'd yet to learn about, let alone appreciate, the lofty perch Mr. Devore occupied on the movie industry ziggurat. His business doubled as an A-list hangout. Danny Kaye and Bob Hope would drop in and, while shoppers looked on, try out new jokes on each other. John Wayne was a regular. Devore dressed Frank Sinatra and his Rat Pack. He tailored suits for Nat King Cole and Rock Hudson. Dean Martin wore custom shirts designed by Devore, wore them so often that the store created a retail version called the Dino. In a strongbox to guard against fires, Sy Devore kept suit patterns for his celebrity customers, which, I'm sure, didn't include my father. My father remained stuck on the B list. Still, one of the salesmen greeted him by name. While the two joked with another actor who'd come in, I wandered down the aisles and ran my fingers along the shoulders of the suits that hung everywhere. They felt soft and soothing. They smelled woolly. I picked up a tie and immediately put it down. I had trouble knotting them.

Sy Devore gave out postcards of his store. I helped myself to three of them—color shots of the storefront with dark blazers on display behind plate glass windows set at an angle to the sidewalk. They wouldn't become the greatest additions to my postcard collection, but now I had extras to trade. Then I visited a travel agency next door and took some brochures, about where I didn't care; any destination intrigued me.

A few minutes later, I walked back into Sy Devore to find my father laughing with a new group of customers. He appeared comfortable, in no hurry to leave. In his Bill Parry jumpsuit and with his hair combed just so, Dad was the archetype of urbanity. He held his cigarette as though he'd been born with it.

If my father bought anything that day, it would have been another jumpsuit; the cost, between twenty and thirty dollars. He couldn't afford Sy Devore's imported Louis Roth suits, priced around $175 to $200.

Back in his car, snared in Hollywood traffic, my father said, "Sometime I'll teach you how to tie a Windsor knot." He'd seen me fiddling with a tie.

As usual, my father and I spent the balance of our day talking about politics, Shakespeare, Europe, the occult, the movie industry, history, radio, television, sex, psychology, the Dodgers—all topics I relished. He didn't mention my appearance, never a "You'd look good in this."

My father's economics didn't impact me thanks to Stan. His Dashew Business Machines stock earned top mention in *You*

Only Have To Get Rich Once. Then he and Bank of America's vice president had started another company, which in 1965, they'd sell to American Express. So on a warm Saturday during my junior year at Beverly Hills High School, my mother interrupted my homework. Dressed in a white top and blue slacks, both garments spotless, she stood over my desk and urged me to go shopping.

"You need some more clothes," she said, not for the first time.

"Mine look fine," I said, not for the first time.

"No, they don't. You need better-looking things. I don't want you to poor-boy it."

I dragged myself out of the house and walked up Rodeo Drive to Carroll & Co., Stan's clothier of choice.

The place brimmed with dark mahogany partners' desks, console tables, leather upholstered chairs, and English-style clothes. On the oak walls hung color drawings of fox hunts and English public-school boys punting on a river, perhaps the Cam. No jumpsuits here. I had no idea Carroll & Co. considered itself Sy Devore's competitor, albeit for stars with conservative taste. Steve McQueen, Cary Grant, Clark Gable, Paul Newman, Frank Sinatra, Gregory Peck, and others looked to Mr. Carroll to dress them. The store would launch a studio division to outfit popular shows. Its founder, Richard Carroll, had been a Warner Bros. publicist.

In one of the fitting rooms, an upperclassman I'd met in summer school auto shop glared at himself in the mirrors, then whipped off his sport coat and tossed it on the floor. Unlike my friends, this boy had miserable grades, but he did have a strong physique topped off by a cleft chin. Someone said his parents had given him a Thunderbird for his sixteenth birthday.

He was too busy donning and doffing to notice me. A cashmere sport coat, a wool sport coat, suits, slacks, blazers. The salesman let him preen in peace. I felt intimidated because during our summer school class, he'd bullied a classmate, a shy campus invisible who hadn't tried to defend himself. I wanted to get away before he saw me. We'd never spoken to each other, and I didn't want to start now.

I grabbed a shirt, put it on my parents' account, and left.

"That's all?" my mother said when I walked into the kitchen. "You didn't get any new pants? Even a tie?" Although she was cooking—a pot roast, bathed in its juices and slowly roasted to tenderize the marbled meat—not one of her brown hairs was out of place.

"I got tired," I said.

"I'm taking you next time," she said, sounding frustrated but good-natured—typical of her. "Next time" wouldn't occur for months. Until then, thanks to my mother, proper shirts and pants showed up in my closet. Every morning I threw something on and left for school, and no one found fault with what I wore.

Appearance constituted one of the few subjects about which my mother, my father, and my stepfather concurred. My mother had gone from one fashionable husband to another. But maybe because his business consumed so much of his time, Stan delegated my appearance to my mother. Or perhaps he was focused on Leslie.

Early in 1959, Leslie arrived for the weekend wearing a mustard-yellow outfit (wrinkled, my mother noticed) with cropped pants and a vest. Acceptable, perhaps, in the San Fernando Valley where she and her mother lived, but not in Beverly Hills. Worse, Leslie had holes in her sneakers, necessary, she said, because of hammertoes.

In the foyer, before she carried her duffel bag up the stairs, Leslie gushed at her dad, hugged him and maybe my mother too. Then she gave me the tentative hello an eleven-year-old offers a new slightly older stepsibling.

"She looks like a ragamuffin," my mother said.

Eyes ablaze, Stan marched his six-foot-two-inch body to the telephone. He grabbed the receiver as though he planned to strangle it.

Stan yelled at his ex-wife, "Is that how you send her to school?" His child support checks had included plenty of money for clothing, and for that reason, Stan refused to take Leslie shopping.

Now I know that the ex wanted Stan to dress Leslie in order to free up funds for her liquor. Leslie never told me how abandoned she must have felt, the pawn in her parents' fight. And since we never talked about clothing, I figured neither of us cared about the topic.

⊙ ⊙ ⊙

Five years later, in 1964, The *Highlights*, Beverly High's student paper, bulged with advertising from local clothing stores like Burdsall's and Joe Rudnick's. Pendleton shirts. Hang Ten slacks and surf jackets, A-1 slacks, A-1 peggers, A-1 Racer pants, Levi's slim-fits, stretch Levi's, blue Levi's corduroys, slim continental slacks. I ignored them all, even when I became coeditor-in-chief of the paper, obligated to approve everything on its pages. I had better things to do with my time than pay attention to clothes—like attacking the Girls' League Modes and Manners Committee.

The Modes and Manners Committee had just sent a confidential checklist to every teacher with a request that they report—anonymously—any girl they felt needed counseling in a number of areas, leading off with a fashion faux pas: *Skirt too short or too tight.* Eight more categories followed: *2. Extreme hairdo 3. Overly made up 4. Nails poorly groomed 5. Body odor 6. Sitting in unladylike position 7. Uses foul language 8. Lack of courtesy 9. Other.*

"We have to expose this," I complained to our faculty sponsor. "I want to write an editorial."

In a nasty tenor, Mr. Gelms snapped back. He had a beak for a nose. The red hair on his head had worn down to stubble, and his eyes were too small. "We want our girls to look good," he said. "Don't you?"

It was a late-fifties-early-sixties question, a product of a culture that valued a girl's looks above all else, and naturally I was as tone deaf about the subject as Mr. Gelms. I'm sure I said yes, but that wasn't the point. What the committee proposed to do brought back memories of my parents shushing me so they could watch Joseph McCarthy during "the morning session." Now the Girls League wanted teachers to start naming names.

On his desk the most recent *Highlights* lay open to a photograph of "October's Good Grooming Girls of the Month"—four girls, one from each grade, all wearing their honor club smiles. One was a movie star's child. Each wore a tailored dress, or a skirt with a sweater, or a skirt with a tailored blouse. The Modes and Manners Committee had anointed each of them. No such laurel existed for the boys. I returned to my desk and muttered something about Big Brother watching us.

Mr. Gelms barked, "What was that?"

"Nothing," I said.

I reacted to the Girls' League questionnaire by confronting them and saying I knew they wanted teachers to answer their questionnaires and throw girls upon the mercy of their committee. I threatened an editorial. They abandoned the project.

This was not the first time I'd fought the school. I'd tried to editorialize about cliques in student government and a student election in which ballot-stuffing had occurred. But at home I avoided battles with Stan and my mother, especially my mother, due perhaps to an irrational fear that my stitched-together family could fall apart if I rebelled too harshly. At worst I baited them, knowing I'd immediately retreat, like the time my classmate David called on a Saturday morning in May 1964. "Want to come up tonight and play some pool?" His parents had installed a table in their attic.

I knew we wouldn't play pool. My friends were planning a surprise birthday party for me. The signs had been obvious, but when I dressed for the evening, I chose a battered madras shirt and faded blue jeans. This was a test, the brat in me seeking a reaction from a parent, and I got it.

My mother begged me to change into something better. "You're visiting one of your nicest friends," she said, standing in the hall. "At least put on a decent pair of slacks." My mother knew David's parents, Beverly Hills civic leaders who'd been married for twenty-two years and would stay married another forty-nine. Of course, she'd wanted me to appear stylish. Children of divorced families dressed sloppily, someone told her once.

Without any back talk, I trailed my mother up the stairs and let her produce an outfit from my closet. Maybe Stan could have helped me through a Windsor knot, but I didn't ask him. Learning to tie a Windsor remained my father's promise.

On cue, everyone yelled "Surprise" and sang "Happy Birthday," and I did a good job of acting surprised as I surveyed the room—Larry, Howard, Richard, Gary, and Joe, all in dark slacks, ties, and dark sport coats, buttoned in front because that's how boys—at least my crowd—dressed for parties in 1964. And that night, I'd dressed like them.

As for the girls: Jacquie, the date they'd picked for me, wore a pink short-sleeved dress. The others came in knee-length sleeveless dresses of all colors.

The party flowed across David's library, a roomful of boiserie that his parents had purchased, complete with sconces and lighting, from Cordhaven, a 32,000 square foot Beverly Hills mansion that a developer had torn down in order to subdivide the lot. For one evening, I felt wanted—and wanted to look wanted. I didn't think about the fact that neither of my fathers had taken my hand and led me to a suit.

In 1968, my father died without ever teaching me to tie a Windsor knot.

⊙ ⊙ ⊙

What I didn't know—wouldn't know for years—was that during school, Leslie had started working in order to afford decent clothes for herself. She babysat and she filed for a freight bill company, an ordeal she still refers to as "the most boring job ever." Although good grooming awards didn't exist at her high school, Leslie acknowledged clothing's importance long before I did. It took a phone call from Stan to start the process with me.

Stan called in January 1975, the morning after a law firm asked me to leave. Rapidly, without prelude, before I'd shaken myself awake, he said, "I want you to take two thousand dollars from your checking account and go buy a new wardrobe. I want you to go today. You need new clothes. You don't look good the way you dress. I'm sure that's why they let you go. I want you to get some new clothes." He carried on like that for at least another ten seconds. I guess this was the best Stan could do—send me there, not take me there. By then I'd accepted his style. At least he was more instructive than my father had been.

I thought my law firm had let me go because the work bored me, and I'd let it show. But on the off-chance Stan was right, I dragged myself back to Carroll & Co.

⊙ ⊙ ⊙

In May 1994, two salesmen at Carroll & Co. measured me for a judicial robe. I knew I'd never possess their sartorial elegance. The suits each man wore were impeccably tailored; their gray hair, exquisitely coiffed. They looked almost as polished as my father.

"I'm so proud of you, Tony, I mean *Your Honor*," one of them said. I'd known him for years, starting with my January 1975 visit.

"Stretch your arms," the other said. "Drop your shoulders."

I duly obeyed.

As the man ran a measuring tape across my shoulders, down my back, and along my arms, a warm feeling took hold. I was in no hurry. I felt satisfied, arrived. Light as it was, the touch of the tape felt bracing. I wanted the process to last forever. This was part of my transition to the bench, and I relished every second of it.

"Shoulders, nineteen inches. Sleeves, twenty-one and a half," the salesman told his colleague, who wrote my measurements on a form.

After they finished, one of the salesmen offered me a small bottled water and an oatmeal cookie. He said, "Some wonderful Chester Barrie suits just came in. Do you have time to try one on?"

The store felt comfortable, its furniture and drawings unchanged, its odor still woolly. I had plenty of time but declined. After all, nobody knows what judges wear under our black robes. It could be a sweater or a T-shirt, tails or a gorilla suit. Part of me still didn't care how I dressed.

In 2017, I got around to watching *Come Blow Your Horn*, the 1963 movie adaptation of Neil Simon's play. Midway through the story, Frank Sinatra, who plays a bachelor man-about-town, leads his naive kid brother, Tony Bill, into at least four clothing stores and a fancy barbershop in order to make him look elegant. During Tony's haircut, a man shines his shoes, and a woman gives him a manicure. As the movie's theme song, a guide for living life large, plays across the soundtrack ("I tell ya, chum, it's time to come blow your horn"), Sinatra picks out the right shirts, suits, and slacks, the right overcoat, the right everything for Tony, down to a perfect Stetson. Meanwhile, Frank keeps singing his instructions until the final "I tell ya, chum . . ."

Cut to the new Tony Bill, a slow pan from his lustrous shoes up to his flawlessly trimmed hair. Frank turns him around, places the hat on his kid brother's head, clasps Tony's shoulders, and gives him a pinch on the cheek. Tony has become 1963's good grooming man of the year.

Per Frank Sinatra's request, one of the exterior sets designed for *Come Blow Your Horn* was a replica of Sy Devore's storefront.

The scene caught in my throat. I'd misheard the lyrics. I thought Frank Sinatra had sung, "I tell ya, *son.*"

EPILOGUE

My father died in Europe, a heart attack, they said, hours after he'd enjoyed a dinner of oysters. The TV series pilot he'd filmed in 1968 was in the can, a story set in an apartment house starring him as Jeff Landers, the urbane owner through whom the tenants' lives would crisscross. They'd titled it *Private Entrance*, perfect for a series about people—according to the treatment, "each with his own private entrance" into their little homes, "the world packed into small containers."

He'd never displayed signs of heart disease; he always told me that according to his doctor, he was "sound as a dollar." But for years my father smoked over two packs a day, ate nothing but steak, eggs, and burnt bacon, and worried about money. *Foreign Intrigue. Rough Sketch. Holiday For Hire.* They'd all fizzled. His B movies were middling. Residuals had yet to take hold in the industry. He was far from his goal, expressed to me in a 1963 letter, written during an overseas trip in search of work: "If I succeed in establishing myself here in Europe, I can fulfill a dream I have always had of being an international actor, flying back and forth, happily working all over the world."

Mai couldn't afford a funeral for him. My father left without a will. She had no money to bring him home from Sweden, so she said a month later. The little crypt she purchased sits at ground level in a cemetery on one of Stockholm's islands. The inscription gives my father's name, date of birth (June 11, 1914), date of death (November 9, 1968), and nothing more. To read it thirty years on, I had to clear away the shrubbery and wipe my eyes.

A decade passed before I could talk about it. Dad's last movie, *Funny Girl* (1968), was released six weeks before he died. I didn't go then because I was waiting for Christmas vacation, when I'd be home from school, Dad would be back from Sweden, and we'd see the movie together, sitting next to each other in the theater, as we had years earlier with *Terror in the Haunted House* and *The Angry Red Planet*.

◉ ◉ ◉

Stan died at home in April 2013, forty-five years after my father. He was ninety-six and a half. The celebration of his life overflowed the ballroom at UCLA, next to the international student center, which bore his name. One by one, friends and colleagues praised his talents, his drive, his generosity. They called Stan a mentor. His youngest niece compared him to a magician. Leslie fought back tears long enough to say how much she missed his presence and advice. We buried him next to my mother, as Stan had arranged—two grave sites, each with a view of the Hollywood Hills.

Even into his dotage, Stan embraced change with zest, ordering every new gizmo on the market. The habit fed his success during middle age. It was a trait I admired, but never mimicked. I'd endured too much of it as a child, moving to Sweden, moving to New York, moving to Beverly Hills, and shifting families. Maybe that's why I pouted the day Walt Disney dialed back *The Mickey Mouse Club* from one hour to half an hour. Maybe that's why I like the law. The law lags progress. It trails behind everything, as do most judges. Some of my colleagues still use their computers as nothing more than paperweights. Still, thanks to Stan, my mind remains more ajar to change. Our court's information technology staff says I'm a heavy computer user. But they have to keep explaining how to navigate the special software they install for us.

Watching my fathers' trajectories made me cautious, like most judges I know. After vicariously riding the Stan and Gerry roller coaster, I opted for a calm life on the bench, growing old with steady, modest government pay along with the opportunity to help people resolve their battles and move on with their lives. In addition, judging has provided the ability to watch my own private movies, otherwise known as trials. Some are funny; others, tragic. They've made me laugh or cry, but always privately, in chambers. And regardless of the verdict, I'm not facing personal disaster.

⊙ ⊙ ⊙

As he got older, Stan changed. The man who'd yanked me out of Beverly Hills to make me spend time with the crew on his boat became hungry for renown, to be Stan the entrepreneur, Stan the tycoon, Stan the man. By his late eighties, Stan had become gullible, prey to people like Andrew, an alleged producer. They met at a party. How Andrew got to that party, I don't know. The host claims he didn't know him. Andrew said he wanted to cast Stan in a movie. He started dropping by nightly at nine or so, to cadge hundred-dollar bills with each visit. Skip, Leslie, and I managed to stop him, and the night we did so was the last time he visited Stan.

It hurt to see Stan yearning for the tinfoil version of fame. I'm not sure what I did about it was right. Skip and Leslie didn't approve when I announced my idea, but at the time I was sure it would please Stan. It did. For Stan's ninety-fifth birthday, I hired Arlene Howard, a publicist.

"I love your stepfather," Arlene said after their first meeting. She had a take-no-prisoners tone of voice, and within days she'd hatched a plan. Stan found himself being interviewed and featured in, among other places, *Forbes, The Huffington Post*, and the *Los Angeles Times*. Upon his death, *TIME* would give him a mention in *Milestones*, and the *Los Angeles Times* would splay his obituary across the top of the page. Arlene made Stan's final year a little happier.

Did she make Stan famous? Not if you measure fame by autograph hounds. Yes, if fame includes respect, the quality that flowed through all the articles Arlene planted in which Stan offered advice for those in business. ("If you can't find a job, then make your own" and "If you don't have all the skills or resources to implement an idea, team up with someone who has what you lack.") Stan was imparting to readers lessons he'd taught me and many that he'd learned too late. Reading his quotes made me proud, but they failed to satisfy my stepfather. He wanted more notice and more success; his age be damned. I can only hope that at the end, some part of Stan believed he'd lived a good life, for he did, by any legitimate measure of success.

⊙ ⊙ ⊙

As Stan would ask me after school, what have I learned? I wasn't sure what I'd learned then, other than Metternich's diplomacy and the symbolism in *Arrowsmith*. That's not what Stan wanted to hear, and the reluctant teen in me didn't care to accommodate him. Had I, I would have said that the faculty was teaching me to think.

What's unfortunate—which I didn't think about then—is that almost none of my friends met both of my families. The few girls I dated in high school didn't, nor did anybody from college. I'm not even sure Skip or Leslie ever met my father, nor did Tommy or Timmy meet Stan. If they did, the encounter lasted seconds. I wasn't embarrassed to make the introductions—far from it. The opportunity never surfaced, with the result that hardly anyone knew me as well as they thought they did.

At times I ask myself how life would have unspooled had I lived with my father. Maybe more classmates would have known I was an actor's son, but so what? If the Beverly High campus didn't swoon over the likes of Julie (Lee J.) Cobb, Larry (Joey) Bishop, Amanda (Oscar) Levant, and over twenty more like them, hardly anyone would have treated me differently.

It was good to live with Stan. I witnessed a storybook marriage, not the shouting matches that plagued my father and Mai, nor the tense silences that lurked under my parents' marriage. What's more, had we lived together, my father may have overshadowed me more than he did, even though he didn't mean to. One example should suffice: In 1967, I spent the summer in Peru with a college service project, and when I returned, I wrote an article about it for our local paper, the *Beverly Hills Courier*. Within hours of submitting it, the editor called to ask if Gerald Mohr was my father.

They published me, all right, under a headline that opened, "BH Actor's Son . . ." They featured a photo of my father, not me. The night the article ran, I had a date with a girl I liked, and the moment I met her mother, she gushed, "I've always had a crush on your father."

And it was good to live with my mother. At every critical juncture, she sat me down and talked. Each time I failed at something, she reassured me. "You have a tremendous resilience. It's one of your best qualities, the ability to bounce back. And that's what you'll do." And she knew how to react to the triumphs, like the day I became coeditor-in-chief of the paper: "Don't get mixed up in the rivalries. Just tell them that all you want to see is *the page*."

Maybe living between two worlds helped me in my eventual life as a judge. We of the bench are trained to suspend conclusion until the end, to weigh both sides, to inhabit all points of view. Only then must we decide, and I use the word *must* deliberately. Embedded in California law is the *duty to decide*—"A judge has a duty to decide any proceeding in which he or she is not disqualified." To say I had practice weighing lifestyles is an understatement. And when they say a trial is a search for the truth, well, spending childhood in the dreamlike realm of Hollywood helped prepare me to separate fact from fiction. As Valory recently said over dinner—we've kept in touch over the years—"I learned early on that things were not always as they appeared to be." So did I, though back then I may not have realized it.

I wish my mother had seen me become a judge. She died the day the governor appointed me, missing the event by hours. She was a constant through the years, not mercurial like Mai, flamboyant like my father's lover Miriam, alcoholic like his leading lady in *Invasion USA*, Peggy Castle, or daring like the nineteen-year-old model who showed up at midnight, naked, on my father's doorstep. Come to think of it, the woman I married embodied the spirit of my mother.

Based on what my mother told me every time I had a success, I can guess the advice she would have offered me upon taking the bench. Be fair. Go to Carroll's and buy a new suit. Listen to everyone. Get a haircut. Read the briefs. Clean up the backseat of your car. Be you. She would have commented on the opportunity to meet different people, hear their stories, ferret out their truths, and "be challenged again, something you have not been for some time now, have you?" Mom would have said all of that. To be a judge requires the ability to listen, and on the day that title became mine, I realized I would have to listen harder than before in order to hear her words.

⊙ ⊙ ⊙

On the last day of my sophomore year at Beverly, with about three minutes to go before the bell rang, Mr. Occhipinti leaned against a table near the blackboard and addressed his modern history class. As calmly as I'd ever heard him, he said, "In the forty-five or fifty years that are left to you . . ."

Who knows what Mr. Occhipinti said after that? He'd just made me realize how few years I had left to live. Forty-five or fifty didn't sound like much. Fifty years plus the sixteen behind me constituted the human life span for Americans born in 1947. That's what I was thinking when Mr. Occhipinti took a step forward and urged us to enjoy the rest of our lives. "Go out there," he said in a voice softer than he'd used all year. "Give it a whirl."

None of us jumped up when the bell rang. Summer vacation may have been hours away, but I took more time than usual to close my notebook and leave Room 121. High school was half over, a scary thought. Beverly was my fulcrum between two homes.

⊙ ⊙ ⊙

I'm risk averse, but I'm satisfied. On many levels, being a judge resembles the movie industry, only better. A trial can become my own private soap opera, and sometimes I can direct the action, stop the action, or call for a second take.

What's more, I look the part. Judges don't need chiseled features. The judicial security unit urges us to Google ourselves at least monthly and report anything that suggests a threat. During one of my searches, I stumbled across my name in a chat room. I vaguely remembered the woman who posted the comment:

"Anthony Mohr is now a Los Angeles Superior Court judge! He was born in 1947. I went out with him once, a long time ago. Why? Duh! I loved watching his dad!"

A post from someone else asked the woman if I resembled my father.

"No, sorry," wrote the girl. "He looks NOTHING like his dad! He is short and stocky."

⊙ ⊙ ⊙

Periodically in the judges' lunchroom, colleagues remark that we have the best job in the world. I agree. Although at times I've wisecracked that it would be fun to edit *The Atlantic* or become the assistant secretary of defense for special operations and low-intensity conflict, I've spent over a quarter of a century trying cases ranging from wrongful deaths to contracts, from malpractice to murder, from class actions to drunk driving. They're all different, and they all matter. I have to struggle with them. Sometimes the choices are horrible; whatever I do is wrong. But I rule. Then, after court recesses, I drive home to my wife, a Midwesterner whose only resemblance to Sweden is her blond hair. Often after dinner, we curl up with our Lhasa Apso and watch spy movies.

ACKNOWLEDGMENTS

To bring a book into the world takes more than a village; a small town is more like it. That was the case with *Every Other Weekend*, and the thanks I give here hardly conveys the gratitude I feel.

Portions of several chapters in this book previously appeared in various literary journals. My thanks and appreciation to all their editors for their votes of confidence. *Brevity's blog, DIAGRAM, Diverse Voices Quarterly, Eclectica, Hippocampus Magazine, Los Angeles Daily Journal, Maryland Literary Review, Mojo, North Dakota Quarterly, Prick of the Spindle, Rappahannock Review, The Broken City, War, Literature & the Arts, ZYZZYVA,* and these anthologies: *California Prose Directory 2013, Christmas Is a Season 2008, Freckles to Wrinkles, Golden State 2017.*

Some writers refuse to let anybody suggest changes. I'm not one of them. When editors want revisions, that tells me they care; they want to curate my work into the best version possible. Almost every time their input improves the piece. Among the editors I worked with, the best of the best was Leslie Schwartz. She stayed with me for the duration. She had the patience and the talent to spot the soggy middles, tag the non sequiturs, kill the darlings, and in short, bring my sentences to a level worthy of publication. Others who gave me their time and advice include Sarah Einstein, who helped shape the work, and Dani Shapiro, who at the Wishing Stone Workshop, helped bring two of the chapters to life. At the Kenyon Review Writers Workshop and onward since then, Allison K Williams and Dinty W. Moore provided valuable pointers. Will Allison helped me through a difficult chapter. Nicole Walker suggested a killer ending to another. Also providing encouragement and advice along the way were Bernard Cooper, Sonia Baku, Melissa Ballard, Laurie Ember, Rebecca Forster, Kenneth Lagstrom, Edan Lepucki, Clif Leonhardt, Jake Morrissey, Beatrice Motamedi, Andrew Weiner, and Yasmin Tong. And from my California Judges Writing Group, these honorables: Kenneth Freeman, Michelle Rosenblatt, and Elizabeth White. Also John Kralik, author of *A Simple Act of Gratitude* and *Three Bodies by the River*. He steered me to Koehler Books. Working with them, especially John Koehler, Becky Hilliker, and Christine Kettner, was a pleasure.

A number of friends and classmates shared impressions and memories of my fathers, as well as places and events. Special thanks to my muse Merel Grey Nissenberg. Also to Larry Ach, Carl Borack, Susan Diskin, Lesley Geiger, Edwin Girard, Al Goodman, Robbie Long, Candy Mannis Schulman, Alice Matzkin, Valory Mitchell, Diane Murphy, Paul Peterson, Robert Post, Liz Weller, and Jack Yellin. Thomas Quinlan provided excellent feedback, as he did half a century ago when he was my English teacher. I wish Mr. Occhipinti had been alive to do the same.

Bill Geerhart, master of the Conelrad website http://www. conelrad.com/features/invasionusa/mohr.html), led me into aspects of my father's fanbase and biography that I didn't know.

Special thanks to the master of grammar, Kenneth Kaufman, for all his help.

Then there's my family: both sets of stepsiblings, Skip and Leslie Dashew, their spouses Linda Dashew and Jack Salisbury, and Tommy and Timmy Dietrich. We've had endless conversations about Gerald and Stan. The same with my cousins on both sides:

Jeff and Warren Adler, and Lisa and Herve Pauze. They, as well my nieces Elyse Dashew, Sarah Dashew, and Baleigh Isaacs, shared stories as well as feelings, and any factual errors in this book are mine alone.

And finally, my wife Beverly. She has made the final third of my life the best. Without her support, this book would not exist. I might not either.

CPSIA information can be obtained
at www.ICGtesting.com
Printed in the USA
JSHW020151250323
39467JS00004B/11